D0719318

☞ MR. HARTSTON'S
MOST EXCELLENT
ENCYLOPEDIA OF USELESS
INFORMATION

☞ MR. HARTSTON'S
MOST EXCELLENT
ENCYLOPEDIA OF USELESS
INFORMATION

THE SUPREME MISCELLANY
OF FANTASTIC FACTS

WILLIAM HARTSTON

metro

Published by Metro Publishing
an imprint of John Blake Publishing
3, Bramber Court, 2 Bramber Road,
London W14 9PB, England

www.blake.co.uk

First published in Hardback in 2006

13-digit ISBN 978-1-84358-160-4
ISBN 1 84358 160 4

British Library Cataloguing-in-Publication Data:

A catalogue record for this book is available from the British Library.

Design by www.envydesign.co.uk

Printed in Great Britain by CPD

1 3 5 7 9 10 8 6 4 2

Papers used by Metro Publishing are natural, recyclable products made from
wood grown in sustainable forests. The manufacturing processes conform to
the environmental regulations of the country of origin.

Every attempt has been made to contact the relevant copyright-holders,
but some were unobtainable. We would be grateful if the appropriate
people could contact us.

'What I want is information; not useful information, of course; useless information.'
OSCAR WILDE, *THE PICTURE OF DORIAN GRAY*, (1891)

'It is a very sad thing that nowadays there is so little useless information.'
OSCAR WILDE, *MAXIMS FOR THE USE OF THE OVEREDUCATED*, (1894)

PREFACE

Have you noticed how dull encyclopedias have become in recent years? The trouble is, their compilers feel obliged to include so much noble and worthy information that it squeezes out all the really interesting stuff. Even worse, they all seem to have reached an agreement on the level of dullness to which they aspire. If a particularly interesting fact is absent from one of them, you can be fairly sure you will not find it in another encyclopedia of comparable size.

This standard of stultifying worthiness was the first reason for my setting out to write this book. Over the past decade or more, I have had to hunt through many obscure sources of information to find the answers to questions that intrigued me. On many other occasions, snippets of fascinating knowledge have caught my attention and I have reeled them in, just in case I may have use of them in the future. The net result of this habit is a series of huge files on my computer packed full of the cherished snippets of information that have

WILLIAM HARTSTON

passed my way which are not to be found in the standard sources of reference.

The second justification for this book came as a result of approaching the problem from the other side. There is, after all, no shortage of trivia books, but they are, almost universally, not encyclopedic in their content or format. Collections of startling facts can educate and amaze, but as a source of enlightenment they can be depressingly random. I have so often been infuriated by half-remembering something I have seen in a trivia book, and even recalling which book it was in, but then finding that there is no way anything can be looked up. What was the name of that fellow who had his first wife embalmed and used to ride round Hyde Park on a pony painted with purple spots? Where can you find a museum of umbrella covers? What do you call a point on your body that you cannot reach to scratch? In this encyclopedia, you can find out these things. Just look up 'embalming', 'umbrella' and 'scratching' and the cross-references will lead you to the right spot in no time.

Finally, there is another reason for my deciding to write this book, which far outweighs the two mentioned above. Because of my passion for absorbing odd pieces of information, I frequently find myself co-opted on to quiz teams, yet somehow my teams never seem to do as well as they ought. I have analysed the reasons for this and reached an inevitable conclusion: I would do far better if the people setting the questions knew the same things that I do. Often – and I can only presume it is because they are unacquainted with the really interesting facts in this book – the question setters ask mundane questions relating to popular culture, or chemistry, or medieval Peruvian poetry, which leave me completely at a loss.

Why can they not ask me instead the names of the goats that drew Thor's chariot, or who was the only US president to hold a patent, or what colour a Gentoo penguin's feet are? These and countless other facts are lodged in my head waiting for a quiz setter knowledgeable enough to demand them as answers. Now, finally, in one volume, all the facts have been put together to allow quiz setters to ask the sort of questions that will fascinate, challenge and allow my team to win.

In 1851, the painter John Ruskin said: 'Remember that the most beautiful things in the world are the most useless, peacocks and lilies, for instance.' I hope that, after browsing some of the entries on the pages that follow, you will agree with me that, as far as facts go, the most useless and pointless are also often the most beautiful.

Symbols used in this book:
Important dates are indicated by the symbol ★
Important statistical or numerical information is preceded by ☛
Cross-references are indicated with a signpost ☞

AA
As all good Scrabble players know, Aa is a type of volcanic lava. There are also rivers called Aa in France and Germany. Whether these are alphabetically the first places on earth depends on how you treat the accent on the town of Å in Norway.

AARDVARK
The aardvark (which means 'earth-pig') has specialised in eating termites for about the past 35 million years. They have only 20 teeth and their ears may be 10in long. The first aardvark born in captivity in the western hemisphere weighed 4lb 2oz.
★ It was born on 24 September 1967 in Miami.

ABORIGINE
In 1957, a research project at Darwin University attempted to discover why Aborigines stand on one leg to rest. In the course of the project, an orthopaedic surgeon interviewed several Aborigines, and some white

Australians were trained in techniques for standing on one leg. No firm conclusions were reached and further research is clearly needed.

In several Aborigine tribes, the traditional punishment for manslaughter was to be stabbed in the thigh by a tribal elder.

☞ ALBERT I, KOALA

ABORTION

The first country to legalise abortion was the USSR, which did so in 1920. In 1984 China had about 18 million births and nearly 9 million abortions.

In North America, beavers' testicles were once thought to be useful for procuring an abortion.

ACCIDENTS

More people suffer fatal falls in December in the UK than any other month, though you are most likely to drown in July, and most likely to be shot in November. You are also most likely to be killed in a road accident in December.

Research in the USA has shown that the average American is more likely to die from an asteroid hitting earth than as a result of a flood, but is more likely to die in an aircraft accident than from an asteroid impact. The precise probabilities of each event are: aircraft accident – one in 20,000; asteroid impact – one in 25,000; flood – one in 30,000. The chance of dying from food poisoning is one in 3 million.

☞ ALBERT I, AUSTRALIA, CALIFORNIA, CANADA, DEATH, DENTISTRY, DONKEY, ELEPHANT, HORSE, MENSTRUATION,

MOTORING, OPERA, PORTER, SKIING, TEETH, TRANS-
PLANTATION, TURKEY (country), WATER-SKIING

ACCORDION
The accordion was patented by Anthony Faas of
Philadelphia on 13 January 1854.

ACNE
According to a survey in 2004, 73 per cent of acne
sufferers would turn down a fortune if they could have
a perfect complexion.

ACNESTIS
The point on a mammal's back where it cannot reach to
scratch is called the 'acnestis'.

ADDAMS, Charles (1912–88)
The cartoonist Charles Addams, creator of The
Addams Family, liked to reply to fan mail on headed
notepaper that claimed to be from 'The Gotham Rest
Home for Mental Defectives'. He married his third
(and last) wife in a dog cemetery, with both bride and
groom dressed in black.

ADDRESS
In 1463, Paris became the first city to adopt house
numbers. London followed suit 300 years later.
☞ TAIWAN

ADMIRALTY ISLANDS
Natives of the Admiralty Islands in the Pacific are said to

3

have made cricket bats for generations from the wood of a tree grown from the artificial leg of the missionary Elisha Fawcett, who taught them to play cricket.

ADOLESCENCE

A study lasting 34 years at Northwestern University Medical School in Chicago confirmed that middle-aged men cannot remember their adolescent years. The research involved 67 men who were questioned first at age 14 and again at 48 regarding family relationships, home environment, dating and sexuality, religion, parental discipline and general activities. Their answers the first time were correlated with their memories 34 years later. The researchers reported that results showed that the likelihood of accurately remembering events from adolescence is no greater than chance.

ADULTERY

In ancient Greek, the meaning of the verb *rhaphanizo* is 'to thrust a radish up the fundament'. It was a punishment for adulterers. The penalty for an adulteress in Britain at the time of King Canute was to forfeit both nose and ears. In ancient India, however, an adulterer or adulteress only lost their nose.

AESCHYLUS (525–456BC)

The Greek writer of tragedies, Aeschylus, is reputed to have been killed when a tortoise fell on his head. An eagle carrying the tortoise is believed to have mistaken Aeschylus's bald head for a rock, and dropped the tortoise on it in an attempt to crack its shell.

AFGHANISTAN

From 1918 until 1991, Afghanistan was the only country on earth whose name began with A but did not end in A. After the Soviet Union collapsed, it was joined by Azerbaijan. However, Afghanistan still comes first if you arrange the nations of the world in alphabetical order.

The minaret of Jam in Afghanistan is the second tallest minaret in the world.

A traditional sport in northern Afghanistan is Buzkashi, a sort of polo without ball or polo stick in which horsemen try to dump a headless calf in the enemy goal. Buzkashi players are allowed to whip or kick the man holding the calf, but off-the-calf fouls are penalised.

Afghanistan is four and a half hours ahead of Greenwich Mean Time.

Between 80 and 90 per cent of the heroin sold in Europe comes from opium grown in Afghanistan.

☛ There are 47 airports (of which 10 have paved runways) and five heliports in Afghanistan. The average woman in Afghanistan gives birth to 5.64 children. There are 10 men over 65 in Afghanistan to every nine women.

AGATHOCLES (361–289BC)

Agathocles, the 'Tyrant of Syracuse', was the son of a potter. He is said to have died through using a toothpick poisoned by his enemies, at the age of 71.

Agathocles is also the name of a heavy metal band from the Belgian city of Mol.

AGE OF CONSENT

In England in 1576, 10-year-olds were allowed to marry.

This is the lowest the age of consent has ever been. In 1875, it rose from 12 to 13; in 1885 it went up from 13 to 16, where it has stayed ever since. The current age of consent for sexual activity between a man and a woman varies around the world from 12 in Mexico to 20 in Tunisia.

AIR HOSTESSES

Although air stewards had been operating since 1922, the first stewardess did not take off until 15 May 1930. She was Miss Ellen Church, of Iowa, who had herself written to United Airlines to suggest that suitably qualified young ladies might perform a useful function on flights. The airline was so impressed, they not only employed her but also gave her the job of drawing up qualifications for further recruits. Miss Church's specifications were clearly modelled on what she considered her own best points: applications would only be considered from registered nurses aged no more than 25. They must weigh no more than 115lb and not be more than 5ft 4in tall.

Britain was slow to follow the lead set by America, perhaps fearful of a repetition of the strong hostility to the air hostesses shown by US pilots' wives. The first British air hostess was Miss Daphne Kearley, who made her first flight on 16 May 1936. Typing and cocktail-mixing were among the skills required, though her own account of the job suggested that the work consisted mainly of calming down anxious passengers and turning down marriage proposals.

By the time BOAC began to recruit stewardesses in 1943, the principal qualifications were already less demanding. At the top of the list were 'poise' and an 'educated voice'.

'Stewardesses', incidentally, is the longest word that is typed entirely by the left hand of a competent typist on a standard keyboard. However, it is two letters shorter than the distinctly uncommon 'aftercataracts' (an eye condition that may follow an operation for cataracts) and 'tesseradecades' (groups of 14).

ALASKA

Alaska is the only state in the USA whose name can be typed on a single row of letters on a keyboard (cf PERU).

The Nenana Ice Classic is an Alaskan sweepstake that has been running since 1917. It started when bored railway engineers erected a wooden tripod on the frozen Tenana River and placed bets on the exact moment in spring when it would fall through the ice. It has taken place every year since and now attracts entrants from around the world, which has boosted the jackpot from an original $800 to around $300,000. A paper in the journal *Science* in 2001 was devoted to demonstrating that the records of the Nenana Ice Classic are a valid measure of global warming.

Alaska was purchased by the USA from Russia in 1867 for $7,200,000. This was less than the cost of making the film *North to Alaska* in 1960.

Until 1995 it was illegal to keep an elephant in Alaska. In that year, however, they changed the law regarding exotic pets specifically to allow an ex-circus elephant to stay there.

Under the Alaskan penal code 'wanton waste of a moose' is a class-A misdemeanour, equal in seriousness to drunken driving.

ALBANIA

In 1995, drivers in the northern Albanian city of Shkodra refused to pay a newly imposed traffic light tax of 2,000 lek (about £14) because their city had no traffic lights.

Albanian tennis player Imed Sejati laid a claim to be considered one of the least successful international sportsmen in history at the Mediterranean Games in Bari, Italy, in 1997. After watching his first-round Moroccan opponent serve four straight aces past him in the opening game, Sejati replied with four successive double faults. Then he retired, smiling.

There is only one heliport in Albania.

ALBERT I, King of Belgium (1875–1934)

King Albert I was killed in a climbing accident near Dinant in Belgium. His last reported words were: 'If I feel in good form, I shall take the difficult way up. If I do not, I shall take the easy one. I shall join you in an hour.'

ALCHEMY

The art and science of alchemy, which thrived from around 200BC until the 18th century, was founded on rational principles. Plato and Aristotle had developed a theory of matter that held everything to be made of earth, air, fire and water. Each of those in turn combined two of the primary qualities: hot, cold, wet and dry. Earth is cold and dry, air is hot and wet, fire is hot and dry, water is cold and wet. When fire loses its heat, it becomes earth – in the form of ash; when water is heated, it becomes air – in the form of steam. In principle, anything can therefore be turned into anything else by stripping it down to its basic components, then remixing them with a little heating, chilling, wetting or drying.

But to do it properly, it was necessary to have the Philosopher's Stone, which has the power to turn all things to gold. 'I have seen and handled more than once the Stone of the Philosophers,' said J.B. van Helmont. 'In colour it was like powder of saffron but heavy and shining even as powdered glass.' Van Helmont, incidentally, was a noted chemist who invented the word 'gas'.

The Stone, however, did not only turn base metal to gold. It was also believed to have the power of giving eternal life and transforming a person from earthly impurity into heavenly perfection. Here, however, we must make a distinction between exoteric (outward) and esoteric (hidden) alchemy. The former was concerned with the practical business of finding the Stone, concocting an Elixir of Life, making gold and living for ever. Esoteric alchemy, however, was a mystical and religious concept linked to the belief that only the pure of soul would be granted the divine grace needed to discover the Philosopher's Stone. Thus, the first objective became not so much transmuting metal into gold, but transmuting the sinful towards purity.

There are 15 alchemists listed in the *Dictionary of National Biography*, of whom the following deserve special mention:

Sir Thomas Ashton and **Sir Edmund de Trafford** who, in 1446, were given special privileges by Henry VI to continue their experiments. The King also forbade any of his subjects from molesting them.

Thomas Charnock (1526–81), who was bequeathed the secret of the Philosopher's Stone by an alchemist in Salisbury but was frustrated when his equipment perished in a fire in 1555. Two years later he again believed he was on the verge of success when he was called up for the relief of Calais.

Edward Kelley (1555–95), who claimed to have discovered the Philosopher's Stone among the ruins of Glastonbury Abbey. He had his ears cropped in the pillory at Lancaster after a conviction for forgery.

John Dee (1527–1608), who employed Kelley, never noticed the latter's mutilated ears (which were hidden beneath a skull cap). Dee sent Queen Elizabeth a piece of gold that he said he had made from metal cut from a warming pan, and gave his son quoits supposedly made from transmuted gold.

John Damian, who was court alchemist to James IV of Scotland. In 1507, he built himself a pair of wings and tried to fly from the ramparts of Stirling Castle but fell to the ground and broke a leg. He blamed the feathers he had used, which came from barnyard fowl unaccustomed to flying. Despite this failure, James IV still paid £15.16s.0d for his alchemist's gown of damask and £4 for his velvet socks.

Alchemy began to fade when Robert Boyle published *The Sceptical Chymist* in 1661, in some ways fulfilling Isaac Newton's prediction that science would lead away from alchemy and theology towards materialism and atheism. Its scientific respectability, however, was partly restored in the 1950s when Carl Jung represented the whole of alchemy as a basis for depth psychology. More recently, Beethoven's piano sonata Opus 110 has also been compared in structure to the symbolic patterns of alchemy, while J.K. Rowling's Opus 1, *Harry Potter and the Philosopher's Stone*, was called *Harry Potter and the Sorcerer's Stone* in the American edition, presumably because American children were thought unlikely to know what a philosopher was.

The French alchemist Nicholas Flamel, whose search for the Philosopher's Stone inspired much of Rowling's story, lived from 1330 to 1418. The house he built in 1407 is now considered the oldest building in Paris and is the site of a restaurant, the Auberge Nicolas Flamel. A set lunch there was priced at 11 euros in 2004.

ALCOHOL

Licensing laws are nothing new. Recent research has shown that, around 4,500 years ago, workers on the pyramids had three drink-breaks each day during which five types of beer and four varieties of wine were available.

Alcoholic drinks, however, date back still earlier. The sediment found in a pottery jar recently excavated in the Zagros mountains of northern Iran indicates that man was swigging a retsina-like wine in 5000BC. There is also evidence of beer-drinking in Mesopotamia around 8000BC, which is about the time that the woolly mammoth died out.

The word 'alcohol' has a curious history. Its original meaning, in the early 17th century, was a fine metallic powder, ore of antimony, used as eye make-up. The *OED* suggests a derivation from the Hebrew *ka-khal*, 'to stain'. By extension, alcohol came to mean any fine powder produced by grinding or distillation, then finally took on the meaning of a distilled liquid. Samuel Johnson's *Dictionary* defined alcohol as: 'an Arabic term used by chymists for a highly rectified dephlegmated spirit of wine, or for any thing reduced into an impalpable powder'. For chemists, however, an alcohol may be any of a wide class of organic compounds of which ethyl alcohol, C_2H_6O, is the one some of us know all too well.

Alcohol begins to interfere with the brain's ability to function properly when the blood–alcohol concentration exceeds 0.05 per cent – that is, 0.05g of alcohol per 100cc of blood. About half a pint of whisky will produce a concentration of 0.2 per cent, at which level the imbiber has difficulty in controlling his or her emotions and may tend to cry or laugh a lot and fall over if not prostrate already.

The Empress Catherine I of Russia banned women from getting drunk. This law has been cited as the main reason for the large numbers of female transvestites who attended Moscow balls, where wine ran freely. Catherine's husband and predecessor, Peter the Great, had the lover of one of his mistresses executed and his head preserved in alcohol and kept by his bedside.

Research on both humans and goldfish has shown that anything learned in a state of mild inebriation is liable to be forgotten when sobriety is restored. But a subsequent return to the inebriated state may be accompanied by a return of the forgotten memories. In other words, if you have forgotten something important that you learned when you were drunk, your best policy may well be to get drunk again. If you drank so much that you blacked out, however, all memories of what you said, did or learned while intoxicated are liable to vanish for ever, whether you are human or goldfish. (For further information, the reader should consult the paper 'The Use of Goldfish as a Model for Alcohol Amnesia in Man', by R.S. Ryback, in the *Quarterly Journal of Studies on Alcohol*, vol 30, 1969.)

Why some heavy drinkers become alcoholics and others appear not to develop an addiction is a matter still not fully understood, though recent studies of animal and human twins suggest a genetic predisposition to alcoholism. A particular gene on chromosome 11 is the thing to watch out for. Chronic alcoholism shrinks the left side of the brain.

There are fewer reliable studies of possible beneficial effects of alcohol, though mildly inebriated goldfish have been shown to learn simple tasks more quickly than sober goldfish.

As to the effects of alcohol on lechery, a Porter explains all to Macduff in Shakespeare's *Macbeth*: 'It provokes the desire, but it takes away the performance.' This has been confirmed in studies which show that alcohol increases subjective estimates of sexual arousal but diminishes physiological symptoms. (You may think you're aroused, but you're not really.)

According to a paper by W.H. Gantt in 1952, however ('Effect of Alcohol on the Sexual Reflexes or Normal and Neurotic Male Dogs', *Pyschosomatic Medicine*, vol 14), regulated doses of alcohol may have a therapeutic effect on premature ejaculation in a neurotic dog.

☞ BEQUESTS

ALDRIN, Edwin Eugene ('Buzz') (b. 1930)

In 1963, Buzz Aldrin received a doctorate from MIT for his thesis on orbital mechanics. He acquired the nickname 'Buzz' from a little sister's attempt to pronounce the word 'brother', which came out as 'Buzzer'.

☞ MOON

ALEXANDER I (1777–1825)

Tsar Alexander I of Russia considered trousers – instead of knee-breeches – to be subversive.

ALEXANDER III 'the Great' (356–23BC) King of Macedonia

Alexander the Great forbade his soldiers to wear beards, on the grounds that they were too easy to get hold of in a fight. Alexander slept until noon, could not swim and named a town after his favourite dog, Peritas. It was one of the now-extinct Mollosian breed, a sort of giant Rottweiler, used for fighting. Alexander's pet, according to legend, won fights against a lion and an elephant. Among the ruins of Pompeii, archaeologists have found mosaics depicting Mollosians outside people's homes with the message '*cave canem*'– 'beware of the dog'.

ALEXANDRA, Queen (1844–1925)

Wife of Edward VII, Queen Alexandra was left with a limp after an illness in 1867. Ladies at court copied the limp to be fashionable.

ALLIGATOR

In the US state of Michigan, it is illegal to chain an

alligator to a fire hydrant. This has often been cited as a curious law, but in fact it is illegal to chain anything to a fire hydrant in Michigan. There is no specific mention of alligators in Michigan's statutes.

ALPACA

The alpaca is a sort of soft-haired llama and comes mainly from Peru. Alpaca wool comes in 22 natural colours, the most of any wool-producing animal. A baby alpaca is called a cria.

ALPHABET

The dot above a letter 'i' is called a tittle.
☞ EZRA

AMERICA

Although America is generally believed to have been named after the explorer Amerigo Vespucci, recent evidence has been unearthed to suggest another claimant. Richard Amerike, a Bristol merchant, certainly knew about North America long before Columbus and Vespucci 'discovered' it. The Bristolians had been trading for years with Icelanders, buying salted cod that had been caught in Newfoundland. Not wanting to spread the word about their new fishing grounds, they kept it a secret. But Amerike was one of the major sponsors of John Cabot's voyages to North America, and recently found documents suggest that Cabot gave a map – perhaps with Amerike's name on it – to Columbus. A final piece of strong circumstantial evidence is Amerike's family banner: a flag in red, white and blue, depicting stripes and stars.

The first person to call the New World 'America' was the cartographer Martin Waldseemuller, who inscribed the new name on his map of the world engravings in 1507. Later in life, Waldseemuller is said to have changed his mind about the name, coming to the view that 'Columbia' might have been a better name, but by then the name of America had established itself too well to be altered. The country Colombia was given its name in 1819 by Simon Bolivar. In 1825 Bolivia was named after Bolivar, who was Venezuelan anyway.

☞ UNITED STATES

AMMONIA

The gas ammonia (NH_3) takes its name from the Egyptian god Ammon. In classical times, sal ammoniac (Ammonium Chloride) was discovered by accident through burning the dung of camels in the temple of Jupiter Ammon at Siwa oasis in Libya. The marine fossils known as ammonites also take their name from Ammon, in their case because their spiral structure is reminiscent of the ram's horns that Ammon is supposed to have had.

AMPUTATION

☞ CRICKET, LATVIA, NAPOLEON BONAPARTE, PORTER, SANTA ANNA, WIMBLEDON

ANAESTHETICS

In 2002, researchers at the University of Louisville reported that people with ginger hair require 20 per cent more anaesthetic before surgery than people with hair of another colour.

ANAGRAMS
Notable people whose names are anagrams of a single word include the actress Meg Ryan (Germany), former vice-president Al Gore (gaoler), the politician Clare Short (orchestral), the singer Roger Daltrey (retrogradely) and the actor Tom Cruise (costumier).

☞ FIZZY DRINKS, FOOT-AND-MOUTH DISEASE, LEWINSKY, RAILWAY, RUSEDSKI, SCOTT, SEA LION, SHAKESPEARE, SPEARS

ANCHOVY
Anchovy-flavoured popcorn was among the bedtime treats offered to cats at the Sutton Place Hotel in Vancouver, Canada, when it started its 'Pampered Pets' service in 1998.

The first screenplay Quentin Tarantino ever wrote was called 'Captain Peachfuzz and the Anchovy Bandit' written in 1985.

☞ CARUSO

ANDERSEN, Hans Christian (1805–75)
The great Danish writer of fairy tales, Hans Christian Andersen, was born two months after his parents married. He himself never married, but carried a letter from his first love, Riborg Voigt, in a pouch around his neck until he died. He had a big nose and parted his hair on the right. He never ate pork and when staying in hotels always carried a coil of rope with him in case he needed to escape from a fire.

ANDORRA

Andorra has no unemployment, no airports, no US Ambassador and the world's highest life expectancy at 83.51 years.

☞ INCOME TAX

St ANDREW

Andrew, the patron saint of Scotland, is also patron saint of Greece, Russia, Amalfi (Italy), fishmongers, fishermen, gout, spinsters, singers and sore throats.

He was the son of Jonah (according to St Matthew) or John (according to St John) and was a fisherman.

He was crucified in Greece by order of the Roman governor Aegeas or Aegeates, on 30 November AD60. According to a tradition that apparently began in the 14th century, the cross on which he was bound (not nailed) was decussate, i.e. x-shaped, from which the cross of St Andrew takes its form.

His relics were taken to Constantinople about AD357 and moved to the Cathedral at Amalfi in the 13th century, where most of them still remain.

According to legend, a Greek monk called St Rule was directed by an angel in AD357 to take what remains of St Andrew he could carry to the 'ends of the earth' for safekeeping. So he took them to Scotland. The place where St Rule came ashore later became St Andrews.

St Andrews University has no apostrophe in its name because it is the University of the town of St Andrews (without an apostrophe) rather than the University belonging to St Andrew.

St Andrews in Nova Scotia does not have an apostrophe, but St Andrew's in Newfoundland does.

ANIMAL NOISES
In Denmark pigs go 'knor'; in Germany horses go 'prrrh'; in ancient Greece, dogs went 'au au'.

Italians sneeze 'ecci ecci'.

☞ UKRAINE

ANORAK
The word 'anorak' comes from the Canadian Inuit *annuraaq*, meaning 'a piece of clothing'. It first appeared in English in 1924. The first recorded use of 'anorak' in its more recent sense of (as the *OED* puts it) 'a boring, studious, or socially inept young person' was in 1984.

★ On 23 September 1996, the Swedish artist Ann-Kristin Antman presented her design of an anorak made from salmon skins toughened and made waterproof by soaking in human urine. 'It is a method used in the Stone Age in Sweden,' she explained. 'The smell disappears when you rinse the skins in water.'

ANTARCTICA
Antarctica was given its name by the ancient Greeks, who called it 'Anti-Arktikos'. The literal meaning is 'opposite the bear': the Great Bear (Ursa Major) is above the North Pole. So, while the South became Anti-Arktikos, the North became identified with the bear, Arktikos. Until 1840, nobody was sure whether the Antarctic was a genuine continent or just a collection of islands linked by ice. In that

year the matter was resolved by the American explorer Lt
Charles Wilkes. After that, the name of Antarctica became
universal and the alternative name, Terra Australis Incognita
(the unknown southern land), faded away.

Present-day Antarctica contains between 1,000 and
4,000 people (depending on the season) from 27 nations
(the signatories to the Antarctic Treaty), around 100
million penguins and one active volcano, Mount Erebus.
The average annual precipitation (rain or snow) in the
interior of Antarctica is less than two inches, making it
drier than the Sahara desert.

In summer, almost the entire continent is covered by
ice with an average thickness of almost a mile. When
Antarctica freezes in winter, newly formed ice almost
doubles its area to about 30 million square miles. There
is about eight times as much ice in Antarctica as in the
Arctic. If all the ice in Antarctica melted, the global sea
level would rise by about 200ft.

★ On 14 October 1899, the Norwegian zoologist Nicolai
Hansen became the first person to be buried in Antarctica.

St APOLLONIA

St Apollonia is the patron saint of dentists and toothache
sufferers. Her martyrdom by the Romans in AD249
included having her teeth knocked out. In the Middle
Ages, relics claimed to be Apollonia's teeth were peddled
as cures for toothache. During the reign of Henry VI in
the 15th century, several tons of her alleged teeth were
collected in a bid to stop the scam.

APPLE

More than 40 million tons of apples are produced in the world each year. The largest producer is China, followed by the United States. Apples are the second most valuable fruit crop in the USA behind grapes.

There are over 7,000 varieties of apple in the world. The one that is said to have struck Isaac Newton and inspired the Theory of Gravity is a large green-skinned variety called 'Flower of Kent'.

☞ BURNT FOOD, HALLOWE'EN, HEDGEHOG, PUMPKIN, SCHILLER, SWAT, TWELFTH NIGHT

ARCHERY

The science of archery is known as toxophily, after a treatise on archery called *Toxophilus* written in 1545 by the English scholar Roger Ascham. Unscientific archery, however, is far older than this. The earliest known use of bows and arrows in warfare was in 2340BC, when Sargon of Akkad in Babylonia defeated the Sumerians with an infantry of archers.

In the 1900 Olympic archery, live pigeons were used as targets.

Useful archery vocabulary:

- *kisser button*: a device attached to a bowstring that touches the archer's lips when the string is drawn fully back.
- *gakgung*: the traditional bow in Korean archery. It is made out of buffalo horn, cow sinew, bamboo, mulberry wood, oak wood, fish bladder and white birch bark.
- *quarrel*: a crossbow arrow.

- *a Robin Hood*: The feat of firing one's arrow into the shaft of another which is already in the target.

Great archers:

- Lottie Dod (1871–1960) won Wimbledon when she was 15, won the English Ladies Golf Championship in 1904; and took silver in the Olympic archery in 1908.
- Geena Davis, the Oscar-winning actress, reached the semi-finals of the US women's archery championship in 1999 and was eventually placed 24th overall.

☞ FOOTBALL, St GEORGE, GOLF, OLYMPIC GAMES

ARGENTINA

Argentina has become a popular venue for unusual international congresses. In 1995, the first International Housewives Congress was held in Buenos Aires, and in 1966 the Free Tramps Federation staged the first World Tramps Congress in the seaside resort of Mar del Plata. Among the proposals suggested at the latter event was the official introduction of an International Day of Idleness on 2 May as a response to Labour Day on 1 May.

The Argentine lake duck has the largest penis of any bird.

☞ CHANNEL, PERU, SHOES

ARISTOTLE (384–322BC)

'There was never a great genius without a tincture of madness' – Aristotle.

☞ ALCHEMY, FISH, HAIR, PREGNANCY, SEX, TEETH, UNICORN

ARMADILLO

The nine-banded armadillo is the only animal other than the human that can suffer from leprosy.

☞ DINOSAUR

ARMOUR

Under a statute of 1313, it is illegal for a British Member of Parliament to enter the House of Commons wearing full armour.

☞ HENRY VIII, SPIDER

ARTICHOKE

Castroville, California, calls itself the Artichoke Capital of the World. The first Artichoke Queen of Castroville, crowned in 1947, was Marilyn Monroe.

ASCOT

Ascot Racecourse dates back to 1711, when Queen Anne decided a patch of land in an area called East Cote was ideal for 'horses to gallop at full stretch'. In 1813, Parliament passed an 'Act of Enclosure' ensuring that Ascot Heath, though crown property, would be kept and used as a public racecourse in perpetuity. However, some of the regulations for the week of Royal Ascot are still very strict:

In the 1920s women in the Royal Enclosure were forbidden to smoke. Divorcees were first banned from the Royal Enclosure until 1955, but convicted criminals and undischarged bankrupts are still banned.

Traditionally, when the reigning monarch finishes lunch in the Royal Box, everyone else must stop eating.

The late Princess of Wales is the only woman to have been allowed in the Royal Enclosure bare-legged.

ASHES, The
The concept of the Ashes cricket trophy dates back to 1882, when England's first home cricket defeat by Australia led to a mock obituary in the *Sporting Times*: 'In affectionate remembrance of English cricket, which died at the Oval on 29th August, 1882.' A note at the end added: 'The body will be cremated and the ashes taken to Australia.' Until the following year, however, there were no physical ashes. Those now found inside the urn at Lord's Cricket Ground in London are from the bails burned after an English victory in Australia in 1883. Mindful of the obituary the previous year, two Australian sisters burned the bails to give the English some ashes to return to the motherland.

ASH WEDNESDAY
Until 1715, Ash Wednesday was marked in the royal household in Britain by an officer called the King's Cock Crower imitating a cockerel, in remembrance of St Peter being called back to repentance by a cock crow. The tradition was dropped when the Prince of Wales (later George II), whose English was far from perfect, took the display as some form of offensive lunacy.

ASTROLOGY
According to a survey by Touchline Insurance in the UK in 1998, people born under the sign of Sagittarius make fewer insurance claims than those born under any other

sign. Cancer, Aquarius and Aries make the highest number of claims, but people born under Capricorn were revealed as the clumsiest, with the highest number of claims for accidental damage.

According to a more recent survey, Australians born under the sign of Gemini are most likely to be involved in road accidents.

ASTRONAUTS
According to NASA, the items most missed by astronauts on space missions are pizza, ice cream and fizzy drinks.
☞ POTATO

ASTRONOMY
The sun contributes 99.87 per cent of the weight of the entire solar system. If you want to remember the order of the planets around the sun, one recommended mnemonic is the sentence 'MEn Very Easily MAke Jugs Serve Useful Nocturnal Purposes' (Mercury, Venus, Earth, Mars, Jupiter, Saturn, Uranus, Neptune, Pluto). If the 2004 discovery of the so-called 'tenth planet' Sedna is accepted, this may be modified by adding the word 'Sometimes'.
☞ COMPUTATION, HOLES, MARS

ATHLETICS
The word 'athlete' comes originally from a Greek verb meaning 'to compete for a prize'. The Welsh athlete Griffith Morgan ran 12 miles in 53 minutes in 1732. He won a prize of 100 sovereigns, but fell and died when slapped on the back in congratulations.

On 24 April 1909, Harry Hillman and Lawson Robertson set a record that has still not been broken: they ran the 100-yard three-legged race in 11.0 seconds. It is illegal to run a three-legged race for money in British Columbia, Canada.

☞ St KITTS and NEVIS, OLYMPIC GAMES, SEX TEST, SPORT, TRANSPLANTATION

ATLANTIC

The word 'Atlantic' originally referred to Mount Atlas in Libya. It was subsequently applied to the sea near the west coast of Africa, and finally to the whole ocean.

There are as many molecules in a teaspoon of water as there are teaspoons of water in the Atlantic.

In 1957 the US air force completed a survey of the Atlantic Ocean but refused to divulge its width on the ground that the information might be of military use to the Russians.

In 1995, two Englishmen – Jason Lewis and Steve Smith – became the first to cross the Atlantic from east to west on a pedalo.

● The Atlantic Ocean contains 23 per cent of the world's seawater. The Pacific contains 48 per cent.

☞ LINDBERGH, PANAMA, QUEEN MARY, TEETH

ATOMIC ENERGY

The word 'atom' comes from a Greek word *atomon*, meaning 'that which cannot be divided'. The name was proved inaccurate in 1932 when John Cockcroft and E.T.S. Walton split the atom. In 1933, Ernest Rutherford said, 'Energy produced by the breaking down of the atom is a very poor kind of thing. Anyone who expects a source of power from the transformation of these atoms is talking moonshine.'

The first atom bomb released 1,000,000,000,000,000,000,000 ergs of energy. Einstein commented, 'The release of atom power has changed everything except our way of thinking.' He went on to say, 'If only I had known, I should have become a watchmaker.'

AUGUSTUS (63BC–AD14)
The Roman Emperor Augustus was 5ft 7in tall and wore thick-soled shoes so that he would look taller. According to the historian Suetonius, his teeth were small, few in number and decayed. He softened the hairs on his legs by singeing them with red-hot walnut shells and he carried a seal-skin amulet, which he believed protected him from his greatest fear – lightning.

AUSTEN, Jane (1775–1817)
Jane Austen was the earliest known writer to use the expression 'dinner party'. According to her niece, she always wore a cap.
☞ BASEBALL, LAVATORIES, MARRIAGE

AUSTRALIA
In Australia, December is the least common month for births but the most common month for conceptions to occur.

The highest mountain and the largest city in Australia are both named after men who never visited the country. The highest mountain is Mount Kosciuszko, named after a Polish patriot who fought alongside Washington in the American Civil War, and the largest city is named after Lord Sydney.

The first man to fly an aeroplane in a public display in Australia was the escapologist Harry Houdini.

The Indian cobra is the 15th most deadly snake on earth; the top 14 are all found in Australia.

The first Australian animals in space were spiders that perished on the US shuttle *Columbia* in 2003.

☞ ABORIGINE, ASTROLOGY, CAMEL, CHEESE, CROCODILE, DINGO, DINOSAUR, DUBLIN, ECHIDNA, FIDGETING, ICE CREAM, IRELAND, KANGAROO, KOALA, NAVEL, OCTOPUS, PENGUIN, PIZZA, PLATYPUS, QUEENSLAND, SARDINE, SWIMMING, TEETH, TORTOISE, TOURISM, TRANSPORT

AUSTRIA

The first international tennis tournament for over–85s was held in Austria in 1998.

The world's biggest liver dumpling was cooked in the Austrian village of Zams on 16 September 1996. It weighed 1.8 tonnes.

☞ GEORGE II, THIRTEEN, WIMBLEDON

AZERBAIJAN

The first time Pope John Paul II stayed in a hotel was during his visit to Azerbaijan in 2002.

☞ AFGHANISTAN

AZTECS

☞ CELIBACY, CHOCOLATE, MONTEZUMA II

BABBAGE, Charles (1792–1871)

The mathematician and computer pioneer Charles Babbage wrote to Alfred Lord Tennyson to express annoyance at the poet's lines 'Every moment dies a man, every moment one is born.' Babbage argued that, if this were true, the world population would remain constant. As he pointed out, the correct version should, at the time of writing, have said: '... every moment one and one-sixteenth is born'.

☞ COMPUTATION

BABIES

Research has shown that men are better than women at detecting the smell of newborn babies. Trials at the Munich Institute of Medical Psychology in 2001 showed that men were more successful than women at correctly identifying from the smell whether T-shirts had been worn by babies or older children.

☞ BALI, PREGNANCY, SEX, SMELL, STRAWBERRY, TEETH

BACH, Johann Sebastian (1685–1750)

★ J.S. Bach died on 28 July 1750. Vivaldi died on 28 July 1741.

The last direct descendant of J.S. Bach was his grandson Wilhelm Friedrich Ernst Bach, who died on Christmas Day 1845 at the age of 86. He was the only one of Bach's grandsons to make his living as a composer.

BACHELORS

In ancient Sparta, men who were still unmarried at the age of 30 forfeited the right to vote. This contrasts strongly with 19th-century America, where James Buchanan, despite being a bachelor, was elected President in 1857. While he was in office, his niece, Harriet Lane, served as First Lady. No other bachelor has ever become President of the USA.

☞ ITALY, MARRIAGE, OSTRICH

BACON, Francis (1561–1626)

After being fined £40,000 for accepting bribes while he was Lord Chancellor, Francis Bacon devoted his life to science and knowledge. He died from a severe cold in 1626, which he is said to have contracted while attempting to stuff a chicken with snow in an early attempt to invent frozen food.

☞ URINE

BAGHDAD

☞ PYRAMID

BAHAMAS

There are around 700 islands in the Bahamas, of which only 30 are inhabited. One of those islands was probably the first sight of the New World discovered by Christopher Columbus in 1492.

The first Governor of the Bahamas was a former pirate named Woodes Rogers. He is remembered as the captain of the ship that rescued Alexander Selkirk – the original Robinson Crusoe – from the island of Juan Fernandez.

Perry Christie, who became Prime Minister of the Bahamas in 2002, won a bronze medal in the triple jump at the Central American and Caribbean Games in 1962.

☞ BRANDING, INCOME TAX

BAHRAIN

☞ INCOME TAX

BALFOUR, Arthur (1848–1930)

☞ DAYLIGHT SAVING

BALI

The Balinese traditionally forbid sex to the sick or malformed. Another traditional Balinese belief is that hurried love-making will result in deformed babies.

BALLET

Two thousand ballet-goers were evacuated from London's Royal Opera House one evening in 2001 when a fire alarm was triggered by an exploding baked potato.

☞ EPONYM

BALLIOL COLLEGE, Oxford
☞ CHOCOLATE

BALLOON

The toy balloon owes its invention to Michael Faraday who used balloons to store gases produced in his chemical experiments in 1824.

★ On 4 June 1784, the opera singer Madame Thible became the first woman to fly in a Montgolfier balloon. The King of Sweden was among those watching. She was accompanied by Monsieur Fleurant after whom the balloon was named Le Fleurant.

The first living creatures to fly in a hot-air balloon were a sheep, a cockerel and a duck, sent aloft by the Mongolfier brothers in September 1783. All survived the flight, but the cockerel broke a wing, probably the result of its being kicked by the sheep.

The first recorded manned flight was made two months later by Jean Francois Pilatre de Rozier and the Marquis d'Arlandes. The balloon caught fire but both were unharmed.

Another pioneer balloonist who narrowly avoided disaster was Jacques Charles, who also made a flight from Paris in 1783. When he drifted low over fields, his balloon was attacked by farmers who thought he must be the Devil. He placated them with champagne.

In 1808, two men called de Grandpré and le Pique had a duel from balloons after a dispute over a woman. Le Pique's balloon was shot and he crashed to his death.

Brian Jones and Bertrand Piccard became the first

people to fly round the world in a balloon in 1999. It took them 19 days, 12 hours and 47 minutes.

The US publisher Malcolm Forbes has a collection of oddly shaped hot-air balloons, including one shaped like a Harley-Davidson motorcycle, and another in the shape of a bust of Beethoven.

☞ CHANNEL, WASHINGTON

BALZAC, Honoré de (1799–1850)

Suckled by a wet-nurse, the author Balzac did not meet his rich mother until he was four years old. He owned a huge circular bed and designed his own coat of arms, featuring a naked woman and a cockerel.

He liked to begin work at midnight and write for 18 hours at a stretch, staying awake by drinking 50 cups of coffee. A typical meal for the writer comprised 100 oysters, 12 lamb cutlets, a duckling, two roast partridges, various fruits and – of course – coffee.

BANANA

The banana plant is the largest known plant without a solid trunk. Botanically it is not a fruit but a berry. If we do classify them as fruit, however, bananas are by weight the world's second highest fruit crop, just ahead of grapes but behind oranges. They contain more vitamin B6 than any other fresh fruit. This is the vitamin most commonly associated with creating a good mood and may provide some justification for the latin name for the banana, which is *Musa sapientum*, which means 'fruit of the wise men'.

India and Brazil produce more bananas than any other countries.

Elephants in Burma have been known to silence bells hung round their neck by clogging them with mud so they won't be heard when stealing bananas.

In February 1946, a girl in Bridlington died after eating four bananas from among the first crop to reach Britain's shops after the war.

Mait Lepik won the first Banana-Eating championship in Estonia in 1997 by eating 10 bananas in three minutes. His secret was to save time by eating the skins as well. The world record for the most bananas eaten in one hour is 81.

★ Bananas first went on sale in Britain on 10 April 1633. Three hundred and forty-seven years and one day later, Dr Canaan Banana became President of Zimbabwe.

☞ COLOMBIA, SHOPPING TROLLEYS, TEA

BANGLADESH
Bangladesh is the most crowded country on earth, with 2,639 people per square mile.

In February 1986, Bangladesh launched a campaign to hunt rodents that were destroying food crops worth £350 million a year. The government offered a bounty of about £7 for every 1,000 bodies of dead rodents.

☞ EXAMINATIONS, MUGGING

BARCELONA
In 1997, Spain's first dating agency for pets opened in Gerona, near Barcelona. The manager of 'Happy Animals' said they would concentrate on dogs, cats and birds at first, but may branch out to snakes later.

☛ Statistical information (2004 figures):

- 1,308: number of kilometres of roads in Barcelona.
- 12,650: pounds sterling fetched at auction in 1999 for the rose-pink Lycra corset with satin conical cups worn by Madonna at a concert in Barcelona in 1990.
- 355,671: number of trees in Barcelona.
- 2,412,560: number of square metres of cemeteries in Barcelona
- 3,378,635: number of tourists who visited Barcelona in 2001.
- 7,969,496: number of nights they spent in the city, which is an average of 2.36 nights per tourist.

BAR CODES

The first three digits of a 13-digit bar code (the standard type on products sold in Europe) identifies the country of origin. For example, codes beginning 000 to 139 are from the USA or Canada; 300 to 379 indicate France; 400 to 440 is Germany; 500 to 509 is the UK. And to add a few from further afield, 484 is Moldova, 609 is Mauritius, 740 is Guatemala and 865 is Mongolia. This national identifier, however, gives only the country of origin of the bar code itself, not necessarily the product it is attached to. Irrespective of the nation of origin, newspapers and magazines always have a code beginning 977 and books are 978.

If you add together the first, third, fifth, seventh, ninth, eleventh and thirteenth digits of a bar code, then add to that three times the sum of the second, fourth, sixth, eighth, tenth and twelfth digits, the answer will always be divisible by ten.

For example: a bottle of made-in-England Parker Quink ink has the bar code 5011247021678 (note the 501 at the start, indicating British origin). The sum of the odd digits is $5 + 1 + 2 + 7 + 2 + 6 + 8 = 31$. Three times the even digits is 3 x $(0 + 1 + 4 + 0 + 1 + 7) = 3$ x $13 = 39$. Add this to 31 and we get 70, which is 7 x 10.

★ On 26 June 1974, in Troy, Ohio, a package of Wrigley's chewing gum was the first item to be scanned by a bar-code reader.

BARRIE, Sir James Matthew (1860–1937)

J.M. Barrie, the author of *Peter Pan*, stopped growing at the age of 15. He was impotent, ambidextrous and invented the name 'Wendy'.

BASEBALL

According to the paper 'Life Expectancy of Major League Baseball Umpires', published in the journal *The Physician and Sports Medicine* in May 2000, baseball umpires have exactly the same life expectancy as anyone else.

The earliest recorded use of the word 'baseball' in English is in Jane Austen's *Northanger Abbey*.

☞ BENFORD'S LAW, BUSH, DOLPHIN, St KITTS and NEVIS

BASKETBALL

Basketball was invented by the Canadian physical fitness instructor James Naismith in Massachusetts,

USA, in 1891, supposedly to keep his football players occupied during the winter.

☞ FISHING

BAT

In 1943 the US army developed a new incendiary bomb involving bats with napalm strapped to their wings. The bat bomb project was abandoned in 1944, after the USA pinned their faith on the atom bomb instead.

☞ BAUDELAIRE, DICKENS

BATMAN

In a phone-in poll in 1988, readers of *Batman* comics voted by 5,343 to 5,271 to have Robin the Boy Wonder killed by the Joker.

BAUDELAIRE, Charles Pierre (1821–67)

The favourite foods of the French poet and critic Baudelaire were onion soup and bacon omelette. He kept a pet bat in a cage on his desk and died of syphilis.

BEANS

Every hour, 38.5 tons of baked beans are eaten in Britain. The average Briton eats four times as many baked beans as the average American. It is the Irish, however, and not the British who eat the most baked beans per capita: an impressive 5.6kg (12lb 5oz) each every year.

☞ CHIPS, LIVER

BEARD

The longest ever beard was that of the Norwegian Hans Langseth – it stretched 5.33m (17ft 6in) when measured on his death in Kensett, Iowa, in 1927. The beard was presented to the Smithsonian Institution in Washington in 1967. The average human beard, if left untended, will grow 14cm a year.

☞ ALEXANDER III, HAIR, MERKIN, SANTA CLAUS, SWEDEN, UNITED STATES,

BEAUTY

The scientific unit of beauty is the millihelen, defined as the amount of beauty required to launch one ship. (The argument is that, if Helen of Troy had a face that launched 1,000 ships, a millihelen must be enough for one.) According to research at the Polytechnic University of Hong Kong, the best measurement of a woman's attractiveness is given by taking her volume in cubic metres and dividing it by the square of her height. Sadly the researchers did not give any conversion formula between this measurement and the result in millihelens.

King Philip the Fair of France (1268–1314) had such high standards of beauty that he made skin diseases a punishable offence.

★ The first International Beauty Contest was held in Folkestone on 14 August 1908.

☞ CAMBODIA, CAMEL, CLEOPATRA, COSMETICS, CRUSTACEAN

BEAVER

It has been calculated that a beaver 68ft long with a 51ft tail could have built the Kariba dam. The testicles of a beaver are internal. Despite the difficulties posed by that arrangement, minced beavers' testicles were sometimes added to tobacco in the olden days in North America to sweeten the flavour.

☞ ABORTION, DINOSAUR, PLATYPUS

BED

Research in 2001 showed that couples with beds less than two years old are far more likely to share intimate secrets with each other at bedtime than those whose beds were eight years old or more.

☞ BALZAC, CHRISTMAS, DANDELION, DICKENS, FRANKLIN, LOUIS XIV, LOVE, OBESITY, PHOBIAS, PORTER, SHAKESPEARE, SHOES

BEE

Until the late 17th/early 18th century, queen bees were thought to be kings. Bees cannot see the colour red – it looks the same as black to them.

☞ St BERNARD

BEER

The total amount of beer drunk in the world in 2002 was a record 141.56 billion litres. The United States was the biggest consumer with 23.82 billion litres, followed by China with 23.50 billion litres. The biggest consumers per head of population, however, are the Czechs, who each drink more than 35 gallons of beer a year. The British drink 21 gallons each, and the habit seems to be an old one: records show that the weekly ration allocated to each child in Norwich children's hospital in 1632 included two gallons of beer. Deprivation from beer is also an old British punishment. Among the regulations applying to Officers of the Bedchamber at the court of Henry VIII was this: 'Such pages as cause the maids of the King's household to become mothers shall go without beer for a month.'

Beer also has a fine tradition across the Irish Sea. One of the miracles that led to the canonisation of the 16th-century abbess St Brigid of Ireland was her feat of transforming her bath water into beer for visiting clerics.

There is a type of flea that lives and breeds only in beer mats in Germany. Octopuses in Monterey Bay in California have shown no particular fondness for beer mats but have been observed making their homes in discarded beer cans. The hobby of collecting beer mats is called tegestology.

Louis Pasteur developed pasteurisation for beer more than 20 years before he did it for milk.

The Sumerian goddess of beer was called Ninkasi.

☞ ALCOHOL, DUBLIN, DRUNKEN DRIVING, GHOSTS, OCTOPUS, TWELFTH NIGHT, WIFE-CARRYING, ZAMBIA

BEETHOVEN, Ludwig van (1770–1827)

Beethoven was 5ft 5in tall. When drinking coffee, he insisted that every cup was prepared from exactly 60 coffee beans. His last words are said to have been: 'Pity, pity, too late,' when he was delivered a crate of wine from his publisher.

★ On 26 October 1996, Daniel Barenboim conducted

a curious performance in Berlin's Potsdamerplatz, which involved 19 construction cranes swaying back and forth in time with a tape of Beethoven's Ninth Symphony. The concert was held to celebrate the completion of a building project.

☞ ALCHEMY, BALLOON, MUSIC

BELGIUM

In some parts of Belgium, cabbage is eaten on Shrove Tuesday in the belief that this will save other cabbages from being eaten by caterpillars and flies. Belgium is the only western country never to have imposed film censorship for adults. In 2001, Belgium was the only country in the world whose government had more female ministers than male.

There was no Christmas Day in Flanders in 1582: in that year they made their change from the Julian to Gregorian calendar and omitted the last 10 days of the year from 22 to 31 December.

The Belgian hare is not a hare but a rabbit.

☞ ALBERT I, DEMOCRATIC REPUBLIC OF THE CONGO, EURO, FROGS, HIPPOPOTAMUS, LEGS, METEOROLOGY, STRAWBERRY, St SWITHUN

BELL, Alexander Graham (1847–1922)

Alexander Graham Bell's patent for the telephone modestly titles the invention as 'Improvement in Telegraphy'. When he tried to sell this patent to Western Union in 1876, he was turned down with the words: 'This electrical toy has far too many shortcomings to ever be considered a practical means of communication.'

When President James Garfield was shot in 1881, Bell was summoned to devise a way to search for the bullet. He quickly devised an electromagnet device to locate its position in Garfield's body but it was impossible to save the President's life.

In 1919, Bell collaborated on a hydrofoil design that set a world water speed record that was not broken until 1963.

While those inventions were undoubtedly successful, Bell's claim to have been the first to invent a working telephone is open to challenge on various grounds:

Firstly, he only beat Elisha Gray to registering a preliminary patent in February 1876 by a couple of hours. Subsequent research suggests that the device described in Gray's patent would have worked while Bell's would not.

Secondly, documents unearthed in London's Science Museum in 2003 appear to confirm that the German Philipp Reis had invented a working telephone in 1863.

Thirdly, the US House of Representatives passed a motion in 2002 crediting the Italian Antonio Meucci with the invention of the telephone as long ago as 1849.

★ The date of Bell's patent – number 174,465 – was 7 March 1876. It is supposedly the most valuable patent of all time.

BENFORD'S LAW
First stated by Dr Frank Benford in 1938, this is the law that tells us, paradoxically, that numbers are far more likely to begin with a '1' than any other digit.

Benford first confirmed this experimentally by

looking at tables of statistics from a variety of sources – lengths of rivers, heights of mountains, street numbers in addresses, baseball averages, areas of countries – then reasoned out the process by which so many began with the digit '1'.

Effectively, all numbers arise from a counting process. Counting up to nine uses each digit once (we exclude zero as a possible starting digit). From 10 to 19, everything begins with 1, which puts 1 in a big lead. All the others have caught up by the time we get to 99, but from 100 to 199, the '1' numbers storm ahead again. The same thing happens from 1,000 to 1,999. With all the other digits always playing catch-up, whatever range a group of finite numbers inhabits, those beginning with 1 are likely to be ahead.

In fact, both theory and practice suggest that the percentage of randomly selected statistics beginning with each digit are as shown in the following table:

1	2	3	4	5	6	7	8	9
30.1	17.6	12.5	9.7	7.9	6.7	5.8	5.1	4.6

BENTHAM, Jeremy (1748–1832)

Philosopher and social reformer Jeremy Bentham kept a cat, which he named the Reverend Sir John Langbourne and fed on macaroni. When the cat died, Bentham buried it in his garden, but donated his own body to science, inviting his friends to watch its dissection. He also instructed that the skeleton be later reconstructed as an 'Auto-Icon' – a mixture of mummy and waxwork of himself – dressed in his own clothes, seated in his favourite chair, and holding his favourite walking stick, which he called 'Dapple'. He also suggested that, if his friends would like to meet for the purpose of paying respect to him, he would like his executor to arrange for his body to be wheeled in to join them. His wishes were followed, though the model was made with a wax head rather than Bentham's own skull, which had deteriorated too badly. In 1850, the body was moved to University College, London, where it can still be seen.

BEQUESTS

When David Davis of Clapham, London, died in 1778 he left five shillings to Mary David 'to enable her to get drunk for the last time at my expense'.

☞ CAT

BERGMAN

The 1978 film *Autumn Sonata* was the last film made by the great Swedish actress Ingrid Bergman (1915–82). It was directed by the great Swedish film-maker Ingmar Bergman (born 1918, no relation) and was shot in Norway after accusations of tax evasion forced the director out of his native country.

★ Ingrid Bergman died on her 67th birthday on 29 August 1982.

St BERNARD of Montjoux (c.923–1008)

St Bernard of Montjoux, after whom the dog is named, is the patron saint of Alpinists, mountaineers and skiers and should not be confused with St Bernard of Clairvaux, who is patron saint of beekeepers, bees, candlemakers, chandlers, Gibraltar, Queens College Cambridge, wax melters and wax refiners. St Bernard of Montjoux founded hospices for climbers and organised patrols to rid the Alps of robbers.

BHUTAN
The official language of Bhutan is Dzongkha. The currency is the ngultrum, which is composed of 100 cheltrum.

BIBLE
The 46th word of Psalm 46 is 'shake' and the 46th word from the end of the same Psalm is 'spear'. William Shakespeare was 46 when the King James Bible was being translated; the above 'coincidence' in Psalm 46 was presumably a birthday present from the translators.

The animal most frequently mentioned in the Old Testament is the sheep, followed by the lamb, lion, ox, ram, horse, bullock, ass, goat and camel. The most common name is David, which occurs over a thousand times. The longest name in the Bible, however, is that of Isaiah's son Mahershalalhashbaz.

The words 'girl' and 'girls' each occur only once in the entire Authorised Version. The word 'eternity' also occurs only once in the Bible.

☛ In the 19th century, theologian Thomas Hartwell Horne counted word frequencies in the Bible and announced that the word 'and' occurred 35,543 times in the Old Testament and 10,684 in the New Testament.

He miscounted the Old badly: the true figure is 40,975; but he was only 37 short in the New.

☞ BOOKS, BRAIN, CEMETERIES, CHEESE, COW, ETHIOPIA, EZRA, HIPPOPOTAMUS, PRUNE, RAIN, ROULETTE

BILLIARDS

The first definite account of the existence of a billiard table was found in a 1470 inventory of the possessions of King Louis XI of France. His table was said to have comprised a bed of stone, a cloth covering and a hole in the middle of the playing field, into which balls could be driven. Mary, Queen of Scots, was also a keen player and complained when she was not allowed use of her billiard table when she was imprisoned. After her execution, her body was wrapped in the cloth from her billiard table.

The only mention of billiards in Shakespeare is in *Antony and Cleopatra* (Act II, scene v) when Cleopatra says to her maid: 'Let's to billiards, come Charmian.'

In 1873, billiards became the first game or sport to hold an official world championship. It was won by a Frenchman called Gamier. The second recreation to have a world championship was chess in 1886.

★ On 7 December 1873, 'The quaintest billiard match ever played' is said to have taken place between Mr Jefferson of America and William Dufton of England. Dufton played with his cue, as normal, but Jefferson played the balls with his nose and won by a margin of 47 points.

BIRMINGHAM

A survey in 1999 revealed that holiday-making Britons

who make love on a foreign beach are more likely to be from Birmingham than any other part of the country. Asked to explain this, a researcher said, 'There aren't many beaches in Birmingham, so it's a bit of a novelty.'

In French slang, 'être de Birmingham' means to be bored to death.

☛ There are 22 more miles of canal in Birmingham than in Venice.

☞ WINDOW

BIRTH
Every 17 seconds, an American is born.

BIRTHDAY
'Happy Birthday to You' was composed by Mildred and Patty Hill in 1936. It is therefore still in copyright and should not be sung in public without the payment of a royalty.

☞ BIBLE, BOWIE, MANDELA, MICKEY MOUSE, NEEDLE, NOBEL PRIZE, ROSSINI, SONGS, SWEDEN

BISCUITS
The word 'biscuit' comes from the French for 'twice cooked'.

In September 2001, a biscuit taken from the *Titanic* before her ill-fated maiden voyage fetched £3,525 at auction in London. Sotheby's catalogue described the biscuit as 'in almost perfect condition with signs of moulding'.

The World Biscuit Throwing Championship is held annually at the Glendale Country Show near Wooler,

Northumberland. Contestants have to throw a McVitie's Rich Tea Biscuit as far as they can. The biscuits must be perfectly round and un-nibbled. All biscuits are examined closely before they are tossed. The winner receives the Biscuit Medal, a Rich Tea thickly dunked in varnish.

In 1991 a VAT tribunal ruled that a Jaffa cake is not a biscuit, thus saving Jaffa 17.5 per cent tax.

The reason biscuit tins are not square is to enable them to be stacked inside each other to save space when being transported.

☞ FOOD, TELEVISION

BLANKET
The first weaving looms in Bristol were established by Thomas Blanket in 1337. However, the story that he gave his name to bedclothes is probably untrue, since the word 'blanket' dates back even earlier. It is more likely that his family took their name from the industry.

☞ GHOSTS

BLINDNESS
In 1985, a policeman in Chesapeake, Virginia, who was almost run off the road by a weaving car stopped the vehicle expecting to find a drunken driver. He was right, except that the driver was also blind. He was aged 24 and had lost his sight at the age of 12.

☞ BULGARIA, CAT, EVEREST, GOLDFISH, MOUNTAINEERING

BLUEBOTTLE
☞ BUCKLAND

BLYTON, Enid Mary (1897–1968)

With over 700 books and 10,000 short stories to her name, Enid Blyton (born Enid Darrell-Waters) is probably the most prolific author of all time. One of her daughters said that Blyton was so busy writing about happy children in pretty, sunlit worlds, she had no time for her own children; her other daughter described her as a mother who picked her up from school, took her on a wonderful walks and read her the adventures of the Famous Five direct from the typewriter.

Enid Blyton created Noddy in 1949 and the Noddy books remained unchanged for 40 years until 1989 when the golliwogs were changed to goblins to avoid charges of racism. Scandinavian countries then protested, taking the change as an insult to trolls. Political correctness intervened again when Noddy went to America, as Big Ears had his name changed to Whitebeard to avoid offending the aurally advantaged.

Noddy is known as Oui Oui in France, Doddi in Iceland, Purzelknirps in Germany and Hilitos in Spain.

BOB
☞ COLORADO

BODY

The average adult human body contains 15lb of hydrogen, 27lb of carbon and 97lb of oxygen.

Parts of the body that you may not have realised have names include the following:

• *Columella*: the partition between the nostrils.

- *Glabella*: the smooth part of the forehead above the eyebrows.
- *Nasion*: the point where your nose meets your forehead.
- *Niddick*: the nape of the neck.
- *Philtrum*: the groove down the middle of your upper lip.
- *Popliteal*: the hollow at the back of the knee.
- *Rhinarium*: the tip of a nose, especially a mammal's cold, wet nose.

BODYGUARD

The first meeting of the World Association of Bodyguards was held in Budapest, Hungary, in September 1995 and attracted 130 delegates from 40 countries.

BOGART, Humphrey (1899–1957)

★ Humphrey Bogart was born on Christmas Day 1899.
☞ BURIAL

BOLEYN, Anne (c.1507–36)

Henry VIII's second wife, Anne Boleyn, had six fingers on her right hand and is often described as having three breasts, though more prudish sources refer to the extra one as a cyst on her neck.

After Anne Boleyn was executed in 1536, her heart was stolen. It was discovered exactly 300 years later, buried under a church organ in Suffolk.

BOLIVIA

Bolivia has a 4,000-man navy but no coastline. The only

other totally inland country in South America is Paraguay.
★ Bolivia also had three different presidents in one day
on 3 October 1970.
☞ AMERICA, BRAZIL

BOMB
☞ ATOMIC ENERGY, BAT, BUTCHELL, CAPITAL
PUNISHMENT, SOAP OPERAS

BOOKS
Every published book is assigned a unique 10-digit
ISBN (International Standard Book Number). The final
digit of any ISBN is included as a way for computers to
make an instant check for incorrectly entered numbers.
The check works like this: you multiply the first digit by
10, the second by 9, the third by 8 and so on until you
reach the final, tenth digit, which is multiplied by 1 and
thus stays unchanged. Then you add all the answers
together. The total will always, if no mistake has been
made, be divisible by 11. For example, the ISBN of the
first edition of Jon-Stephen Fink's book *Cluck! The True
Story of Chickens in The Cinema* is 0907080154. The
above process gives us $(10 \times 0) + (9 \times 9) + (8 \times 0) +
(7 \times 7) + (6 \times 0) + (5 \times 8) + (4 \times 0) + (3 \times 1) + (2 \times 5) +
(1 \times 4)$, giving a total of 187, which is 11×17. The final
digit of the ISBN is calculated specifically to make this
happen. That is why some ISBNs end in X, signifying
10, in order to provide a total divisible by 11.

The average person in the UK borrows almost seven
books a year from public libraries, while his or her
household spends £1.50 on books every week. The

average British male aged 15 to 24 spends only 3.1 minutes a day reading books.

The Japanese spend more on books than any other nation. Norway comes second.

The top three best-selling books of all time are: 1. The Bible; 2. *Quotations From The Works Of Mao Tse-Tung*; 3. *Lord Of The Rings*.

The top three countries for winning the Nobel Prize for Literature are France, the USA and Britain.

☛ There were 119,001 different books published in Britain in 2002, which works out at one new book every 4 minutes 25 seconds. Of these titles, 43,357 were classified as 'academic or professional' while another 18,277 were 'scientific, technical or medical'.

☞ CHAUCER, DIAGRAM, ELASTIC, RHUBARB, SHOPPING TROLLEYS, BAR CODES, BLYTON

BORDEN, Lizzie Drew (1860–1927)

'Lizzie Borden had an axe,
Gave her mother forty whacks.
When she saw what she had done,
She gave her father forty-one.'

★ In fact, on 19 June 1893, Lizzie Borden the alleged axe murderess was acquitted of killing her parents in Fall River, Massachusetts. Her great-great-great-great-great grandfather, Thomas Cornell, however, was executed in Rhode Island in 1673 for killing his mother. He was almost certainly innocent, as the main evidence against him was the testimony of a man who said that the late Mrs Cornell had come to him in a dream and accused her son of having killed her.

BOSNIA
☞ STAMPS

BOSWELL, James (1740–95)
Samuel Johnson's biographer, James Boswell, suffered from gonorrhoea, of which between 12 and 17 episodes are recorded. He also had an ingrowing toenail. His family surname was spelled with only one final L when he was born, but he added another later.
☞ CELIBACY

BOUNTY
Fletcher Christian, who led the mutiny on the *Bounty* in 1789, named his first son Thursday October Christian, apparently because he was born on a Thursday in October 1790.
☞ BANGLADESH

BOWIE, David (b. 1947)
Born David Robert Jones, he adopted the stage name David Bowie to avoid confusion with Davy Jones, who later became lead singer in the made-for-TV band the Monkees. David Bowie was born on Elvis Presley's 12th birthday.

BOWLING
A pin in a tenpin bowling alley has to tilt only 7.5 degrees to make it fall over.
☞ FISHING, WHITE HOUSE

BOWLS
☞ PARROT

BOXING
The longest gloved boxing match on record was the contest between Andy Bowen and Jack Burke in New Orleans on 6 April 1893. After 110 rounds lasting seven hours and 19 minutes, the referee ruled 'no contest' when both men were unable to continue.

More dramatic, however, was the 77-round fight between Harry Sharpe and Frank Crosby for the Missouri lightweight championship in the same year. Both men knocked each other down simultaneously in the 76th round, Crosby banged his head, got up dazed and was knocked out in the following round. The referee, Willie Green, had been taking nips of whisky for a cold and passed out in the 65th round. After that, the fight had continued without a referee.

At the end of the fight, the winner gained the title, a $500 side bet, and an 11-month jail term for violating an anti-prizefight law.
☞ SHAKESPEARE

BRAIN
The Nobel Prize-winning author Anatole France (1844–1924) was found after his death to have one of the smallest human brains ever recorded.

The word 'brain' (or 'brains') does not occur at all in the Bible.
☞ ALCOHOL, CHOCOLATE, COSMETICS, DINOSAUR,
FIZZY DRINKS, LOVE, OSTRICH

BRANDING

In 1844, Jonathan Walker had the initials SS (for 'Slave Stealing') branded into his right palm for helping American slaves escape to the Bahamas.

This was the last instance of branding as punishment in the USA.

BRASSIERE

The word 'brassiere' comes from an old French word originally meaning an upper-arm protector, then a bodice or child's vest and finally a life-jacket. Although Mary Phelps Jacob is widely praised as the inventor of the modern bra, that honour seems to be best deserved by Marie Tucek, whose 'Breast Supporter' came more than 20 years earlier in 1893. The 'Backless Brassiere' of Mary Phelps Jacob was made from two handkerchiefs, a ribbon and cord. The first bras of all, however, were garments worn by Minoan women on Crete around 2500BC.

The bra industry was boosted in 1917 when the US War Industries Board asked women to stop buying corsets in order to save metal. The resulting switch from corsets to bras provided enough metal to build two battleships. The next significant advance came when the A-to-D cup-sizing system was introduced by Warner Corset Company in 1935.

The world's biggest bra was made by Triumph International Japan in 1990 with a bust measurement of 28m (91ft 10in). San Francisco held an Anti-Bra Day in 1969.

In April 2001, the American personal security consultant Paxton Quigley announced her invention of the world's first combined brassiere and gun holster. The garment is designed to hold a .38 calibre snub-nose revolver on one side, and a pepper spray on the other. Ms Quigley called her invention the Super-Bra and said that the chest area is a good place to conceal a weapon.

December 2001 saw another advance in brassiere technology with the launch of the 'Frequent Flyer's Bra' by Triumph International (Japan). With resinous wires and non-magnetic hooks replacing the usual metal fasteners, the garment was developed in response to reports that the metal parts of conventional bras had been setting off detectors at airports.

BRAZIL

Half the people in South America live in Brazil, but most Brazil nuts come from Northern Bolivia. The weight of coffee produced in Brazil, however, is twice the weight of tea produced in India.

A major traffic jam was caused in Brazil in 1964 when a couple kissed in a car and their dentures became inextricably locked together.

In 1969, a gang of Brazilian bus drivers was charged with training beetles to climb into fare boxes and take out coins. The beetles were also arrested.

In December 2001, Ellen Gracie Northfleet was sworn in as Brazil's first female supreme court judge, but there was one small problem: the Supreme Federal Tribunal building still had no women's toilet in the judges' chambers. 'If she has to go to the bathroom, she'll have to do it before the ceremony or wait until after it's over,' a spokesman explained.

In 2002, Brazilian weight-training instructor Edmar Freitas set a world record by doing 111,000 sit-ups in 24 hours. In the same year, scientists in Sao Paolo cloned a bull accidentally. They were trying to clone a cow. The world's largest commercial cattle herd is in Brazil and consists of 170 million head of cattle.

In 2002, Brazilian model and actress Susana Alves received an unusual insurance deal: in exchange for letting them put her image on its billboards, a company insured her buttocks, knees and ankles for $2 million. In Brazil, insurance policies on celebrity rear ends have become so common that insurers have a special term for them: bumbum policies.

☞ BANANA, EGG, GOATS, LOVE, PIZZA

BREAD

In 1984, a man who still vomited at the sight of bread four years after finding a dead mouse in a loaf, was awarded £1,900 damages in the Tasmanian Supreme Court.

According to an old Cornish superstition, a loaf with holes in it foretells a death in the family.

Another equally old superstition, however, says that a loaf with holes in it is a sign that the woman who baked it is going to have a baby.

The word 'lady' derives from an Old English expression for someone who kneads bread: *hlaefdige*, from *hlaef*, a loaf; *dig-*, to knead.

☞ DOUGHNUTS, REMBRANDT, SANDWICHES, SMELL, TELEVISION, TOAST, TURKEY (bird)

BREAST

Mammarism was invented around 1940 by the American Patrick Cullen. It is a form of divination or character assessment from the crinkles around nipples.
☞ BOLEYN, BRASSIERE, DIVORCE, FOX, LOVE, MELON, PHILLIPPINES, PREGNANCY, RENOIR, SANTA CLAUS, SEX

BRONTE, Charlotte (1816–55)

Charlotte Brontë, author of *Jane Eyre*, was only 4ft 9in tall. She had a cat called Tiger.

BRUMMELL, George Bryan 'Beau' (1778–1840)

Trend-setter and dandy Beau Brummell never ate vegetables, on principle, but said that he once ate a pea. Byron considered Brummell to be the greatest man of the 19th century, ahead of Napoleon and himself.

BRUNEI

☞ INCOME TAX

BRUSSELS SPROUTS

An analysis of whether young people liked or disliked Brussels sprouts was undertaken by John Trinkaus of New York and reported under the title 'Taste Preference For Brussels Sprouts: An Informal Look' in the journal *Psychological Reports* in December 1991. A survey of 442 business students revealed that about 50 per cent reported a dislike of sprouts, 10 per cent liked them and 40 per cent were indifferent. Older students were more likely to like them than younger ones.

BRUTUS
☞ SHAKESPEARE, UNIVERSITIES

BUCKLAND, William (1784–1856)
The first dinosaur fossils in Britain were found in 1819 by William Buckland, Canon of Christ Church and later Dean of Westminster. Buckland's passion for geology also incorporated a taste for the unusual – literally. In his opinion, the only thing that tasted worse than a mole was a bluebottle. He died shortly after swallowing an object that may or may not have been the embalmed heart of King Louis XIV of France. He also reputedly once identified his location when lost in the fog on the outskirts of London by the taste of the local earth, which he maintained with certainty was Uxbridge.
☞ DINOSAUR, JONSON

BUDGERIGAR
Research published in 1997 showed that male budgerigars are more likely to be unfaithful to their mates when their mates are not watching. For full details, see 'Extra-pair courtship behaviour of male budgerigars and the effect of an audience' by A.P. Baltz and A.B. Clark, *Animal Behaviour*, vol 53, 1017–1024.

BUFFALO
The world buffalo population is around 150 million, with 53 per cent of them in India.

The Swamp buffalo (*Bubalus carabensis*) has 48 chromosomes; the River buffalo (*Bubalus bubalis*) has 50.

The North American buffalo (*Bison bison*) is not, strictly speaking, a true buffalo at all.

Estimates of the number of buffalo (also known as bison) in North America 20,000 years ago vary between 30 million and 200 million. By the early 1900s, thanks to indiscriminate slaughter and poaching, the number had dwindled to little more than a hundred, but now it is back to around 200,000.

Buffaloes are good swimmers, and so buoyant that their head, hump and tail remain above the water.

The mating ritual of male buffalo involves a display called 'flehmen', which consists of curling the lip back and extending the neck.

A three-day funeral was held in Thailand in January 2001 for a buffalo that had starred in a hit film. Boonlert, a 32-year-old water buffalo with 10ft-long horns, was a leading character in *Bangrachan*, a Thai film based on an 18th-century battle between Thailand and Myanmar. Part of the film's success was credited to Boonlert's unusually long horns. A Thai opera was performed in front of the body of the buffalo to pay respect.

Buffalo milk has 25 per cent more protein than cow's milk.

☞ ARCHERY, PREGNANCY

BUGANDA

African kingdom, of which the native language is Luganda. The word for a second of time in Luganda is 'tikitiki'.

BUGS BUNNY
Mel Blanc, who voiced the part of Bugs Bunny, could not stand the taste of carrots.
☞ STAMPS

BULGARIA
According to an old Bulgarian peasant custom, coins are placed over eyes of a corpse at a funeral then washed in water. The liquid is then added to wine and given to men to make them blind to their wives' faults. Bulgaria is one of the few places on earth where nodding your head means 'no'.
☞ UMBRELLA

BULL
S-W-D Valiant, a Holstein bull owned by American Breeders Service of Madison, Wisconsin, died aged 11 in August 1984. Its semen sales had produced $25 million for the company, and 35,000 offspring.
★ The first matador to appear in a bullring with an advertiser's logo on his suit was Luis Reina on 2 August 1987.
☞ BRAZIL, EUROPE

BULLET
An Alphonsin is a surgical appliance designed to remove bullets.
☞ BELL, FASHION, FORTY-SEVEN, GUATEMALA, GUNS

BULLOCK
The word *taghairm* means inspiration sought by lying in

a bullock's hide behind a waterfall. Sir Walter Scott uses the word in his *Lady of the Lake*.

☞ BIBLE

BUNKER, Chang and Eng (1811–74)

Chang and Eng, the original Siamese Twins, were brought to America by the promoter P.T. Barnum. They adopted the surname Bunker in honour of the battle of Bunker Hill, during the American War of Independence. Joined at the breastbone by a 5in ligament, they were never separated and lived to the age of 62, dying within hours of each other. After a successful circus career, they married sisters and lived as farmers. Eng and his wife had 11 children, and Chang and his wife had 10.

The Battle of Bunker Hill was actually fought on Breed's Hill in Massachusetts.

☞ SIAM

BURIAL

Sir Walter Raleigh was buried with his favourite pipe and a tin of tobacco. Wild Bill Hickok was buried with his Sharps rifle. Rudolph Valentino was buried with a slave bracelet. Bela Lugosi was buried in his black Dracula cape. Humphrey Bogart was buried with a small gold whistle. Elvis Presley was buried with a diamond ring.

☞ ANTARCTICA, BOLEYN, DAVIDSON, DUCK, FERRARI, GOLF, JACKSON, JONSON, LEGS, SANTA ANNA, St SWITHUN

BURMA

The Burmese word *ma* has many meanings according to pitch changes. One sentence composed entirely of *ma* repeated at different pitches can mean 'Get the horse, a mad dog is coming.'

☞ BANANA

BURNS, Robert (1759–96)

Robert Burns's father was a landscape gardener called William Burnes – the poet changed the spelling of his surname after his father died. Burns had a pet sheep called Poor Mailie and a dog named Luath. He was engaged to Mary Campbell, a dairymaid, fathered a child by Anne Park, a servant, and had twins by Jean Armour, whom he later married. Burns worked as an excise officer in Dumfries and was nearly sacked for selling cannons to the French. He died in 1796 of rheumatic fever, which he apparently caught after falling asleep in the open air following a drinking session.

BURNT FOOD

The Museum of Burnt Food is located in Arlington, Massachusetts, and is home to around 50,000 specimens of charred food including over two thousand items in the Hall of Burnt Toast alone. It was founded by Dr Deborah Henson-Conant after an accident in 1981 involving apple cider and a long telephone call. The museum attracts around 25,000 visitors a year.

BUSH, George Walker (b. 1946)

In 2000, George W. Bush became the first right-handed president since Jimmy Carter: Reagan, Bush senior and Clinton were all left-handed.

While at Phillips Academy, Massachusetts, George W.

Bush was known as 'The Lip' for his sarcasm and ready wit. George W. Bush is the second son of a president to become president himself. The first was John Quincy Adams, son of John Adams, second president of the United States. George Bush's dog Spot is also the son of a former First Dog: its mother was Millie, Barbara Bush's dog.

George W., however, is the only US president to be the father of twins – just like Margaret Thatcher and Cleopatra. In 1989, George W. Bush became the co-owner of the Texas Rangers baseball team.

'I know the human being and fish can coexist peacefully.' George W. Bush, speaking in Michigan in September 2000.

'They misunderestimated me.' George W. Bush, speaking in Arkansas in November 2000.

☞ GUITAR, TWELFTH NIGHT, UNITED STATES

BUTCHELL, Martin van (1736–1814)

Reputedly London's most expensive dentist, Martin van Butchell was a man of curious habits, including the practice of riding through Hyde Park on a pony that had been painted with purple spots. He also carried a large white bone, probably the jawbone of an ass, with which to defend himself. His most celebrated possession, however, was the body of his wife.

When Mary Butchell died on 14 January 1775, her will stipulated that her husband was entitled to a stipend from her fortune for as long as her body remained above ground. Butchell therefore decided to have her body embalmed and turned this to further advantage by putting it on display in his London home where he practised. The celebrated physician Dr William Hunter, under whom he had studied, and Dr William Cruikshank performed the task, injecting the body with preservatives and finishing the job with a pair of 'nicely matched glass eyes'. The body was then dressed in a fine lace gown and embedded in a thin layer of plaster of Paris in a glass-topped coffin with curtains.

Butchell introduced her to visitors as 'My dear departed' and allowed strangers to see her by appointment only, 'any day between Nine and One, Sundays excepted'.

When van Butchell remarried, his second wife, Elizabeth, was less than enthusiastic about the corpse and it was removed to the College of Surgeons, where it was later described as a 'repulsive-looking object'. Mary's body was finally destroyed by a German incendiary bomb in 1941.

BUTE, John Stuart & Marquis of (1713–92)

In 1750, John Bute was appointed lord of the bedchamber to Frederick, Prince of Wales; in 1756, he became Groom of the Stole to Frederick's son, the future George III. He became Prime Minister in 1762. The office of Groom of the Stole lapsed in Victoria's reign. The role was to carry the royal chamber pot on long journeys ('stole' means stool or privy).

BUTTERFLY

Despite frequent assertions to the contrary, the butterfly never was called the 'flutterby'.

Butterflies taste with their feet.

☞ CALIFORNIA, NABOKOV, SWIMMING

BUTTOCKS

The word 'buttock' comes from the Old English 'buttuc', meaning a short ridge of land.

The *Oxford English Dictionary* lists 49 words to describe buttocks, which is the same as the number of words for snow listed in Michael Fortescue's 1984 book on the Eskimo language of West Greenlandic. (But see SNOW for a more detailed discussion of this matter.)

Among the English buttock-related vocabulary are the following:

- *Callipygous*, or *callipygean*: fair-buttocked.
- *Dasypygal*: hairy-buttocked.
- *Steatopygous*: fat-bottomed, especially as a medical condition.

In 1998, a ferry in Seattle cut its maximum seating from 250 to 230 because US bottoms had become larger. 'Eighteen-inch butts are a thing of the past,' a spokesman said.

☞ BRAZIL, CARUSO, DIAGRAM, MOLE, RENOIR, RHYME

BYRON, Ada (1815–52)

Countess of Lovelace and daughter of Lord Byron. The programming language ADA was named after her.

☞ COMPUTATION

BYRON, Lord George Gordon, 6th Baron Byron of Rochdale (1788–1824)

Byron was born lame and developed a club foot. Despite this, he played cricket at Harrow, using a runner, and was a fine swimmer. He kept a pet bear in his rooms at Cambridge, because he was not allowed a dog. He wore his hair in curlers at night. When Byron's coffin was opened in 1938, his lame right foot was found to be missing.

☞ BRUMMELL, SWIMMING

CABBAGE

The word 'cabbage' only occurs once in the works of Shakespeare, in Act I, scene i of *The Merry Wives of Windsor*, when Falstaff exclaims: 'Good worts! good cabbage. Slender, I broke your head: what matter have you against me?'

☞ BELGIUM, GERMANY

CALAIS

☞ ALCHEMY, PYRAMID

CALENDAR

According to the International Standard Organisation's ISO 8601, week 1 of any year is the week including 4 January.

It is a curious consequence of the rules underlying the Gregorian calendar that the thirteenth of the month is more likely to fall on a Friday than any other day of the week. Here is the reason:

The Gregorian calendar operates on a 400-year cycle with a Leap Day added every fourth year, except for three out of every four century years. That results in exactly 146,097 days every 400 years. But $146,097 = 7 \times 20,871$. In other words, 400 years comprise exactly 20,871 weeks. So, whatever the date is, you can be sure that date will fall on the same day of the week in 400 years' time. Since there are 4,800 months in 400 years, there will be 4,800 thirteenths of the month, and whatever days of the week they fall on will be repeated during all subsequent 400-year cycles. Since 4,800 is not divisible by seven, the thirteenths cannot be equally divided among the seven days of the week. When you work it out, it turns out that every 400 years, there are 685 Monday the thirteenths, 685 Tuesday the thirteenths, 687 Wednesday the thirteenths, 684 Thursday the thirteenths, 688 Friday the thirteenths, 684 Saturday the thirteenths and 687 Sunday the thirteenths.

☞ BELGIUM, FEBRUARY, St GEORGE, OCTOBER, OLYMPIC GAMES, SWEDEN

CALIFORNIA

The Californian legal system seems to have a soft spot for animals. For one thing, anyone molesting a monarch butterfly in Pacific Drive, California, is liable to a $500 fine. For another, in 1972 the owner of an elephant named Bimbo was awarded $4,500 damages by the Californian Supreme Court after a road accident. (See WATER-SKIING.) It is worth mentioning also that more turkeys are raised in California than in any other state in the United States.

Plants also have a good time: a creosote bush called King Clone in the Mojave desert in California may be the world's oldest living organism. Its age has been estimated as 11,700 years.

One out of every eight United States residents lives in California, but this is not without its hazards. Records show that more than one Californian a day claims to have been abducted by aliens.

If California were a country, at its current rate of industrial performance it would have the seventh largest economy in the world. The state motto of California is Eureka! (Greek for 'I have found it!'), relating to the discovery of gold in the Sierra Nevada in the 1840s.

The music for the state anthem of California, 'I Love You California', was written by a man named Frankenstein.

★ On 30 July 1968, the Public Defender of California State, Don Jones, was fined for being too fat. His weight at the time was 238lb.

☞ ARTICHOKE, BEER, CHEESE, DIVORCE, DOLPHIN, ELEPHANT, FEET, QUEEN MARY, REVOLVING DOORS, TUESDAY, WATER-SKIING

CALIGULA (AD12–41)
After Caligula's death in AD41, his favourite horse, Incitatus, which he had raised to the rank of senator, was deprived of its privileges.

CAMBODIA
Cambodia's first transvestite beauty contest was held in 2001, when a 19-year-old dancer from Phnom Penh was

crowned the country's most beautiful 'ladyboy' of the 30 entrants. 'We wanted to help the ladyboys be happy in society and not be neglected because they cannot change their ways,' a spokesman from the sponsoring TV station said. No women were permitted in the contest, but contestants were required to be pretty, charming and similar to real women. The winner, Pop Pi, received a trophy, 500,000 riel (about £80) and a tiara.

In November 2002, a Cambodian woman was sentenced to 15 years' imprisonment after murdering her husband by hitting him repeatedly in the groin with an axe, then running off with her son-in-law. Passing sentence, the judge said, 'It is totally unacceptable in Cambodia that a wife should kill her husband by smashing his genitals.'

It is illegal to use water pistols during New Year celebrations in Cambodia.

CAMBRIDGE
☞ St BERNARD, BYRON, CELIBACY, CREATION, FOOTBALL, MARS, NOBEL PRIZE, SHEEP, TIE KNOTS, TROUSERS, UNIVERSITIES

CAMEL
The camel has no gall bladder and, despite the hump, the backbone of a camel is perfectly straight. A camel can drink 35 gallons of water in 10 minutes but rats can survive longer than camels without water.

In the village of Garissa, in north-east Kenya, in October 1987, an elderly man who got a schoolgirl pregnant while supposedly giving her private tuition was ordered in court to pay four camels in compensation.

There are more camels in Somalia that any other country, but more wild camels in Australia.

In 1995, Emir Sultan ibn Mohammad ibn Saud al-Kebir gave $500,000 in prize money to Saudi Arabia's first beauty contest for camels, called Miss Dromedary. Saudi Arabia also led the world in opening the first commercial dromedary dairy in Riyadh in 1986 selling camel milk at £1.20 a litre. One potential bonus from camel's milk is that cream made from it is supposedly one of the best ways to get rid of fleas. Just smear the milk on anyone else and the fleas will desert you for them. There's nothing a flea likes as much as camel's milk.

A cross between a camel and a llama is called a cama. Only two have ever been bred, in 1998 and 2002.

According to Alan Davidson's *Oxford Companion to Food*, 'It is generally considered that the best part of the camel for eating is the hump.' He mentions, however, that the Greeks spoke of whole roast camels at banquets and the Roman Emperor Heliogabalus was particularly fond of camel's heel.

★ On 27 August 1997, a camel at Knowsley Safari Park on Merseyside was struck by lightning and killed. This is the only recorded case of a camel being killed by lightning in England.

☞ AMMONIA, BIBLE, LIBYA, OSTRICH, PAKISTAN, SEX EDUCATION, SOMALIA, VOWELS

CAMP DAVID

The rural retreat of American presidents was established in 1942 and called 'Shangri-La' by President Roosevelt.

In 1953, it was renamed Camp David by President Eisenhower after his grandson David.

CANADA

Canada not only has an area greater than that of Europe but its coastline is longer than that of any other country. Indonesia is second.

In Canada, 0.3 per cent of all road accidents involve moose. Whether or not you have been involved in a collision with a moose, it is illegal to remove bandages in public in Canada.

Canada has the highest proportion of university students, with 6 per cent of adults at university. There is a town in Newfoundland, Canada, called Dildo.

☛ A survey in 1995 reported that 38 per cent of Canadian women preferred chocolate to making love.

☞ ANCHOVY, ATHLETICS, BAR CODES, ELEPHANT, EUROPE, HALITOSIS, JIFFY, ROBBERY, SANTA CLAUS

CANARY

The Canary Islands have nothing to do with canaries. They are named after dogs: *Insulae Canariae* – the islands of dogs.

CAPITAL PUNISHMENT

Around 1500, there were eight crimes for which a person could be hanged in Britain: treason, petty treason (killing of a husband by a wife), murder, larceny, robbery, burglary, rape and arson.

In 1671, after Sir John Coventry had been attacked in Covent Garden and had his nose slit, an act was passed making it a capital crime to lie in wait with intent to put out an eye, disabling the tongue or slitting the nose. In 1699, shoplifting to the value of five shillings or more was added to the list for which one could be put to death.

In the 18th century the number of capital offences grew rapidly, with poaching, damage to forests and parks, cutting down an orchard, blacking the face or using a disguise while committing a crime among those boosting the number. Between 1779 and 1789 there were 531 hangings in London and Middlesex but the number dropped rapidly as transportation began to replace hanging. All the same, in 1810, British law recognised 222 capital crimes.

Between 1818 and 1861, less serious crimes began to be removed from the list of capital offences. Sheep, cattle and horse stealing were the first to go, followed by sacrilege, letter stealing, returning from transportation, forgery and coining, burglary and theft from a dwelling house and finally rape and attempted murder. Finally in 1861 the Criminal Law Consolidation Act reduced the number of capital crimes to four: murder, treason (including arson in Royal Naval dockyards), mutiny and piracy.

In 1965, capital punishment was suspended for five years, and in December 1969 Parliament confirmed its abolition for murder.

Nobody has been burned at the stake in Britain since 1786.

★ Important dates in the chronology of hanging in Britain:
  • 23 June 1649: Twenty-three men and one

woman are executed at Tyburn for burglary and robbery. This was probably the largest number of ordinary criminals put to death in a single execution in Britain.

- 5 May 1760: Lawrence Shirly, the Fourth Earl of Ferrers, is hanged at Tyburn for the murder of a servant, the only Peer of the Realm to hang for murder.
- 2 April 1868: Last public hanging of a woman – Francis Kidder at Maidstone for murder.
- 26 May 1868: Last public hanging in England – Michael Barrett at Newgate for the Fenian bombing at Clerkenwell.
- 3 January 1946: William Joyce – alias 'Lord Haw Haw' – is the last to be hanged for treason.
- 13 July 1955: Ruth Ellis is the last woman to hang.
- 13 August 1964: Peter Allen (at Walton Prison, Liverpool) and Gwynne Evans (at Strangeways Prison, Manchester) are the last to be hanged. The executions take place simultaneously at 8.00am.

☞ EXECUTION, GUILLOTINE, HANGING, SWEDEN

CAPONE, Alphonse (1899–1947)

Al Capone's business card described him as a used furniture dealer.

★ On 20 June 2000, his toenail clippers were sold for £5,000 at auction in San Francisco.

CARBON

☞ BODY, FART, FIZZY DRINKS

CARROLL, Lewis (Charles Lutwidge Dodgson, 1832–98)

Lewis Carroll was over 6ft tall and never wore an overcoat.

Queen Victoria loved *Alice in Wonderland* and requested a copy of Lewis Carroll's next book. It was *Syllabus of Plane Algebraical Geometry*.

☞ In the last 37 years of his life, Lewis Carroll wrote 98,721 letters to his friends, usually in black ink, though he preferred violet when writing to young girls.

★ The original story from which *Alice in Wonderland* grew was told by Carroll to amuse the Liddell sisters on a boat trip in Oxford on 4 July 1862.

☞ MOZART

CARS

Pound for pound, a new car is cheaper than a hamburger.

☞ BLINDNESS, BRAZIL, DRUNKEN DRIVING, GENETICS, LICENCE PLATES, LOVE, MONKEY, MOOSE, MOTORING, NIGERIA, ROBBERY, SANTA CLAUS, SHOES, SHOPPING TROLLEYS, SOMALIA, SPEED LIMIT, SUICIDE, TRANSPORT

CARTER, James Earl (b. 1924)

☞ BUSH, FLYING SAUCERS, UNITED STATES

CARUSO, Enrico (1873–1921)

The opera singer Enrico Caruso was convicted and fined in 1906 for pinching a woman's bottom in the monkey house of New York Central Park Zoo. He was probably innocent. He also hung anchovies around his neck, which he believed helped prevent damage from smoking 40 cigarettes a day.

When his wife ran off with another man in 1908, he was quoted as saying: 'It was the very thing I desired.'

CASANOVA, Giacomo Girolano (1725–98)

Seducer of an estimated 10,000 women, Casanova generally used a pig's bladder as a condom. He was awarded the Order of the Golden Spur by Pope Clement XIII.
☞ OYSTER

CAT

Eighteen thousand mummified cats were sold at one auction in Liverpool in March 1890. They went for an amount equivalent to about ten cats a penny, and were intended to be used as fertiliser. A cat needs three matings for ovulation to occur; an egg is produced 26 hours after the third mating.

In 1995, a survey showed that one in three British children believe that their mum prefers the cat to their dad.

In Bangkok, in October 1996, a wedding celebration costing £18,000 was held for two 'diamond-eye' cats called Phet and Ploy. Diamond-eye is a form of glaucoma that causes a thick blue film over the lens and is believed in Thailand to bring good luck. It is an open question whether it brought good luck to the cats. They were supplied with gold rings specially made for their paws, but the glaucomas had left both of them blind in one eye.

The top ten names for female cats in Britain are:
1. Lucy   3. Cleo
2. Poppy   4. Holly

5. Daisy	8. Misty
6. Molly	9. Amber
7. Tabitha	10. Chloe

The top ten names for male cats are:

1. Charlie	6. Ben
2. Sammy	7. Smokie
3. Billy	8. Tigger
4. Oscar	9. Sooty
5. Oliver	10. Leo

★ On 16 June 1995, Kitty Cat, the richest cat in the state of Oregon, died at the age of 19. She had been left a $250,000 mansion by her late owner, John Bass, in 1983.

☞ ANCHOVY, BARCELONA, BENTHAM, BRONTE, HYENA, LAVATORIES, NEWTON, PARAPSYCHOLOGY, WEATHER

CATARACT

The first successful operation for removal of a cataract from the eye of a giant panda was performed in 1985 in China. The panda was 12 years old and female.

☞ AIR HOSTESSES

CATERPILLAR

☞ BELGIUM, HEDGEHOG

CATHERINE I, Empress of Russia (1684–1727)

Born Martha Skavronsk, but rechristened Katarina Alexeyevna when she became the mistress of Peter the Great, whom she later married.

☞ ALCOHOL

CELIBACY

Celibacy, which has been the cause of so much introspection within the Catholic Church for 17 centuries, all began as a case of neo-Platonic Manichean dualism. The distinction between lower desires and spiritual aspirations was an important plank in building ethical thought. Plato believed that bodily desires should be suppressed in order to leave the soul free to search for knowledge. This view fitted easily into the dualist belief that all reality is composed of two parts, one spiritual (good), the other physical (bad).

The Manichees (followers of the religious doctrines set down by the third-century prophet Mani) adopted an extreme form of dualism, dedicated to restoring Light (goodness) from the molestation of Darkness (evil). A true, first-degree Manichee would do no work (which delays the distillation of light), abstain from the pleasures of the flesh and live mainly on radishes and melons. Fortunately, they could call upon the services of second-degree Manichees, who were permitted to work and even to marry.

The asceticism and ritual purity of the Manichees had taken firm root by the time the Christian Church drew up its own rules, but St Paul himself had adopted a more ambiguous position. While clearly favouring a state of non-marriage (which is all that 'celibacy' literally means) – as implied in his statement 'I wish that all were as I myself am' – he recognised that marriage could be a good way to avoid the temptation of fornication, 'for it is better to marry than to be aflame with passion'. Paul had even instructed Timothy that a bishop was to be the husband of one wife.

The first formal steps to legislate on the matter were taken at the Council of Elvira in Spain (around AD306). While accepting that priests could be married, the Council issued a decree saying that all priests, married or not, should abstain from sexual relations. The Council of Nicaea (AD325), however, issued a compromise: lower orders of the clergy could marry, but bishops must remain celibate. Finally, the first and second Lateran Councils (1123 and 1139) put an end to the idea of sex-free marriages among clergy. Priestly orders were declared to be incompatible with marriage.

The extreme Manichean position, however, survived in certain sects at least until the 18th century, with the Russian Skoptsy ('the castrated') one of the most recent manifestations. Even Origen of Alexandria (185–253) was supposed to have castrated himself in order not to feel temptation when instructing girl students, so the Skoptsy were merely carrying on a long tradition.

Other ascetics, however, found less damaging ways to prove their faith. Robert of Arbrissel, it is said, founded nunneries at which he slept with the nuns – chastely – in order to test himself. For similar reasons, St Swithin liked to sleep with two beautiful virgins, though he was criticised by St Brendan for the habit.

Celibacy, however, has by no means been confined to the Christian Church, or even to religious organisations generally. Rome had its vestal virgins, the Aztecs had celibate priests, followers of Isis were also required to practise sexual abstinence and, until the late 19th century, dons at Oxford and Cambridge colleges were not permitted to marry.

The Oxbridge rules may have had more to do with a reluctance to provide married quarters than a Platonic belief that sex damaged one's thinking powers, but donnish celibacy was overturned in the 1860s, thanks largely to the efforts of Henry Fawcett, who, among other notable achievements, was perhaps the first person to coin the phrase 'proportional representation'.

For the most profound comments on the subject, we must go to the work of Samuel Johnson and his biographer. As Boswell succinctly put it: 'Even ill-assorted marriages are preferable to cheerless celibacy,' while Johnson himself put it with characteristic relish: 'Though marriage has many pains, celibacy has no pleasures. The unmarried are outlaws of human nature. They are peevish at home and malevolent abroad… a state more gloomy than solitude: it is not retreat but exclusion from mankind.'

The US government spent $9,500,000 in 1990 to encourage celibacy among teenagers.

CEMETERIES

In 2001, the Israeli airline El Al rejected a request to allow certain passengers to zip themselves into body bags when their planes passed over a cemetery. Under Ultra-Orthodox Jewish law, Jews descended from the biblical priests must not enter a cemetery. The request to El Al came after a recent interpretation extended that ruling to cover the airspace above cemeteries too. If they were in plastic body bags, however, they would no longer be deemed unclean if they flew over a cemetery. The religious authorities dropped the idea when told it was not safe to zip yourself inside a body bag. They adopted instead an alternative solution of taking night flights from Tel Aviv, when noise pollution regulations forced them to alter their usual flight path to one that avoided cemeteries.

☞ ADDAMS, BARCELONA, FISH

CENTAUR
According to the Roman poet and philosopher Lucretius, a centaur is impossible since horse and man live to different ages, so one half would be dead when the other was still in its prime.

CENTIPEDE
The zoological name of the centipede is Chilopoda (from the Greek 'kheilos', meaning 'lip' or 'jaw' and 'pous', meaning 'foot'. The name refers to the poisonous fangs made from its front legs). Millipede is Diplopoda (from 'diploos', meaning 'double').

CENTRAL AFRICAN REPUBLIC
When Jean-Bedel Bokassa was crowned Emperor of the Central African Republic in 1977, only one of his 17 wives was permitted to attend the ceremony.

CEZANNE, Paul (1839–1906)
☞ PIGEON

CHAMOIS
Most chamois leather does not come from the chamois,

a type of mountain antelope. True chamois skin was used in the 18th century by the French glove-making industry. Workers found that, by tanning the skin in cod oil from Biarritz, they produced the ideal qualities of water absorption for the soft white gloves. The word 'chamois' (pronounced 'shammy') then came to be used for the process of tanning in cod oil. Nowadays most chamois leather comes from sheep.

☞ YODELLING

CHAMPAGNE

Champagne was invented by Dom Perignon, a monk at the Benedictine abbey of Hautvillers in the region of Champagne, northern France. On sipping the first results of his doubly fermented brew he is said to have called out: 'Come quickly, brother. I am tasting the stars.' He was the cellar master at Hautvilliers for 47 years until his death in 1715.

★ The discovery is said to have been made on 4 August 1693.

☞ BALLOON, COFFEE

CHANNEL

The English Channel did not exist 10,000 years ago, when Britain was still joined to France.

The first cross-Channel flight was made in 1785 by Jean Pierre Blanchard and Dr John Jeffries in a balloon. Blanchard, a French balloonist and the inventor of the parachute, did everything he could to stop Jeffries, an American doctor who financed the trip, from sharing the honours with him. His tricks included wearing lead weights in his belt to try to convince Jeffries that the two of them were two heavy for the balloon.

As they approached the French coast, the balloon lost height and the balloonists jettisoned everything, including their clothes, to keep it in the air. Neither of them could swim.

The first person to swim the Channel was 'Captain' Matthew Webb, who coated himself in porpoise fat and swam across in 21hr 45min in 1875.

The current record for the fastest swim is 7hr 17min set by Chad Hunderby of the USA in 1994.

Alison Streeter MBE holds the record for the most Channel swims, having achieved the feat 39 times. No man has swum the Channel more than 32 times, a figure reached by both Michael Read and Kevin Murphy. Altogether, fewer than 600 people have swum the Channel. More than twice as many have climbed Mount Everest.

The Channel was first swum by a grandmother in 1951, by a legless person in 1990, and first swum underwater in 1962. The first non-stop swim both ways was made by Antonio Abertondo of Argentina in 1961. ★ On 25 July 1959, fifty years to the day after Louis Bleriot's historic first successful cross-Channel flight, the first Channel crossing by hovercraft was made.

☞ EUROPE, SWIMMING, THIRTEEN

CHARLES I, King of England (1600–49)
Even before his head was cut off, Charles I was only 4ft 7in tall.

☞ HUDSON

CHARLES II (1630–85)

Charles II was known to his lover Nell Gwyn as Charles the Third, because she had two other boyfriends named Charles. The king kept King Charles spaniels as pets in his bedchamber. According to John Evelyn, they 'rendred it very offensive and indeede made the whole court nasty and stinking'.

★ According to Samuel Pepys's diary, on 15 October 1666 Charles II became the first man to wear a waistcoat. He had apparently introduced the garment in England though royal proclamation eight days earlier.

☞ DIANA, EDWARD VIII

CHAUCER, Geoffrey (1340–1400)

► Chaucer owned 60 books.

☞ St VALENTINE

CHEESE

The word 'cheese' occurs only twice in the King James Bible: once in the Second Book of Samuel and once in the Book of Job.

The Wisconsin Cheese-Makers Association has hosted the biennial World Championship Cheese Contest since 1957. An Australian brie was voted World Champion Cheese in 2002; a Dutch Old Gouda won in 2004. You cannot make cheese in Wisconsin without a cheese-maker's licence; Limburger cheese-makers require a master cheese-maker's licence.

According to a British study, the optimum thickness of cheese to be put into a cheese sandwich varies according to the cheese: 7mm for Wensleydale; 5mm,

Cheshire; 4.5mm, Caerphilly; 3mm, blue Stilton; 2.8mm, cheddar; and 2.5mm for double Gloucester or red Leicester. Using an aroma-measuring device, Dr Len Fisher of Bristol University was able to show that, once a cheesy smell has reached a certain level, increasing the amount of cheese makes no difference.

His results are listed in a report entitled: 'Optimum Use of Cheese in a Cheese Sandwich', which he prepared for the British Cheese Board in 2003.

★ The first recorded sighting of the word 'cheeseburger' was on 23 December 1941 over a shop in Burbank, California.

☞ COW, CRISPS, FORTUNE-TELLING, HOLES, MARS, MOON, OYSTER, PIZZA, REMBRANDT, SANDWICHES, TELEVISION, UMBRELLA

CHERRY

The world record distance for spitting a cherry pip in an official competition is 82ft 9in, set by Thomas Steinhauer in 2000. The Roman general Lucullus is said to have committed suicide in 56BC when he realised he was running out of cherries.

☞ ICE CREAM, SHOPPING TROLLEYS, TOMATO

CHESS

In January 2004, the Russian Orthodox Church ruled that chess is not a sin. A young churchgoer had led a campaign and organised a petition claiming that chess was the work of the devil but Archbishop Wikenti from Yekaterinburg rejected the request. He said that 'passionate games and arousing games that cause confusion, anger and irritation' are banned by the Church, but chess was 'a quiet, intelligent game that encourages people to think'.

☞ BILLIARDS, D'EON, THAILAND

CHEWING GUM

In 1997, Hong Kong businessman Leung Ka-Ching successfully appealed against a fine imposed on him for chewing gum in court. His explanation was that he had been chewing the gum to show respect for the court by having fresh breath.

★ The first commercially available chewing gum, State of Maine Pure Spruce Gum made by John Curtis, was introduced on 23 September 1848.

☞ BAR CODES, SINGAPORE

CHICKEN

According to the Book of Genesis, Chapter 1, verses 20–22, the chicken came before the egg.

In 1975, the Atmospheric Science Research Center in New York conducted a series of experiments to see if chickens could help in the estimate of wind velocities during a tornado. The idea was simple: chickens would be placed in a wind tunnel and, by varying the conditions, the researchers would discover what wind speed was necessary to remove a chicken's feathers from their follicles. Valuable information would then be immediately known about any tornado which left a trail of plucked chickens behind. Sadly, they discovered that the removal of chicken feathers in high winds operates according to complex and unpredictable rules depending on the chicken's condition and various environmental factors as well as wind speed. They concluded that: 'Chicken plucking is of doubtful value as an index of tornado wind velocity.'

On average, six chicken sandwiches are eaten every second in the UK.

➦ Jon-Stephen Fink's 1981 book *Cluck! The True History of Chickens in the Movies* lists 182 films in which chickens or their eggs have played a role.

☞ BACON, BOOKS, CRISPS, KANSAS, SANDWICHES

CHILE

★ On 28 November 1996, the former Chilean dictator Augusto Pinochet gave three pieces of advice to officers in the Chilean army: don't gossip about the military; watch your drink; and don't grow sideburns if you are visiting London.

CHILLI

The strength of chilli peppers is measured in Scoville Units.

CHIMPANZEE

In 1999, *New Scientist* magazine identified chimps in Madrid Zoo as the first non-humans seen to mash food simply because they prefer the taste and texture.

☞ HAIR

CHINA

If the entire population of China jumped as high as they could and landed at the same time, the resulting thump would not, as some have suggested, be enough to knock the Earth from its orbit, or set off a tidal wave lethal to the world, but it would be equivalent to about half a megaton of TNT.

In 2001, Beijing announced a decision to raise the quality of its public lavatories to enhance the chances of a successful bid for the 2008 Olympic Games. Toilets would be awarded one to four stars, with four-star toilets having granite floors, good lighting, lively music, facilities to wash hands, tissues, automatic flush, hand dryers and bathrooms specially designed for disabled and old people. According to a Beijing newspaper announcing this decision, the Chinese capital still lagged far behind other cities in terms of its public toilets.

The 'Dog-Meat King' restaurant in Beijing serves more than 50 dog dishes, including braised dog paws, stir-fried dog chops and boiled tail. In 2001, a petition signed by 11,000 dog breeders and owners was delivered to the Chinese urging an end to the breeding of St Bernards for their meat.

☞ ABORTION, APPLE, BEER, CATARACT, DINGO, DUCK, GOATS, GOLDFISH, LAVATORIES, MUSHROOM, OLIVE, OSTRICH, PEANUT, PERU, RAT, TRANSVESTITES

CHIPS

One of the earliest references to 'chips' is in Charles Dickens's *A Tale Of Two Cities* (1859) where he mentions: 'husky chips of potatoes, fried with some reluctant drops of oil'.

One in four of all potatoes consumed in Britain are cooked as chips. Around seven per cent of the potatoes grown in the USA end up in chip bags sold by McDonald's. The average Briton eats just over 7lb of chips a year; the average American eats 16lb, although the Americans call chips 'French fries'. The verb 'to french' means 'to cut in thin lengthwise strips before cooking'. It was originally applied not to potatoes but to green beans. The Belgians call chips 'Belgian fries' and claim to have invented them.

☞ CRISPS, FISH, RESTAURANTS, SMELL

CHOCOLATE

Montezuma started the myth about chocolate being an aphrodisiac. His cup of cocoa at bedtime was a cold drink whisked from crushed beans. And Aztec women were not allowed to drink it.

Even earlier, however – probably from the third century – the Mayan civilisation had been roasting beans from the pods of the cacao tree and grinding them to mix with water for a luxury drink. There is even evidence dating back to AD750 of a frothy Mayan cappuccino, made by pouring chocolate from a great height.

The drink was so highly valued among the Aztecs that cocoa beans became a form of currency – four beans for a rabbit or 100 for a slave. When Cortés conquered the Aztecs in 1520, he found that cocoa beans were prized even higher than gold.

There is probably no truth in the popular belief that Columbus brought back chocolate from the New World. Cortés or his followers appear the likely culprits. By the first half of the 16th century, it was established as a luxury drink at the Spanish court, but, although the word 'chocolate' is first recorded in English use in 1604, chocolate itself took a long time to reach Britain. According to *The True History of Chocolate* by Sophie and Michael Coe, England's first cup of chocolate was brewed at Balliol College by a student from Crete in 1647.

Exactly 200 years later the world of chocolate changed completely. In 1847, the Quaker firm J.S. Fry's of Bristol invented the chocolate bar. Twenty-one years later, another Quaker firm, Cadbury's, produced the first box of chocolates. Cadbury's, incidentally, had been founded in 1831 and, according to a price list of 1842, were already offering 16 varieties of drinking chocolate and 11 different cocoas.

Among the Aztecs, only nobles, soldiers and sacrificial victims were allowed chocolate; in Spain, it had been reserved as a luxury for state occasions; but in Britain, thanks to the Quakers, anyone could become a chocoholic.

Samuel Pepys drank his first cup of chocolate on 24 November 1664; he noted in his diary: 'To a Coffee-house, to drink jocolatte, very good.' On New Year's Day 1900, Queen Victoria sent 100,000 boxes of chocolates as a personal gift to soldiers in the Boer War.

In 2004, the British spent £3.2 billion on chocolate – an average of £1.06 a week for every man, woman and child in the country. Londoners, surprisingly, spend least on chocolate, while the Scots spend most. And all the chocolate buttons sold in a year would be enough to go round Britain 20 times.

The nature of chocolate craving has only recently begun to be understood. In 1982, researchers in New

York discovered that falling in love correlated with high levels of phenylethylamine (PEA) in the brain. Chocolate also contains PEA, which appeared to support Montezuma's theory of chocolate as an aphrodisiac, or at least as an anti-depressant. A controlled study in 1995, however, suggested that the moods of chocolate addicts are not at all improved by their eating chocolate.

A possible link between chocolate consumption and 'dysphoric mood' (a state of general unease or discomfort) was confirmed by a study in 1991 that showed higher suicide and lower homicide rates in countries with the highest chocolate consumption.

The true nature of chocolate addiction was finally revealed in 1994. Previously, there had been a strong belief that we ate chocolate for the caffeine-like effects of theobromine. (Linnaeus had named the cocoa bush Theobroma cacao – 'food of the gods' cocoa.) Experiments showed, however, that chocolate cravings cannot be satisfied by theobromine alone, nor by chocolate with its chemicals removed. The conclusion seemed inescapable: we eat chocolate because we like eating chocolate. Research in 2002, however, added another dimension. Three German psychologists showed that an individual's liking for chocolate may vary according to his or her mood.

After dividing their 48 male subjects into four groups, they showed each group a film designed to create a specific emotion: joy (*When Harry Met Sally*), sadness (*The Champ*), anger (*Cry Freedom*) or fear (*The Silence of the Lambs*). Then they offered them chocolate, asked how much they liked it and whether they wanted more.

Reporting the results in a paper entitled 'Chocolate Eating in Healthy Men During Experimentally Induced Sadness and Joy' (by Macht, M., Roth, S. & Ellgring, H.; *Appetite*, 39, 147–158), they concluded that men are more likely to reach for chocolates when they're happy than when they are sad. The results with fear and anger, however, were inconclusive. People eat chocolate because they are happy, as well as to make them happy, say the team. They suggest that people may divide into those who eat chocolate to avoid misery and those who eat it to get pleasure.

☞ CANADA, ICE CREAM, LOVE, PARAPSYCHOLOGY, SARDINE, SHOPPING TROLLEYS, SLOANE, SWITZERLAND, TELEVISION

CHOPSTICKS

Thirty per cent of the world's population generally eat with chopsticks. Japanese and Chinese chopsticks, however, are of slightly different design: Japanese chopsticks are usually tapered or pointed at the eating end, and Chinese chopsticks tend to be longer with a blunt or square end.

According to research published in the journal *Applied Ergonomics* in 1996, the perfect chopstick is 240mm long (180mm for children) and tapers from 6mm diameter to 4mm, with a two-degree tip angle.

Japanese etiquette strongly forbids licking the ends of chopsticks, a piece of rudeness known as *neburibashi*. Other chopstick taboos include waving them indecisively over your food (*mayoibashi*) and stuffing food into an already full mouth (*komibashi*).

According to scientists Dr Jim Al-Khalili and Dr Qiang Zhao at the University of Surrey, the comfort of using chopsticks is given by the equation:

$$C = [C_0 \sqrt{N} \eta^\propto d(2-d)]/[mt(1+\propto)].$$

where:

C = comfort factor

C_0 = a constant taken, in the absence of other information, to be equal to 30 (incorporates unknown information, e.g. length of chopsticks and angle of chopsticks)

N = number of Chinese meals eaten with chopsticks

η = texture parameter including shape, softness and crumbliness (a piece of meat is easy to pick up and has a texture parameter close to 1, a grain of rice is not so easy and would have a tiny value of 0.05)

$\propto$ = slipperiness of food (the stickier it is the closer the value to 1)

d = diameter of food (in centimetres)

m = mass of food (in grams)

t = plate-to-mouth transit time (seconds)

What this says is that slippery or crumbly food in small heavy pieces brought slowly to your mouth is most difficult, but you'll improve with practice. One way of raising the value of N (your measure of chopstick experience) could be to visit the Kuaizi Museum in Shanghai, which contains over a thousand pairs of chopsticks. *Kuaizi* is the Chinese word for chopsticks, meaning 'quick little fellows'.

Fear of using chopsticks is called consecotaleophobia.

CHRISTIANITY

According to a survey in 1999, the 10 best-known Christians in Britain were:

1. Sir Cliff Richard
2. The Archbishop of Canterbury
3. The Prince of Wales
4. Terry Waite
5. The Queen
6. Bob Geldof
7. The Pope
8. Billy Graham
9. Frank Bruno
10. Sir Harry Secombe

☞ CELIBACY, EASTER, SCOTLAND

CHRISTMAS

Fixing the date of Christmas was first proposed by the Council of Nicaea in AD325, when one of those present is believed to have been St Nicholas himself, but the earliest record of a celebration on 25 December was in AD354.

According to the 16th-century mystic Godfridus, when Christmas falls on a Thursday, winter shall be good and 'He that falleth in his bed shall soon recover.'

In 1647 the English Parliament abolished the celebration of Christmas. Eating mince pies and plum puddings was also made illegal.

The earliest known Christmas card was produced in 1842 and is preserved in the British Museum.

In 1913, a New York couple were arrested and fined $15 for kissing in the street on Christmas Day.

'Jingle Bells' was composed by James Pierpont in 1857, not as a Christmas song but for Thanksgiving. Its original title was 'One Horse Open Sleigh'.

Happy Christmases include Christmas Day 1066, when William the Conqueror was crowned King of England, and Christmas Day 1989, when President Ceausescu of Romania was executed.

☛ Around £1 million a year is staked on snow falling in Britain on Christmas Day. Weather records suggest the chances are around 10 to one.

☛ The average Christmas tree has about 30,000 bugs and insects on it according to Mr Arne Fjellberg, a Norwegian scientist. Microscopic examination of Christmas trees revealed midges, fleas, lice, parasitic wasps, spiders and beetles.

☛ The total number of gifts given by 'My true love' in the song 'The Twelve Days of Christmas' adds up to 364.

☞ BACH, BELGIUM, BOGART, DWARF, GUATEMALA, PAPER, SANTA CLAUS, SEXUAL HARASSMENT, SMELL, SOAP OPERAS, SONGS, SPAIN, SWEDEN

CHURCHILL, Winston (1874–1965)
Churchill's mother was one-eighth Iroquois Indian.

CICADA
The American cicada lives 17 years, mates only once and dies immediately afterwards.

CICERO, Marcus Tullus (106–43BC)
☞ SLAVERY

CIGARETTE
The cigarette lighter was invented before the match.
☞ CARUSO, GREECE, SMOKING

CINDERELLA
The glass slippers in the Cinderella story were originally fur. The change came through confusion among translators between the mediaeval French *vaire* – 'fur' – and *verre* – 'glass'.

CINEMA
★ On 16 September 1997, the state of Kelantan in Malaysia announced that lights would be kept on in cinemas in order to deter people from kissing and cuddling. 'If we can watch television at home with the lights on, then why not in cinemas?' a minister commented.

☞ ICELAND, INDIA, WHITE HOUSE

CIRCUMCISION
Egyptian male mummies were all circumcised.

☞ PENIS

CIRCUS
The patron saint of circus workers is St Julian the Hospitaller. According to legend St Julian killed his own father and mother through a case of mistaken identity.

☞ ALASKA, BUNKER, COW

St CLARE of Assisi (1194?–1253)
A follower of St Francis of Assisi, St Clare once saw a vision as though it was projected on her bedroom wall. For that miracle, she was declared patron saint of television in 1958. She is also patron saint of embroiderers, eye disease, eyes, gilders, goldsmiths, gold

workers, good weather, laundry workers, needle workers, telegraphs, telephones and television writers.

CLEOPATRA (69–30BC)
Daughter of Ptolemy XII, the famous Egyptian queen was in fact Cleopatra VII. According to Plutarch: 'Her beauty was not of that incomparable kind which instantly captivates the beholder, but the charm of her presence was irresistible… it was delight merely to hear the sound of her voice.'

☞ BILLIARDS, BUSH

CLEVELAND, Grover (1837–1908)
Grover Cleveland is the only American president to have regained the presidency after being voted out of office.

CLINTON, William Jefferson (b. 1946)
William Jefferson Clinton and Richard Milhous Nixon are the only two presidents of the United States whose names contain all the letters needed to spell out the word 'criminal'.

Bill Clinton is the only left-handed president of the United States to have served two full terms.

☞ BUSH, CLEVELAND, LEWINSKY, SEXUAL HARASSMENT

CLOONEY, George (b. 1961)
Actor George Clooney has a pet pot-bellied pig called Max, which he acquired some time around 1988.

☞ NOSE

COCKEREL
☞ ASH WEDNESDAY, BALLOON, BALZAC, PANCAKE

COCOA
'Tea, although an oriental,
Is a gentleman at least.
Cocoa is a cad and bounder
Cocoa is a vulgar beast.'
(G.K. Chesterton)
☞ CHOCOLATE

COCONUT
The only natural habitat of the coco de mer tree is on Praslin in the Seychelles. The sex of the tree cannot be determined until it is 25 years old. More coconuts come from Indonesia than any other country.

The danger of coconuts was analysed by P. Barss in a paper in the *Journal of Trauma* in 1984 entitled 'Injuries Due to Falling Coconuts'. As he points out, 'Falling coconuts can cause injury to the head, back, and shoulders', and an analysis of four years' admissions to a hospital in Papua New Guinea revealed that 2.5 per cent of injuries were due to the victims being struck by falling coconuts. He points out that mature coconut palms are between 24m and 35m high and an unhusked coconut may weigh 1–4 kg. This means that blows to the head from a falling coconut can produce a force exceeding one metric tonne. Of four coconut-related case studies in his paper, two of the victims needed brain surgery. Two further cases were reported of falling coconuts causing instant death.
☞ QUEENSLAND

COFFEE

It is said that coffee was introduced into Europe in 1683, when the Turkish army left sacks of coffee behind as they hurriedly retreated from the gates of Vienna. The Turks were certainly serious about their coffee: in the late 15th century, Turkey passed a law making it possible for a woman to divorce her husband if he did not keep the coffee pot full.

Over 400 billion cups of coffee are drunk around the world every year, which means that the average person on earth drinks about one cup of coffee every six days.

The world's most expensive coffee is probably Kopi Luak coffee, made from beans that have been eaten and excreted by the luak, or palm civet, of Indonesia. They pass almost unchanged through the digestive system of the animal, and it is not known whether the unique flavour of the coffee is due to the civet's digestive juices or its ability to select the ripest beans.

Frederick the Great of Prussia (1712–86) took coffee made with champagne as a calming drink.

Expenditure on coffee in Britain first overtook the amount spent on tea in 1998. Four years later, scientists discovered that sprinkling coffee grounds in the garden helps to deter snails and slugs.

☞ BALZAC, BEETHOVEN, BRAZIL, CHOCOLATE, COLOMBIA, COMPUTATION, GARLIC, ITALY, MARRIAGE, MOTHER TERESA, PINEAPPLE, PUCCINI, SHOPPING TROLLEYS, SMELL, SUICIDE, SWEDEN, TENNIS, VOLTAIRE

COFFEE (decaffeinated)

Decaffeinated coffee owes its invention to a batch of

beans that had been spoiled by seawater before being delivered to German coffee importer Ludwig Roselius in 1903. Research showed the beans had lost their caffeine content and three years later Roselius launched decaffeinated coffee.

COLOMBIA

Colombia is the size of France, Spain and Portugal combined and has the world's highest murder rate as well as being home to around half the total kidnappings in the world. The most deadly thing in Colombia, however, is the Kokoi frog. One millionth of an ounce of its venom can kill a man.

Although best known as a producer of coffee and cocaine, Colombia is also the world's third biggest producer of bananas.

In 1996, the President of Colombia introduced a bill to make drunken walking illegal, and in 1998, officials in the capital, Bogota, introduced poetry reading on buses as a way to reduce stress levels.

There is an average of about one bank robbery a day in Bogota.

☞ AMERICA, FOOTBALL, ROBBERY, SOUTH AFRICA

COLORADO

Between the years 1992 and 1994, the town of Avon, Colorado, held an annual Bobfest for people named Bob. In 1995, however, the series ended. Its founder and organiser, Tom Britz, announced that he was tired of running it. 'I met one bad Bob,' he said, 'and it spoiled the bunch.'

COLUMBUS, Christopher (1451–1506)
☞ AMERICA, BAHAMAS, CHOCOLATE

COMMUNISM
★ The *Communist Manifesto* was first published by Karl Marx and Friedrich Engels on 4 July – American Independence Day – in 1848. Other American disasters on Independence Day include 4 July 1826, which is the only day in history on which two US presidents died (John Adams and Thomas Jefferson), and 4 July 1931, when President James Monroe died. On the plus side, President Calvin Coolidge was born on 4 July 1872, the only president born on the Fourth of July.
☞ CONDOM, DRACULA, INDEPENDENCE DAY

COMPUTATION
Notches on animal bones show that people have been making computations since around 30,000BC. A wolf bone found in France and dated back to the Paleolithic era shows 55 cuts arranged in groups of five, suggesting that we used our fingers for counting even then.

The Babylonians, in 3500BC, had two separate number systems in use at the same time. A decimal system was used for normal business, but sexadecimals (combining sixties and tens) were used for complex mathematical and astronomical calculations. The 60 minutes in an hour and 60 seconds in a minute may have their origins in that system.

The Romans, with their rather cumbersome numerals, put back calculation by several generations, though they did have a good repertoire of calculational tricks to make things easier. They also developed a counting-board, which was the first calculating machine and a precursor of the abacus.

The abacus itself, with sliding balls and all, dates back, depending on which authority you consult, to AD200 (earliest suggestions of possible Chinese development), AD500 (first European abacus) or AD700 (first printed reference to 'ball arithmetic').

The Arabs brought us zero around the eighth century – a rediscovery of an Indian idea of the second century BC – and by the end of the 12th century there were two-tone abacuses, with black beads for positive numbers and red for negative – the origins of the modern bank statement.

Pythagoras, however, had been firmly stuck in the positive world, believing that three was the first proper number, since it had a beginning, middle and end, unlike one and two. Three, however, was where the Yancos tribe of the Amazon stopped their counting system. The word for three in their language was 'poettarrarorincoaroac'. That, at least, was three better than the Vedda, from the forests of old Ceylon, who seem to have had no numbers at all in their language, while, as recently as 1972, a tribe of cave dwellers was discovered in the Philippines who seemed unable to count.

The conceptual father of the modern computer was Charles Babbage (1792–1871), a Cambridge mathematician who was the first to produce a blueprint for a calculating machine. In 1823, the Chancellor of the Exchequer personally agreed a grant of £1,500 from the Civil Contingencies Fund to support Babbage's 'Analytical Engine', which would calculate mathematical tables. By 1842, it had cost £17,000 of public money and the project was abandoned, still incomplete.

Babbage spent his final years an embittered man, harbouring a particular grudge against organ-grinders, whom he blamed for wrecking one-fourth of his entire working life through their audible nuisances.

If Babbage was the father of computing, its midwife was Ada Byron, Countess of Lovelace. A fearless horsewoman and mathematician, daughter of the sixth Baron Byron, she worked with Babbage and prepared notes on the potential of his machine. They were the first to introduce the concept of computer programming, though the ideas were almost certainly Babbage's, not Ada's.

In 1996 the Japanese company Matsushita launched the first laptop computer built to survive coffee being spilled on its keyboard.

☞ MOUSE

CONDOM

In 1995, the authorities in the Philippines threatened to ban fruit-flavoured condoms. A spokesman for the Bureau of Food and Drugs announced this decision explaining: 'You only put a flavour in when it is something to eat.'

★ The musical condom, invented by Ferenc Kovacs, was launched in Hungary on 17 June 1996. While being unrolled, it plays a tune with users able to choose from a selection including a Communist song, 'Arise Ye Worker'.

☞ CASANOVA, INCOME TAX

CONGO
☞ OKAPI, DEMOCRATIC REPUBLIC OF THE CONGO

COOK, Thomas (1808–92)
☞ TOURISM, VANUATU

COOLIDGE, (John) Calvin (1872–1933)
US President Coolidge was famed for being a man of few words. His wife, Grace Goodhue Coolidge, recounted that a young woman sitting next to Coolidge at a dinner party told him she had bet she could get at least three words of conversation from him. Without looking at her, he quietly replied, 'You lose.'

When Dorothy Parker was informed in 1933 that Coolidge had died, she replied, 'How can they tell?'
☞ COMMUNISM, INDEPENDENCE DAY

COPERNICUS, Nicolaus (1473–1543)
☞ UNIVERSITIES

COPYRIGHT
The word 'uncopyrightable' is one of the two longest English words that consists entirely of different letters. It shares first place with the more unusual 'dermatoglyphics'.

CORK
If all the corks from all the wine bottled in France in a year were laid end to end, they would go round the world three times.
☞ PORTUGAL

CORNFLAKES

In 1906 William K. Kellogg founded the Battle Creek Toasted Corn Flake Company to market the breakfast food invented by his brother, John Harvey Kellogg. Cornflakes had originally been conceived as therapy for mental patients at a sanatorium run by the brothers and as a mean of curbing their sex drive.

CORONATION

Edward V (abducted) and Edward VIII (abdicated) were the only English monarchs who never had coronations.
☞ EDWARD VII, SOAP OPERAS

CORTES, Hernan Ferdinand (1485–1547)
☞ CHOCOLATE

COSMETICS

Isabel of Bavaria, a fourth-century French queen, liked to paint her face with a concoction made of boar's brains, wolf's blood and crocodile glands.

In the Middle Ages Japanese women painted their teeth black to look more beautiful.

Lady Coventry died on 1 October 1760 as a result of painting her face with white lead, thus becoming the first martyr to modern cosmetics.

COSTA RICA

The first World Conference of People in Contact with Extraterrestrials was held in July 1995 at Miramar de Puntarenas in Costa Rica. Delegates from 10 countries linked hands to form five concentric circles around three fires and chanted, hoping their focused energy would attract extraterrestrials. After about 40 minutes, it poured with rain, which the organisers said was 'a sign from heaven'. Later it was claimed that four spaceships had appeared nearby, but most of the delegates did not see them.

COW

A cow has four stomachs, the first and largest of which is called the paunch or rumen. The second stomach of a cow may be called the bonnet, king's-hood or reticulum. The third stomach is the omasum, psalterium, manyplies, bible, fardel or fardel-bag, and the fourth stomach is the abomasum, maw, read or rennet-bag.

Cattle can be identified by their nose-prints.

In Somerset in 1841, 737 cows were milked in order to make a 9ft-diameter cheese for Queen Victoria.

In Moscow circuses, cows have been trained to play football.

In Spain, experiments have shown that milk production can be improved by up to 60 per cent by fitting the cows with steel dentures. Elsewhere, however, research has also shown that, if you burst a paper bag near the ear of a Jersey cow, its milk flow will be interrupted for about 30 minutes.

In Paris in 1740, a cow was hanged in public following its conviction for sorcery.

In Switzerland in 1983, a Czechoslovakian was refused Swiss citizenship because his dislike of cowbells was taken as a sign that he had not assimilated successfully, despite having lived in the country for 14 years.

Under the Metropolitan Streets Act of 1867, cows may not be driven down a British roadway between 10am and 7pm unless there is prior approval from the Commissioner of Police.

A group of 12 or more cows is called a flink.

☞ ARCHERY, BRAZIL, BUFFALO, MAY, METHANE, MILK, SWEDEN, TEETH

CRAB

Launce's dog Crab, in *The Two Gentlemen of Verona*, is the only dog required to appear on stage in Shakespeare.

The crab peeler was patented by Harry M. Martin Sr in 1980.

☞ CRUSTACEAN, SEAL

CRANE

☞ BEETHOVEN, EPONYM

CREATION

According to Dr John Lightfoot of Cambridge University, writing in 1644, the world was created on 9am on Sunday, 12 September 3928BC. The date was recalculated in 1650 by the Archbishop of Armagh, James Ussher, who arrived at the date of 23 October 4004BC. Ussher's date was generally preferred for two reasons: first, that both men agreed that the Creation took place on the day of the autumn equinox, which must have been in October not September; and second because Ussher had dated the year of Christ's birth as 4BC (which was the year of King Herod's death) and this gave the millennially convenient period of precisely 4,000 years from the Creation.

CRESS
One ounce of cress boiled down will produce enough cyanide to kill two mice.

☞ PARAPSYCHOLOGY

CRICKET
Frederick Louis, eldest son of George II, is the only Prince of Wales to have been killed by a cricket ball. He was fatally struck on the head in 1751. Forty-five years later, in 1796, a team of one-legged cricketers defeated a team of one-armed players by 103 runs at Greenwich.

Another cricketing fatality occurred in 1976, when an umpire in Pakistan was beaten to death with the stumps by fielders disputing his decisions.

Cricket featured in the 1900 Olympics. Britain took gold, France took silver; no one else entered.

★ The most significant date in cricket history is probably 11 June:

- On 11 June 1907, Nottinghamshire were bowled out for 12, the lowest ever score in the County Championship.
- On 11 June 1952, Denis Compton made his 100th first-class century.
- On 11 June 1953, Len Hutton became the first professional cricketer to captain England.

☞ You can calculate the temperature by timing the chirps of an insect known as the temperature cricket:

- $F = C/40 + 40$ (where F is the temperature and C is the number of chirps per minute).

☞ ADMIRALTY ISLANDS, ASHES, BYRON, FROGS, HUTTON, KARLOFF, OLYMPIC GAMES, RUGBY, SNAIL, WELLS

CRIME

There are 26,294 prisons, penal or correctional institutions in Malaysia, more than any other country.

In terms of prisoners rather than prisons, however, the United States and Russia lead the league tables. Both have 0.64 per cent of their population in jail, with the USA just ahead. Just over 0.1 per cent of the British population are in prison.

In 2001, an Arizona woman was arrested after she phoned 'Guns For Hire' and asked if they could kill her husband. The company, which stages fights for films, gave her details to the police.

The number of crimes recorded by the police in England and Wales in 2004/05 was 5,562,691, of which 36 per cent involved theft. That is one crime every six seconds. There were also about 403,000 bicycles stolen.

In January 2002, the website Convicts Reunited was started to help ex-jailbirds contact former cellmates.

According to a recent study, male scientists and criminals have similar career patterns: both achieve their best results before they get married.

☞ CAPITAL PUNISHMENT, CLINTON, DWARF, KOALA, MARRIAGE, PIG, SWEDEN, WEATHER

CRISPS

What the British call crisps and the Americans call potato chips owe their existence to an irritable chef and a fussy diner. The chef was named Charles Crum and he worked at Moon's Lake House in Saratoga Springs. The fussy diner was, according to some sources, Commodore Cornelius Vanderbilt, who certainly frequented that restaurant, though his connection with the invention of the crisp may well be apocryphal. The story goes that one evening, probably in 1853, a diner who may or may not have been Vanderbilt repeatedly complained that his French fries were not sliced thinly enough. Crum became so annoyed that he sliced them as thin as possible and fried them to a crisp. His intention had been to heap scorn on the diner; instead he found he had invented a delicious new way of cooking potatoes. Crum soon opened his own restaurant and served a bowl of 'potato crunches', as he called them, to each table. They became a favourite of diners and soon spread throughout America under the name 'Saratoga chips'.

If George Crum was the father of potato crisps, however, Laura Clough Scudder was the midwife. For it was she who, in 1926, came up with the idea of selling them in individual portions in sealed, waxed paper bags.

The world's largest bag of potato crisps was made in Ohio in 2003 and weighed in at 1,085lb 8oz.

According to a poll in 2002, the five flavours of crisps British children most liked to find in their lunch-boxes are:

1. Cheese and Onion
2. Salt and Vinegar
3. Pickled Onion
4. Prawn Cocktail
5. Barbecue Beef

And the five least-liked flavours are:

1. Ready Salted
2. Smokey Bacon
3. Beef and Onion
4. Sour Cream and Chive
5. Chicken

☞ TELEVISION

CROCODILE

Artemidorus, the ancient Roman grammarian, is said to have lost his wits when startled by a crocodile. Despite such accidents as this, it was not until July 1996 that the authorities in Queensland, Australia, published their *Workplace Health and Safety Guide*, which included a warning not to 'place any part of one's body in the mouth of a crocodile'.

★ Crocodile wrestling was banned by Israel's Supreme Court on 23 June 1993.

☞ COSMETICS, DINOSAUR, FRECKLES

CRUSTACEAN

Ocean City, New Jersey, has hosted an annual 'Miss Crustacean' beauty pageant every year since 1976. Described as a 'symbol of crustacean comeliness' the coveted Cucumber Rind Cup has been won by crabs with names such as Copa Crabana, Crabunzel, Santa Crab and Crabopatra. Asked to account for the longevity and success of the event in 1996, a spokesman for Ocean City said, 'This makes no sense, has no redeeming social value and offers no prize money.'

CUBA

The tennis player John McEnroe was born on the day Fidel Castro seized power in Cuba.

CUCUMBER

In September 1997, researchers threw 500 cucumbers into the Irish Sea to gain information about the tidal currents. The cucumbers were painted five different colours for identification purposes. The reason for the research was to find out why sheep droppings were being washed up on English beaches. Cucumbers were selected for their hydrodynamic similarity to sheep droppings.

Cucumbers were known to the ancient Egyptians, who enjoyed a drink made from fermented cucumbers. The Roman emperor Tiberius also enjoyed cucumbers, which he grew in carts that slaves wheeled around so that the vegetables could catch the sun.

Cucumbers are about 95 per cent water. The skin is the most nutritious part. The inside of a cucumber can be as much as 11°C (20°F) cooler than the outside temperature.

The word for 'cucumber shaped' is 'cucumiform', not to be confused with 'cuculliform', which means 'hood shaped'.

☛ The world's longest cucumber was grown by John Hammond of Clacton-on-Sea. It was 46in long. The world record for 'Vegetable Cutting' also featured a cucumber: in 1998 Prof. Dr S. Ramesh Babu set a record by slicing a 28cm cucumber into 120,060 pieces in 2hr 52min 21sec.

'A cucumber should be well-sliced, and dressed with

pepper and vinegar, and then thrown out as good for nothing' – Samuel Johnson (1773).

☞ CRUSTACEAN

CURTIS, Jamie Lee (b. 1958)

Jamie Lee Curtis was once engaged to a grandson of Marlene Dietrich.

In both the 1994 film *True Lies* and the 2001 film *The Tailor Of Panama*, Jamie Lee Curtis plays a character married to a man named Harry whom she doesn't know is a spy.

CYCLING

☞ CRIME, DRUNKEN DRIVING, FISHING, PENIS, SWEDEN, TRANSPORT, WRIGHT

CYPRUS

According to tradition, the Archbishop of Cyprus is the only person on the island allowed to write in purple ink.

CZECH REPUBLIC

The Czech for 'a beautiful life' sounds exactly the same as the Russian for 'a red stomach'.

☞ BEER, COW, FORGERY

DANCING

★ On 21 August 1923, the city of Kalamazoo, Michigan, passed a law forbidding dancers to stare into each other's eyes.

☞ CAMBODIA, DAVIDSON, FOXTROT, SONGS, SPAIN, WATER-SKIING

DANDELION

The French for a dandelion is *pissenlit*, or 'piss-in-bed'. The English used to refer to the plant as a pissabed too, referring to its known qualities as a diuretic. Indeed, when apothecaries prescribed dandelion extract for that purpose, it was offered under the name Urinaria.

The English word 'dandelion' comes from the French too: *dent de lion*, or 'lion's tooth', referring to the shape of the leaves.

DANTE ALIGHIERI (1265–1321)

☞ UNIVERSITIES

DARTS

The order of numbers round a darts board was an invention of Brian Gamlin, a carpenter from Bury, Lancashire, who came up with the design in 1896 to minimise the role of luck in darts as a fairground game. The average speed with which a dart hits a dartboard in competition play is 40mph.

DARWIN, Charles (1809–82)

Darwin pointed out that lice which move from Hawaiians to English sailors die within a week. His publisher, John Murray, suggested that Darwin should put more about pigeons into the *Origin of Species*, because everybody is interested in pigeons.

★ Darwin was born on the same day, 12 January 1809, as Abraham Lincoln.

☞ WEATHER

DAVIDSON, Harold Francis (1872–1937)

The rector of the Norfolk village of Stiffkey, Harold Francis Davidson was convicted by the Norwich Consistory Court in July 1932 of disreputable association with women. On 28 July 1937, he was mauled by a lion in Skegness and died two days later.

Davidson had been rector of Stiffkey with Morston since 1906, but voluntarily extended his duties to the West End of London, where he became chaplain to the Actors' Church Union, with a ministry comprising mainly showgirls and prostitutes.

A complaint about his behaviour was finally sent to the Bishop of Norwich, which resulted in five separate charges of immoral conduct. Two of the more bizarre were 'making improper suggestions to waitresses' and 'embracing' a young woman in a Chinese restaurant. After a bizarre trial (one report even mentions him performing a tap dance before the judge) Davidson was convicted and defrocked.

He continued to protest his innocence, however, and soon turned those protests into a lucrative sideshow. On one occasion, he pleaded his case from inside a barrel on the seafront at Blackpool. Another time, he went on a public fast while inside a glass cabinet. Combining his defrocked rector act with that of lion-tamer, however, proved to be a fatal mistake, especially when it came to putting his head in the lion's mouth at Skegness. His parishioners, however, remained loyal and he was buried in the village churchyard. The lion's name, incidentally, was Freddy.

DA VINCI, Leonardo (1452–1519)

Leonardo da Vinci was born in the village of Vinci in Italy, the illegitimate son of a lawyer and a peasant woman named Caterina. His friends described him as the most beautiful man who ever lived.

One of da Vinci's less well-known inventions was an alarm clock that woke the sleeper by gently rubbing his feet.

★ On 21 August 1911, the *Mona Lisa* was stolen from the Louvre Museum in Paris and was not recovered for two years. While it was missing, more people turned up to stare at the empty space than had ever come to see the painting. In the two years the *Mona Lisa* was missing, six

Americans are known to have paid $300,000 each to conmen supposedly selling the painting.

DAYLIGHT SAVING
The UK Parliament passed a bill to introduce daylight saving and British Summer Time in May 1916, but it was not without opposition at all levels of society. Lord Balfour produced one of the most ingenious arguments against putting the clocks forwards an hour during the summer months. Referring to the night when the clocks went back again, he said, 'Supposing some unfortunate lady was confined with twins and one child was born ten minutes before one o'clock… the time of birth of the two children would be reversed… Such an alteration might conceivably affect the property and titles in that house.'

DEATH
There are 50,000 deaths a year in the USA from traffic accidents and 6,000 a year from burns (the second most common accidental cause). The most common fatal natural disaster is being struck by lightning – 400 deaths a year.
☞ CAPITAL PUNISHMENT, COCONUT, CRICKET, DISNEYLAND, DONKEY, EXECUTION, FOOT-AND-MOUTH DISEASE, GOLF, GUILLOTINE, HAIR, HANGING, HEDGEHOG, HORSE, MONDAY, PARAPSYCHOLOGY, POPULATION, QUEENSLAND, SOAP OPERAS, TAIWAN, TAX, TELEVISION

DEER
Men of the Mocoui tribe of South America tie deer hoofs to their ankles and hands to help them run faster.
☞ PREGNANCY, REINDEER, SANTA CLAUS, SINGAPORE

DEMOCRATIC REPUBLIC OF THE CONGO

(Formerly known as the Belgian Congo, 1908–60.) The Belgian Congo was 80 times as big as Belgium.

The Democratic Republic of the Congo is the only country in Africa split into two time zones.

☞ OKAPI

DENIM

Denim has been in existence since 1695 and gets its name from the French town of Nîmes where it was made as '*serge de Nîmes*'.

DE NIRO, Robert (b. 1943)

The real-life character played by Robert de Niro in the film *Goodfellas* would have been eligible for parole in 2004 if he hadn't died in prison in 1996.

DENMARK

When the film *King Kong* was screened in Denmark, it was called 'Kong King'. 'Kong' is the Danish for 'king'.

☞ ANIMAL NOISES, GREENLAND, RUGBY, SKIING, VICTORIA

DENTISTRY

According to figures published in 2002, 29 per cent of British dentists have been involved in road accidents.

The first British dentist to be knighted was Sir Edwin Saunders in 1883.

☞ St APOLLONIA, BUTCHELL, ELEPHANT, ORANGE, TEETH

D'EON, Chevalier (1728–1810)

Charles Genevieve Louis Auguste Andre Timothee d'Eon de Beaumont was a diplomat, spy, dragoon officer, swordsman, lady-in-waiting, chess player and part-time nun. He/she was a celebrated figure in French and English circles of the 18th century, renowned for feats of swordsmanship (including fighting a duel dressed in a pettitcoat in front of an audience that included the Prince of Wales), international intrigue, and the fact that nobody was sure of his/her sex. Indeed, in the 1760s a total of around £120,000 was said to have been wagered on the matter. A dispute over one such bet ended up in court, with the judge ruling that d'Eon was definitely a woman. In royal circles d'Eon was ordered subsequently always to dress as a woman. On his/her demise in 1810, however, the doctor who certified the death pronounced him to be a fully formed male. The woman he had been living with for 20 years promptly fainted and when the news was brought to George III it was said by some to have been the thing that finally drove the king irremediably mad. The term 'eonism' was subsequently used as a technical psychiatric term for transvestism.

DIAGRAM

The Diagram Prize is awarded each year at the Frankfurt Book Fair for the book judged to have the oddest title. The first winner, in 1978, was *Proceedings Of The Second International Workshop On Nude Mice*. Recent winners include:

2000: *High-Performance Stiffened Structures*
2001: *Butterworth's Corporate Manslaughter Service*
2002: *Living With Crazy Buttocks*
2003: *The Big Book of Lesbian Horse Stories*
2004: *Bulletproof Your Horse*
2005: *How People Who Don't Know They're Dead Attach Themselves to Unsuspecting Bystanders and What to Do About It.*

DIANA, Princess of Wales (1961–97)

Diana was the first English bride of an heir to the British throne since 1659. She was a direct descendant of the only sovereigns from whom Prince Charles was not descended: Charles II and James II. In the 55-minute interview she gave to Martin Bashir, which was broadcast on BBC television in 1995 (on the Queen's 48th wedding anniversary, incidentally), she mentioned the name 'Charles' only twice.

☞ ASCOT, FORTY-SEVEN, TELEVISION

DICKENS, Charles John Huffam (1812–70)

Charles Dickens's first job was labelling bottles at a warehouse of Warren's Blacking, a boot polish company. He was 12 years old and was paid six shillings a week. He called his first wife 'Pig' or 'Mouse' and they separated after 22 years' marriage. He combed his hair a great deal, was afraid of bats and hated the game of croquet. He always slept with his bed in a north-south position and had a pet raven called Grip.

☞ CHIPS, POLAR BEAR

DINGO

The Dingo Barrier Fence in Australia is twice as long as the Great Wall of China. With a total length of 2,500km, it is the longest man-made structure on Earth.

DINOSAUR

They finally lost the longest-ever game of hide-and-seek. After roaming the Earth in the Mesozoic Era (between 230 million and 65 million years ago), dinosaurs remained undiscovered until 1822 when Gideon Mantell found a few teeth and bones in Sussex. He called them 'Iguanodon' ('iguana tooth'), but, soon after, a similar discovery was made in Oxford by Rev. William Buckland, who called his teeth and bones 'Megalosaurus' ('great lizard'). The linguistic issue was finally resolved in 1841, when Sir Richard Owen suggested the word 'dinosaur'. Despite all this, the word 'dinosaur' occurs only twice in the entire *Dictionary of National Biography*.

Other useful dates:
- 220 million BC: first mammals
- 70 million BC: first Tyrannosaurus
- 1 million BC: first homo erectus
- 1938: fishermen net a coelacanth, thought to have been extinct for 70 million years
- 1947: birth of Steven Spielberg

Unsung heroes:
- The Stegosaurus ('plated lizard'), whose brain weighed in at 2.5oz, or half of one-thousandth of 1 per cent of its total body weight. This is a record for

a small central processing unit running a large piece of hardware.

- William Buckland (1784–1856) who, quite apart from his pioneering work as a dinosaur hunter, once stole Ben Jonson's heel bone from Westminster Abbey. His day job was Dean of Westminster Cathedral.
- Sir Richard Owen (1804–92) who, apart from inventing the term 'dinosaur', was renowned for his clinical dissections of the beaver, suricate, acouchy, Tibetan bear, gannet, crocodile, armadillo, seal, kangaroo, tapir, toucan, flamingo, hyrax, hornbill, cheetah, capybara, pelican, kinkajou, wombat, giraffe, dugong, apteryx, wart-hog, walrus and great ant-eater.

Extinction:

Although all the other dinosaurs died out suddenly around 65 million BC, the brontosaurus was only officially expunged from the natural history records this century, on the grounds that the Brontosaurus ('thunder lizard'), discovered and named by O.C. Marsh in 1879, was in fact only a grown-up Apatosaurus ('deceptive lizard'), which he had discovered and named two years earlier. The problem was partly caused by his sticking the wrong head on to his Apatosaurus bones. The error had been identified in 1903, after which, according to the rules of the naming game, 'Apatosaurus', as the earlier term, took official precedence. In 1970, the US Post Office was forced to apologise for calling an Apatosaurus a Brontosaurus on a series of dinosaur stamps.

Latest discoveries:

In 1993 it was established that the sound made by a Tyrannosaurus probably resembled, in the words of one scientist, 'The sound made by a human stomach after a bad night in a cheap restaurant.'

Clever theory:

No land animal bigger than a Seismosaurus (100 tonnes and 110ft) can exist, because its legs would need to be so thick to hold it up, it could never move.

Unsolved mysteries:

After cloning the dinosaurs from the blood specimens in the stomachs of mesozoic mosquitoes, how did the architects of Jurassic Park manage to grow the trees for their environment so quickly? That prehistoric tree the heroes hid up when the dinosaur sneezed on them must have been at least 200 years old to get that big.

★ On 14 October 1996, Australia's only known Stegosaurus footprint was reported to have been stolen from Aborigine land north of Broome, Western Australia.

☞ BUCKLAND

DISNEYLAND

Disneyland opened in Florida in 1955 and the first death within its grounds happened in 1964 – apparently a suicide. The first homicide in Disneyland was in 1981 when an 18-year-old was stabbed in a fight that started when one youth touched another one's girlfriend.

DIVORCE

Researchers in Chicago in 2002 reported that unhappily married couples who divorce as just as likely to be unhappy five years later as unhappily married couples who stay together. The town in Britain with the highest rate of divorced people is Blackpool.

The patron saint of unhappy marriages is St Theodore of Sykeon, a seventh-century monk and bishop.

In a divorce case in Leamington Spa in 1997, a woman cited her husband's 'obsession with football and Manchester United' as grounds for divorce. In response, the husband said, 'I have to admit that nine times out of ten I would rather watch the Reds than have sex, but that's no disrespect to Emma.'

Divorce Egyptian style:

An Egyptian court in 1999 rejected a petition from a man who wanted his marriage annulled because his wife had only one breast. He accused his wife of deliberately misleading him by not telling him that she had been born with her right breast missing. He had only just discovered the error after 20 months of marriage.

Divorce California style:

Also in 1999, Californian couple Bonny and Michael Martin visited a psychiatrist for marital counselling. The session did not go smoothly. The problems began when Michael drew a gun, pointed it at Bonny and told her to shut up. She answered by shooting him in the shoulder, then the couple and the psychiatrist took shelter behind furniture while Michael and Bonny continued shooting.

'The only thing that kept them from killing each other was that they both ran out of ammunition,' the psychiatrist said later. He suggested that they ought perhaps to think about divorce, but Mrs Martin said, 'I can't. I really can't. It might sound crazy to you but I really love that man.'

Divorce, Italian style:
In December 1999, an Italian court heard a divorce case between a 94-year-old man and his third wife, who was 52. The court asked the man why he thought the marriage had broken down after five months and he said that it was probably because he wanted too much sex.

☞ ASCOT, COFFEE, ECONOMICS, EDWARD VIII, LEPROSY, LOVE, PALMERSTON, REAGAN, ZAMBIA

DOG
The first mammal to orbit the earth was the Russian dog Laika, sent into space in 1957. No plans were made for its return trip and it burned up on re-entry. The first dogs to return from space alive were Belka and Strelka ('Squirrel' and 'Little Arrow') in 1960. Strelka later gave birth to six puppies, one of which was given to President Kennedy.

Bothy Twistleton-Wykeham-Fiennes, a Jack Russell terrier, is the only dog to have been at both the North and South Poles.

Each day dogs deposit between 4 and 5 tons of excrement on London streets.

In 1875, a Frenchman named Huret patented a three-wheeled vehicle called the Cynophere, whose wheels were powered by dogs on treadmills.

The top five dogs' names in the UK are Max, Ben, Charlie, Molly and Holly.

In January 2003, German inventor Stephan Licht was granted a patent for a 'harness for dog-wearing sunglasses'.

★ On 11 June 1991, Rodney H. Metts and Barry D. Thomas were granted US patent No. 5,023,850 for their invention of a Dog Watch, which they describe as 'A novelty clock, watch, and the like for keeping time at an animal's rate, defined in terms of a multiple of human rate by dividing the average lifetime of a particular animal into the average lifetime of a human being.' In other words, for dogs it multiplies time by seven, because humans live seven times as long as dogs. The first diagram accompanying the patent document shows 'a wristwatch worn by a typical dog'. The record for the largest dog litter was 24 puppies born to a mastiff in England in January 2005.

☞ ADDAMS, ALCOHOL, ALEXANDER III, ANIMAL NOISES, BARCELONA, BURMA, BURNS, BUSH, BYRON, CANARY, CHINA, CRAB, FORD, GHOSTS, HOLES, HOUSEWIVES, HYENA, INDEPENDENCE DAY, IRELAND, KEATS, LAVATORIES, LOVE, MOON, MUSIC, PAKISTAN, PARAPSYCHOLOGY, PARIS, PARKER, PARLIAMENT, PENGUIN, POSTMEN, SNORING, SOUTH KOREA, SWIMMING, TARANTINO, TEETH, TRANSPORT, WASP

DOLPHIN
In 1978, Californian vets were faced with an unusual problem in removing a piece of metal from the stomach of a dolphin that had inadvertently swallowed it. They

solved the problem by enlisting the help of baseball player Clifford Ray, who reached inside the animal's stomach to retrieve the object. The specialist qualification that made Mr Ray so appropriate for the job was an arm length of 3ft 9in.

DONKEY

William Thackeray once referred to a donkey by the word 'cardophagus', meaning 'thistle-eater'. Robert Louis Stevenson, in his *Travels With a Donkey*, reported that the correct word to encourage a donkey to move faster is 'Proot!'

In 2000, a Turkish man was reported to have tried three times to cure his sexual impotence by begging doctors to transplant a penis from a donkey on to him. When he brought a donkey home for the third time, his family were so annoyed with the man that his son shot him in the leg.

Donkey itself is an 18th-century word, and originally rhymed with monkey. More people are kicked to death by donkeys than die in aircraft accidents.

☞ PAKISTAN

DOUGHNUTS

The doughnut began life in Holland as 'oly koeks' ('oil cakes') made by dropping the leftovers from bread-making into boiling oil. The earliest use of the word 'doughnut' in print was in 1809 in Washington Irving's *History of New York*. The first doughnut cutter was patented by John Blondell in 1872.

The hole in the doughnut is attributed to US sea

captain Hanson Crockett Gregory, who, according to one legend, poked out the soggy centres of his doughnuts so he could slip them over the spokes of his ship's wheel. A more reliable version is that the hole in the middle was added to ensure regular baking. Whatever the truth is, Gregory is said to have invented the hole in 1847 and a commemorative centenary plaque was placed on his house in Rockfort, Maine, in 1947.

According to the International Federation of Competitive Eating, the world record for doughnuts is 48 glazed doughnuts in 8 minutes by Eric Booker. Booker also holds other eating records, including one for eating 38 hard-boiled eggs in 10 minutes.

☛ Ten billion doughnuts are made in the USA every year.

☞ PRESLEY

DRACULA

The first book published by Bram Stoker, author of *Dracula*, was called *The Duties of Clerks of Petty Sessions in Ireland*.

The Ministry of Tourism in Romania announced plans to build a Dracula theme park in 2001, but they ran into immediate problems on discovering that the rights to Dracula were held by Universal Studios.

Dracula is often linked to a 15th-century Romanian prince named Vlad the Impaler, though Vlad did not drink blood and there is no evidence that Bram Stoker had even heard of him. In modern Romanian, *drac* means devil or Satan.

Visitors to the Second World Dracula Congress in

1995 in the town of Poiana Brasov in Transylvania, Romania, were given miniature wooden coffins containing earth from beneath Castle Dracula.

When President Ceausescu was in charge of communist Romania, all mention of Dracula was banned.
☞ BURIAL, GARLIC, VAMPIRES

DRIVING
According to a survey conducted in 1997, 7 per cent of lorry drivers think of sex, drink, food and a night out while they are driving; 35 per cent think of their families; and 16 per cent think of nothing at all.
☞ ALASKA, DRUNKEN DRIVING, GARDENING, LOVE, MOTORING, PRAYER, SANTA CLAUS, SHOPPING TROLLEYS, SUPERSTITION, TRANSPORT

DRUGS
In 2001 Jose Antonio Campos–Cloute was arrested at Melbourne Airport after a momentary lapse in concentration: as he was filling out the Customs form, he absentmindedly ticked the 'yes' box to a question asking whether he was carrying illicit substances. The subsequent search revealed that he was a cocaine smuggler.
☞ CONDOM, GRAPEFRUIT, PHOENIX, WASP

DRUNKEN DRIVING
In July 2000, German police arrested a drunken cyclist who had modified his helmet to ensure that he did not have to stop drinking beer while cycling. The helmet had a can of beer attached to each side and straws leading into his mouth. A blood test found that the

cyclist had a blood alcohol level high enough to have had his driving licence taken away if he had been driving a car. Police let him off with a warning and allowed him to keep his helmet – on condition he promised to return it to its original design.

On New Year's Eve 1997, an Ohio judge ordered a chronic drunken driver to move nearer a liquor store or face jail. Dennis Cayse, who already had 18 convictions for drunken driving, was ordered to move within 'easy walking distance' – defined as half a mile or less – of a liquor store within 30 days or face an 18-month jail sentence for drunken driving. He was also sentenced to spend the first week of each of the next five years in jail.

In 2000, a court in Munich, Germany, imposed a three-month driving ban on a man who was arrested for being drunk in charge of his motorised wheelchair.

☞ ALASKA, BLINDNESS, GARDENING, MOTORING, SHOPPING TROLLEYS

DUBLIN

The O'Connell Bridge in Dublin is the only traffic bridge in Europe which is wider than it is long.

Between the hours of 5.30pm on a Friday and 3.00am the following Monday, Dubliners drink an average of 9,800 pints of beer an hour.

There are twelve places called Dublin in the United States and six in Australia.

The original name of Trinity College, Dublin, was Trinity College, near Dublin, but the city grew out to meet it.

☞ PREGNANCY, UNIVERSITIES

DUCK

When swimming, a duck is only a sixth as efficient as an average ship at utilising energy.

There is a statue of a duck at Freiburg in Germany, erected in memory of its alerting the population to an imminent air raid in 1944. The effectiveness of this warning may be judged from the result of a later noise abatement court case in Germany, at which experts testified that 10 quacking ducks make as much noise as three motor lorries with trailers. No research seems to have been done into the question of whether German ducks are noisier than Canadian ducks, but, when Milutin Velkjovic set a new world record in 1970 by being buried for 463 days, he spent his time underground accompanied by two Canadian ducks.

In a storm in Arkansas in 1974, people were pelted by frozen ducks, killed by a sudden blast of cold air across their flight path.

Donald Duck's middle name is Fauntleroy.

☛ The total number of ducks in the world has been estimated as 580 million, which is less than one duck for every 10 people. Around 27 per cent of them are in Vietnam, which is more than in any other country except China.

☞ ARGENTINA, BALLOON, BALZAC, ICELAND, MICKEY MOUSE, PLATYPUS, REINDEER, UKRAINE

DUELLING

The Duke of Wellington was the only British prime minister to fight a duel while in office. It was with Lord Winchelsea in Battersea Park in 1829. Wellington aimed at the legs and missed. Lord W. fired in the air and apologised. In 1809 George Canning (then Foreign Secretary, later Prime Minister) fought a duel with Lord Castlereagh on Putney Heath. Canning was wounded in the leg. Both men resigned.

☞ BALLOON, D'EON, HUDSON

DWARF

In October 1995, the 3ft-10in-tall Manuel Wackenheim petitioned the European Court of Human Rights to take action against France for banning the pastime of dwarf-throwing. The State Council, France's highest court, had ruled that dwarf-throwing was degrading to human dignity, but Wackenheim maintained that the ruling prevented him from earning a living. Wackenheim's lawyer was reported as saying, 'Banning him from his work is a restriction of liberty.' He said that his client, who weighs 97lb (44 kg), had never been injured by being thrown. In dwarf-throwing, the human projectile wears a crash helmet and padded clothes with handles on the back for ease of throwing. The flights are usually about 6ft long and end on an inflatable mattress. 'This spectacle is my life,' Wackenheim wrote to the Court. 'I want to be allowed to do what I want.'

The case was argued for seven years before a final decision was reached by the UN Human Rights Committee in September 2002, which ruled that: 'The ban on dwarf-tossing was not abusive but necessary in order to protect public order, including considerations of human dignity.' The committee also ruled that the ban 'did not amount to prohibited discrimination'.

Even before the matter reached the courts, however, the ethics of dwarf-throwing had exercised the minds of moral philosophers. In 1993, Robert W. McGee published a paper in the *American Journal of Jurisprudence* entitled 'If Dwarf-tossing is Outlawed, Only Outlaws Will Toss Dwarfs: is Dwarf-tossing a Victimless Crime?' This paper also formed the basis of a module in a Harvard University philosophy course. McGee's conclusion was unequivocal: there are no valid arguments to justify outlawing or restricting the practice of dwarf-tossing.

The last court dwarf in Europe was Coppernin, dwarf of the Princess of Wales (Princess Augusta of Saxe-Gotha), who was the mother of George III of England.
☛ Only two dwarfs are known to have lived to the age of 100.

★ On 29 November 1995, a spokesman for the actors' union Equity explained the problems caused by 14 Christmas productions of *Snow White*: 'I think it's clear there are relatively few people who are physically suitable for this work,' he said. 'We have only 37 persons of restricted growth on our register.'

☛ GOLF, HUDSON

EAGLE
☞ AESCHYLUS, MOON, PHOENIX, YODELLING

EARTH
Since the earth is not a perfect sphere, the pull of gravity varies slightly at different points on its surface. A person who weighs 150lb at the equator would weigh 151lb at the North Pole.

☞ AA, ACCIDENT, AFGHANISTAN, ALCHEMY, ASTRONOMY, AUSTRALIA, BANGLADESH, BUCKLAND, BULGARIA, CHINA, COFFEE, DINGO, DOG, DRACULA, EUROPE, EVEREST, GALILEI, GOLD, HAWAII, HITLER, KOMODO, MARS, MOLE, MOON, PACIFIC, PANAMA, PERU, PLINY, St LUCIA, SANTA CLAUS, SECOND, SUN, TROUSERS, UGANDA, WEATHER, WORM, ZYWOCICE

EASTER
The rules for calculating Easter are rather complex. Easter Day falls on the first Sunday after the first full moon that falls on or after March 21, but the 'full moon' referred to

is not the real moon but a theoretical moon that doesn't quite match the one in the sky. In 1928, the British House of Commons agreed to a bill fixing the date of Easter, subject to agreement by various Christian churches. Efforts to secure that agreement, however, have been going on ever since.

The name of 'Easter' is generally believed to be derived from Eostre, the pagan goddess of dawn, though recent research suggests that Eostre may not have been a goddess at all but the name of a season, and the 'goddess' was only a mistranslation by the Venerable Bede in the eighth century.

Easter Island in the Pacific was discovered by the Dutch sailor Jacob Roggeveen on Easter Day 1722.

☞ SANTA CLAUS

ECHIDNA
Small marsupial of Australia. A baby echidna is called a puggle.

☞ PLATYPUS

ECONOMICS
On 20 October 1995, the American economist Robert Lucas gave his ex-wife Rita half of his $1 million award for winning the Nobel Prize for Economics. There had been a clause in their 1989 divorce settlement guaranteeing her half his winnings if he won a Nobel Prize before 31 October 1995.

EDISON, Thomas Alva (1847–1931)
Edison advised answering the telephone with a simple

'hello'. He coined the word 'hello' specifically for that purpose. Before then it had generally been 'hullo'.
☞ ELECTRIC CHAIR, LIGHT BULB, MOZART

EDUCATION
'Education with socialists, it's like sex: all right so long as you don't have to pay for it' – Alan Bennett.
☞ MALAYSIA, POPULATION, SEX EDUCATION, UNIVERSITIES

EDWARD VII (1841–1910)
The coronation of Edward VII in 1901 had to be postponed to allow an emergency appendectomy operation to be performed on the King. When the ceremony finally took place two weeks late, the Archbishop of Canterbury placed the crown back-to-front on the royal head.
★ King Edward VII was born on 9 November, on which date Ramsay MacDonald, Neville Chamberlain, Chaim Weizmann and Charles de Gaulle all died.
☞ ALEXANDRA, EDWARD VIII

EDWARD VIII (1894–1972)
Edward VIII (later the Duke of Windsor) became king in 1936 but abdicated (in order to marry divorcée Wallis Simpson) before any coins could be issued bearing his head. Until then, the directions a monarch's head faced on British coins had followed a strict alternating pattern from the times of Charles II. For example, in the last two centuries: George IV faced left; his successor William IV faced right; Victoria faced left; Edward VII faced right; George V faced left… which would have

resulted in Edward VIII facing right. So, when Edward abdicated and was replaced by his brother, the new coins had George VI facing left again to take account of the missing monarch.

Oddly enough, this avoided a potentially difficult problem. Some coins had in fact been minted, but never released, with King Edward VIII's head on them – and it was facing left. Officially this was the wrong way, but the King always preferred to be viewed from that side.

★ Edward VIII acceded to the throne on the death of George V on 20 January 1936. On that day he also became the first British monarch to fly in an aeroplane.

☞ CORONATION, FASHION, FRUITCAKE

EGG

According to research at the US Agriculture Department, it takes 0.792 seconds to take an egg out of the refrigerator. Since the average American eats 286 eggs a year, he will spend 3min 46.5sec a year taking eggs out of the fridge.

Security guards watching over president Fernando Henrique Cardoso of Brazil spent weeks studying the maximum distance an egg can be thrown. Their conclusion was that the President will be perfectly safe from egg-throwing demonstrators, as long as he stands 60 metres away them.

The hens in Europe produce 85 billion eggs a year.

☞ CAT, CHICKEN, DOUGHNUTS, OSTRICH, PLATYPUS, PREGNANCY, SANDWICHES, TOOTHPASTE, TURTLE

EGYPT

The Great Pyramid of Cheops was the tallest structure

in the world for over 4,000 years. It was built in 2580BC and its 480.9ft height was not overtaken until 1584 when the central tower of Lincoln Cathedral was built.

The conventional greeting in Egypt translates as 'How do you sweat?' Dry skin is an indication of fever; sweating shows health.

☞ AMMONIA, CIRCUMCISION, CLEOPATRA, DIVORCE, GARLIC, HAIR, HAT, HEDGEHOG, MARS, OSTRICH, PHOENIX, PYRAMID, SEX, TATTOO, TOOTHPASTE, UMBRELLA, WATERMELON, WIG

EINSTEIN, Albert (1879–1955)
☞ ATOMIC ENERGY, HAIR, INCOME TAX

EISENHOWER, Dwight David (1890–1969)
President Eisenhower had two pairs of pyjamas with the five stars of a general on them.
☞ CAMP DAVID

ELASTIC
★ On 1 April 1946, wartime restrictions on the use of elastic were dropped on its employment in the making of underwear, nightwear, overwear, hose, shirt armlets, identification bracelets, pocket books, pram covers and umbrellas. Restrictions remained in force on other items.
☞ RUBBER BANDS

ELECTRIC CHAIR
The electric chair was invented by Thomas Edison in 1889 – not as a means of execution but as a way of demonstrating the danger of alternating current (AC)

while he was trying to promote his own direct current (DC) system. Once the world's executioners saw the potential of the machine, however, its value as a warning of the dangers of electricity was forgotten. One of the first outside America to be impressed by the new invention was Emperor Menelik II of Abyssinia (now Ethiopia), who promptly ordered three of them. Unfortunately, Abyssinia had no electricity but undeterred he had one of them converted into an imperial throne.

★ On 6 October 1941, two men were sent to the electric chair in Florida. Their names were Willburn and Frizzel.

ELEPHANT

The manner of copulation in elephants was a matter for speculation in the Dark Ages. Back to back was one theory, suggested by the position of their genitals. Others thought the male dug a pit or floated, to avoid crushing his mate.

- The pulse of a healthy elephant is only 25 beats a minute. Its trunk contains about 40,000 muscles and no bones and can hold a pint and a half of water.
- The elephant is the only animal apart from man that has been taught to stand on its head. Elephants cannot jump.
- It is forbidden to lead an elephant through the approach tunnels of London's Heathrow Airport.
- King James I is said to have kept a menagerie in St James's Park, including an 'ellefant', which was given a gallon of wine every day.

- The original Jumbo the Elephant was killed in 1885 in a railway accident in Ontario, Canada. It took 160 men to remove his body from the tracks.
- The first dental filling on an elephant was performed in South Africa in 1981. A team of 17 doctors and dentists took part, using enough anaesthetic to kill 70 men.

★ On 2 June 1971, the *Sun* newspaper reported that an elephant named Iris had been taught to play 'When the Saints Go Marching In' on a mouth organ.

★ On 17 July 1975, an elephant called Modoc died in California at the age of 78, the oldest known non-human mammal. Twenty-two years later to the day, on 17 July 1997, the science journal *Nature* published a paper showing that the African golden mole is more closely related to the elephant than to the garden mole.

☛ A Boeing 747 Jumbo jet weighs as much as 67 average African elephants. At the beginning of 2002, there were 129 elephants in the UK. The gestation period of an African elephant is 660 days. The food eaten in the life of the average Westerner weighs as much as six fully grown elephants.

☞ ALASKA, BANANA, CALIFORNIA, FENCING, HIPPO-POTAMUS, MOLE, PREGNANCY, TEETH, WATER-SKIING

ELIZABETH I, Queen of England (1533–1603)

The *Dictionary of National Biography* entry on Queen Elizabeth I says: 'she swore, she spat upon a courtier's coat when it did not please her taste, she beat her gentlewomen soundly, she kissed whom she pleased.' She also had black teeth from eating too much sugar. But she did take a bath once a month.

☞ ALCHEMY, HAT, RALEIGH, DE VERE, WIG

ELIZABETH II (b. 1926)

★ Queen Elizabeth married Prince Philip in Westminster Abbey on 20 November 1947; the 10-shilling note went out of circulation on 20 November 1970. General Franco died on 20 November 1975.

➥ Her Majesty takes size-7 gloves.

☞ MOLE, VICTORIA

EMBALMING

☞ BUCKLAND, BUTCHELL

EMU

☞ KANGAROO

ENGLISH

More English words begin with the letter 'S' than any other letter of the alphabet. The longest word in the *Oxford English Dictionary*, however, does not begin with S but P. It is:

pneumonoultramicroscopicsilicovolcanoconiosis

This is a 45-letter lung disease. By contrast, the longest word used by Shakespeare was 'honorificabilitudinitatibus', a 27-letter concoction which is found in *Love's Labours Lost*.

The longest common words that can be typed on

the top row of letters of a typewriter or computer keyboard are 'proprietor', 'repertoire', 'perpetuity' and 'typewriter' itself.

'Aegilops', which can mean either a genus of molluscs or an eye ulcer, is the longest word that has its letters in alphabetical order.

The top three words in spoken English are 'I', 'you' and 'the'. In written English, they are 'the', 'of' and 'and'.

☞ BREAD, BUTTOCKS, CHOCOLATE, COPYRIGHT, DANDELION, GOLDFISH, KISSING, LAVATORIES, LUNCHEON, PORTUGAL, RHYME, SCRABBLE, TATTOO, VOWELS, WIG

EPONYM
A word that derived from a person's name. For example:

- *leotard*: Jules Léotard gave his first performance in November 1859 as the daring young man on the flying trapeze at the Cirque Napoleon in Paris. The ballet leotard is named after his tight-fitting costume.
- *bloomers*: after Amelia Jenks Bloomer, the 19th-century social reformer who advocated wearing such things.
- *boycott*: from Captain Charles Boycott, the Irish land agent whose high rents in 1880 angered the Irish Land League into having nothing to do with him.
- *cardigan*: from James Brudenel, 7th Earl of Cardigan, who led the Charge of the Light Brigade.
- *derrick*: now a crane, but originally a scaffold named after London hangman Goodman Derrick.

- *mausoleum*: from King Mausolus, whose tomb was one of the Seven Wonders of the World.
- *salmonella*: named after the American surgeon Daniel Elmer Salmon.
- *shrapnel*: after General Henry Shrapnel (1761–1842) inventor of shrapnel shells.

… and do remember that, while 'tawdry' refers to shoddy goods bought at St Audrey's Fair in Ely, true 'sleaze' comes only from Silesia.

☞ HAT

ESKIMO
☞ BUTTOCKS, MOOSE, SNOW

ESTONIA
Estonia has one of the greatest discrepancies in the world between male and female life expectancy at birth. For men the figure is 64.36 years, while for women it is 76.57 years. There are only 49 men over 65 to every 100 women. Only Russia and Latvia are worse, each having 48 males for every 100 females among the over-65s.

☞ BANANA, WIFE-CARRYING

ETHIOPIA
Emperor Menelik II of Ethiopia nibbled a few pages of the Bible whenever he became ill. In December 1913 he ate the entire Book of Kings when convalescing after a stroke, and died.

☞ ELECTRIC CHAIR

ETIQUETTE

Raising one's hat is a symbol of subjugation. The gesture dates back to the practice of stripping prisoners as means of emphasizing the conqueror's domination. Between friends it is enough to remove your hat.

☞ CHOPSTICKS

EURO

The launch of the euro provoked varied reactions in different countries:

In Poland, two mathematicians performed experiments demonstrating that Belgian euro coins were more likely to land heads than tails when spun on a table. Their result, however, did not apply to tossed coins.

In Germany, tests showed that euro notes could survive being washed and spun-dry, but ironing ruined them.

In Britain, the Magic Circle appealed for an increase in the size of euro coins, which were too small for a number of tricks.

Meanwhile, replying to reports of toxicity in the ink, the European Central Bank stated that you would have to eat 400 banknotes to make yourself ill.

The initial letters of the 12 countries that joined the euro on its launch spell out the phrase 'Baffling Pigs'.

When the new currency was launched on 1 January 2002, 50 billion coins and 14.5 billion notes were brought into circulation. If all the one-euro coins had been put into a single pile, it would have been 49,000 miles high.

★ The first euro coin rolled off the presses in France on 11 May 1998.

☞ NETHERLANDS

EUROPE

European civilisation began with a beef crisis. Zeus, chief of the Greek gods, fell in love with Europa, daughter of the Phoenician king Agenor. After disguising himself as a white bull, he wandered among her and her handmaidens, and lay down to let them stroke him. Europa found him so sleek and gentle, she climbed on his back, whereupon he galloped off into the sea and carried her off to Crete. After turning back into Zeus, he made love to her either in a cave or under a plane tree (which, according to legend, was rewarded for the shelter it provided by being made evergreen). Before ditching her, Zeus gave Europa three sons and three presents: an unerring spear, Laelaps the inexorable hound and Talos, a bronze man who drove away strangers.

Europa, whose name comes either from the Greek for 'broad face' or a Semitic verb meaning 'to set' (symbolising her riding off into the setting sun on a bull), gave her name to the continent; the bull took its place as the constellation of Taurus.

Geographically, Europe has no real claim to be considered a continent. Its notional boundary with Asia began as a matter of convenience for the Greeks, who wanted a way to differentiate between the land on the two sides of the Hellespont. That local viewpoint extended as European civilisation did, causing great confusion to Herodotus. After his account of the discovery and exploration of Asia, he wrote: 'As for Europe, nobody knows if it is surrounded by sea, or where it got its name from, or who gave it.'

Covering 4 million square miles (roughly eight per cent of the Earth's surface), Europe is much the same area as Canada. Geologically, its oldest part is the Baltic (or Fennoscandian) Shield, covering Scandinavia, which is a relic dating back to pre-Cambrian times of around 600 million years ago. The vast bulk of Europe, from the British Isles to the Urals, was formed during the Hercynian orogeny in the Paleozoic era between 570 million and 225 million years ago. Britain's insularity dates back only 5,000 to 10,000 years, when the seas rose to form the Channel and North Sea.

Man's ancestors, Homo sapiens Neanderthalensis, first appeared in Europe between 100,000 and 50,000 years ago – which is up to 100,000 years after the first hominids in Africa. The earliest artefacts in Europe date back around 30,000 years, with the Willendorf Venus, dated at around 21,000BC, the earliest known European sculpture of a female nude.

According to the *Harmsworth Encyclopaedia* of 1921, there are two main anthropological types in Europe: 'The two extremes are round heads where the width exceeds 85 per cent, and long heads where the width is less than 77 per cent of the length.' Only Portugal, England and areas near the Rhine are inhabited by long heads.

The present population of Europe (excluding the former USSR and the European part of Turkey) is about 500 million.

☞ AFGHANISTAN, BAR CODES, CANADA, COFFEE, DUBLIN, DWARF, EGG, GREENLAND, HIPPOPOTAMUS, MOOSE, NETHERLANDS, OCTOBER, PEANUT, POTATO, SWITZERLAND, TOILET, TOMATO, UNIVERSITIES

EUROVISION SONG CONTEST

Although Norway holds the record for scoring no points most often – a feat it has achieved on four occasions – the country with most last places is Finland, with a total of eight. In 1964, Germany came last with no points despite having the longest ever title: 'Man Gewohnt Sich So Schnell An Das Schone'. By contrast the shortest titles have been 'Si' (Italy, 1974), 'El' (Spain, 1982), 'Hi' (Israel, 1983) and 'Go' (UK, 1988). In 1968, the lyrics of the Spanish entry 'La, La, La' included 138 occurrences of 'la'.

☞ IRELAND

EVEREST

Sir George Everest, after whom the world's tallest mountain was named, pronounced his surname with two syllables, Eve-rest, not three, as in E-ve-rest. The mountain was established as the world's highest by the Great Trigonometrical Survey of 1852 and was named Everest by the British in 1865. They would probably have not done so if they had known that the Chinese called it Qomolangma, after an earth goddess, about a century earlier.

In 1990, Peter Hillary, son of Sir Edmund, became the first son of an Everest climber to follow in his father's footsteps.

Since 1953, on average one person has climbed Everest every three weeks and one has died on its slopes every 14 weeks. If we discount the expeditions that end in neither death nor glory, the odds are therefore slightly worse than Russian Roulette.

★ 10 May 1993 was the most crowded day at the top of Everest, when 40 people reached the summit. On 25 May 2001, the American Erik Weihenmayer became the first blind man to conquer Everest.

☛ Because of movement of the Earth's tectonic plates, Everest grows at a rate of about 4mm a year.

☞ CHANNEL, MOUNTAINEERING, TOKYO

EXAMINATIONS

According to recent news items, cheating in examinations is a worldwide phenomenon:

In 1995, schoolgirls in one area of Nigeria had to remove their underwear before taking exams because so many had been smuggling in crib sheets in their undies.

In 1996, an Italian teacher was suspended for passing students answers hidden in salami sandwiches.

In 1999, thousands of Bangladeshi students were expelled for demanding the right to cheat in exams.

Cheating would not have helped students in Uganda in 1998, when thousands of exam results were lost after rats chewed through computer cables at the National Examination Board.

Exam cheats can be sentenced to 10 years in jail in the Indian state of Andhra Pradesh.

☞ HOMEWORK, SANDWICHES, SLIPPERS

EXECUTION

According to Harold Hillman's classic report 'The Possible Pain Experienced During Execution by Different Methods' (*Perception*, 1993, vol. 22, pp. 745–53), stoning to death is probably the most painful way of being executed.

★ On 15 March 2004, Utah became the last US state to give up executions by firing squad. Until then, their method was to have a five-man firing squad, one of whom was randomly allocated a blank cartridge so nobody would ever know who fired the fatal shot.

☞ BILLIARDS, CAPITAL PUNISHMENT, ELECTRIC CHAIR, GUILLOTINE, HALIFAX, HANGING, MARY QUEEN OF SCOTS

EXTRATERRESTRIALS

☞ COSTA RICA

EYELASH

False eyelashes were invented by the film director D.W. Griffith for the 1916 film *Intolerance* to be worn by Seena Owen. Judy Garland's false eyelashes fetched $125 at auction in 1979 in Beverly Hills.

☞ HAIR

EZRA

The 21st verse of the seventh chapter of the Book of Ezra in the Old Testament contains every letter of the alphabet except J, both in the King James and New English editions. At the time of King James, the letters I and J were the same; they only became distinct letters around 1700.

FART

In 2002, Mitreben Laboratories, based in Osaka, Japan, developed the *hohi kenshutsuki*, which they claimed to be the world's first fart detector. 'In hospitals, it is important for physicians to know if a post-operative patient has been farting,' explained Hideo Ueda, a member of the research team. 'When a patient is coming out from under total anaesthesia, farting is an indication that the digestive tract is returning to normal. After major surgery, patients are still in a groggy state and aren't aware of this themselves ... That is what led to the development of this device.'

☛ The average fart comprises 59 per cent nitrogen, 21 per cent hydrogen, 9 per cent carbon dioxide, 7 per cent methane and 4 per cent oxygen.

☞ METHANE, DEVERE

FASHION

'Fashion' originally meant shape or appearance. Shakespeare may have been the first to use it to imply something that is in vogue. In the 16th century, Catherine de Medici, Queen of France, decreed that all ladies at court must have 13in waists.

In 1994 the American designer Ed Kirko introduced a new fashion by shooting holes through clothes. His best-seller was a Stetson hat with a bullet hole apparently going through the wearer's head.

'Gentlemen never wear brown in London' – Lord Curzon (1859–1925).

★ On 1 March 1934, the Prince of Wales (later Edward VIII) said, 'I can see no reason why women should not wear shorts.'

★On 11 September 1995, white wedding dresses for pregnant brides made their first appearance at a bridal fair fashion show in Harrogate, England.

☞ ALEXANDRA, PARAPSYCHOLOGY, SHOES

FEBRUARY

Before Julius Caesar reformed the calendar, February was the only month with an even number of days. Februarius, as the Romans called it, took its name from februa, 'means of cleansing'. This was the cleansing appropriate to the ushering in of spring and a new year.

Even after Caesar's calendar reform, which brought in leap years, the last day of February was still always the 28th. The extra day every fourth year was gained by counting the 24th twice.

February is the only month that can pass without a full moon. This last happened in 1999 and will next happen in 2018.

Much Ado About Nothing is the only Shakespeare play that mentions February.

☞ SWEDEN, St VALENTINE

FEET

People in the south of England have on average bigger feet than people in the north. Nearly a quarter of all your bones are in your feet.

★ On 17 November 1997, the Californian Supreme Court ruled that feet are not deadly weapons, as defined by the law of aggravated assault.

☞ BUTTERFLY, DA VINCI, MOLE, PEACOCK, PENGUIN, POLAR BEAR, SHOES, SLIPPERS, SWAHILI, TUG-OF-WAR

FENCING

The elephant is the only non-human animal ever to be taught to use a sword.

☞ D'EON, OLYMPIC GAMES

FERRARI

★ The funeral of Mrs Sandra West of San Antonio, Texas, was held on 19 May 1977. According to the terms of her will, she was to be laid to rest: 'next to my husband, in my lace nightgown... in my Ferrari, with the seat slanted comfortably'. It was a light-blue 1964 Ferrari 250GT. The funeral cost $17,000.

FERRET

A male ferret is called a hob; a female is a jill; a baby ferret is a kit. The collective noun for ferrets is a 'business'. The chuckling sound made by ferrets when they are happy is called 'dooking'.

FIDGETING
According to research in 1993 by Prof. Leonard Storlein of Wollongong University, Australia, a compulsive fidgeter may expend 1,000 more calories a day than someone who sits still. This is equivalent to going on a 33km run. The scientific name for fidgeting is Non-Exercise Activity Thermogenesis, or NEAT.

FINGERS
The *Oxford English Dictionary* lists seven names for the second finger of your hand: it is the demonstrator, forefinger, index finger, insignitur, lickpot, teacher or weft finger.

Your middle finger is your middling, your midsfinger or your nameless finger; the ring finger may also be called the leech finger, physician finger or wedding finger; and your little finger is the ear finger, mercurial finger or pinkie. Your thumb is your pollex. Your big toe is your hallux.
☞ BOLEYN, COMPUTATION, FORTUNE-TELLING, FOX, FROG, IRAN, KOALA, MARRIAGE, PANDA, SHOPPING TROLLEYS, TOOTHPASTE, YETI

FINLAND
Ronkainen, a legendary Finnish robber of the 18th century, tested gang members by making them carry a heavy woman over an obstacle course. This selection

ritual is the origin of the annual wife-carrying championships in Sonkajaarvi, Finland.

☞ EUROVISION SONG CONTEST, MARRIAGE, MICKEY MOUSE, SANTA CLAUS, WIFE-CARRYING

FIREWORKS

The West African state of Niger banned the use of fireworks at the New Year 2001 festivities, saying they were making the public less attentive to the sound of real gunfire. The ban was ordered by the interior ministry after people had failed to report armed attacks by criminals, dismissing them as firecrackers.

Meanwhile, the Ivory Coast nearby also banned the use of fireworks, but for precisely the opposite reason: people there, who had been living through a bitter political crisis, tended to panic at the sound of fireworks, taking it to be gunfire.

☞ HENRY VII

FISH

Aristotle recognised 117 species of fish. The first fish in space were South American guppies which spent 48 days in orbit on the Russian Salyut 5 in 1976. Twenty years later, researchers at the University of New Brunswick published their findings that female guppy fish prefer brightly coloured males to drab ones.

Research has also shown that goldfish remember things better in cold water than warm water. Also, if you put a goldfish into water laced with alcohol, then teach it something and put it back into clean water, it is liable to forget what it learned; but if it is then put back into the alcoholic water, it will remember it again. This research is unlikely to have been done in Ohio, where it is illegal to get a fish drunk.

It is also illegal to carry fishing tackle in a cemetery in the town of Muncie, Indiana, and it is illegal to fish on horseback in Utah.

As a useful rule of thumb, it may be helpful to know that the top speed of a fish is generally equal to about ten times its own length per second.

☛ Only 1,506 tonnes of shark and swordfish were eaten in the UK in 2001 compared with 244,366 tonnes of cod and haddock. Every second almost eight portions of fish and chips are sold in the UK.

☞ St ANDREW, ARCHERY, BUSH, DINOSAUR, FISHING, FORTUNE-TELLING, GOLDFISH, JAPAN, LIVERPOOL, PARAPSYCHOLOGY, PARROT, PERU, POLAR BEAR, POMPADOUR, SARDINE, SHOPPING TROLLEYS, SMELL, THAMES, TUNA

FISHING

The most common fishing injuries are sticking a hook through your hand or straining a muscle getting out of a boat. In the league table of sporting injuries in the US, fishing comes sixth behind basketball, cycling, tennis, hiking and bowling.

★ On 19 August 1941, the US Patent Office issued patent No. 22553125 for a firing mechanism in a fishing hook invented by H. Heineke and others. The design is meant to ensure that, when the bait is taken, the gun fires, killing or at least stunning the fish.

☞ AMERICA, FISH, PERU, POLAR BEAR

FIZZY DRINKS

The English chemist Joseph Priestley is best known as the discoverer of oxygen, but he is also the man who invented fizzy drinks when he bubbled carbon dioxide gas into water in 1768. Priestley evidently did not appreciate the commercial potential of his invention, however, and the idea for marketing fizzy drinks originated with a German jeweller called Jacob Schweppe in 1794.

Schweppe's Soda Water was originally promoted as treatment for 'Stone of the Bladder'.

Coca-Cola was created by Dr John Pemberton, an Atlanta pharmacist, in 1886. It was first marketed as a 'brain and nerve tonic' and 'cure for all nervous affections' and takes its name from the coca leaf and Kola nut among its ingredients.

Pepsi-Cola was created by Caleb Bradham, a North Carolina pharmacist, in 1898. The name originally given to it was 'Brad's Drink'. 'Pepsi-Cola' is an anagram of 'Episcopal'.

Britons each drink an average of 149.7 pints of fizzy drink every year; Americans drink 377.9 pints.

According to research published in 1999, the main appeal of fizzy drinks is not the fizz itself but a reaction between the drinker's saliva and carbon dioxide in the bubbles producing carbonic acid, which stimulates the mouth.

☞ ASTRONAUTS

FLAMINGO

The first flamingo to be fitted with an artificial leg was a bird known only as B9720, in Lincoln Park Zoo, Illinois.

★ The operation was performed on 21 August 1997. The leg was plastic.

☞ DINOSAUR

FLEAS

☞ BEER, CAMEL, CHRISTMAS, HEDGEHOG, SWEDEN

FLIES

The musical fly swatter was patented in 1994 by Kathleen J. Spalding and Merrick W. Spalding of the United States. Their 'Fly swatter with sound effects' has two sound circuit boards – one plays a tune at the flick of a switch, while the other is activated by the swatter hitting something.

☞ PARAPSYCHOLOGY, BELGIUM

FLIGHT

★ On 15 June 1928, the train *The Flying Scotsman* beat an aeroplane in a race from London to Edinburgh.

☞ AIR HOSTESSES, BALLOON, CEMETERIES, CHANNEL, DUCK, DWARF, IN-FLIGHT CATERING, LINDBERGH, WRIGHT

FLIRTING

New York State introduced a bill to outlaw flirting in public in January 1902.

☞ PENGUIN

FLYING SAUCERS

The term 'flying saucer' dates from a sighting of disc-shaped craft moving at great speed by US pilot

Kenneth Arnold in 1947. That was 53 years after the first recorded occurrence of the word 'spaceship'.

The first country to depict flying saucers on its postage stamps was Equatorial Guinea in 1975.

US President Jimmy Carter thought he saw a flying saucer in 1973. Research suggests it was probably the planet Venus. Carter, however, was far from alone. A poll in the USA in 1997 revealed that 92 per cent of respondents believed that space aliens are already living among us.

Project Sign, Project Grudge, Project Twinkle and Project Blue Book have all been names of official US investigations into flying saucers and, according to a 1995 report, as many as 5 million Americans may have been abducted by aliens. Pooling the data from those who claim to have been abducted, the details suggest that it takes on average six aliens to abduct one human.

You can insure against alien abduction with the insurance company Goodfellows. Over 40,000 people have taken out Alien All Risks insurance, but no successful claims have yet been made.

☞ STAMPS

FOOD

In a week, the average person in Britain eats 329g of cakes and biscuits and only 229g of fresh green vegetables. Every day America eats more than 70 million cans and jars of food and more than 32 million pounds of frozen food.

In highland Scottish, the word *giomlaireachd* means the habit of dropping in at mealtimes.

'Food is an important part of a balanced diet' – Fran Lebowitz.

☞ ACCIDENT, BACON, BANGLADESH, BAUDELAIRE, BURNT FOOD, CAMEL, CHIMPANZEE, CHOCOLATE, CHOPSTICKS, CONDOM, CORNFLAKES, DRIVING, ELEPHANT, FROG, GHOST, GRAPE, INDONESIA, ISRAEL, MARY QUEEN OF SCOTS, MOOSE, MUSHROOM, PANCAKE, PERU, PHILIPPINES, PIZZA, PLATYPUS, POLAR BEAR, POPCORN, REINDEER, RESTAURANTS, SAUSAGES, SEAL, SHOPPING TROLLEYS, SKUA, SWEDEN, TABLOID, TINS, TUNA, WHALE, WORM

FOOT-AND-MOUTH DISEASE
'Foot-and-Mouth Disease' is an anagram of 'Moo of death is sad tune' and 'Doomed site: fauna shot'.

FOOTBALL
The Romans called it 'pila pedalis', which the English translated as 'foot-ball' and promptly banned. The first use of the word listed in the *OED* is in 1424 in an Act of James I: 'The king forbids that any man play at the fut ball under the pain of jail.' He was not the first king to ban it, however, since Edward III had already done so in 1349 (though he did it in Latin). While Edward's motive, however, was dictated by a desire to abolish anything that might distract men from archery practice, King James seemed to have an objection to football in principle, as he explained in his Basilicon Doron: 'From this court I debarre all rough and violent exercises, as the foot-ball, meeter for lameing than making able the users thereof.'

The general violence of the game is confirmed by

Joseph Strutt, in his *Games and Pastimes of the People of England* (1876): 'It was formerly much in vogue among the common people of England, though of late years it has fallen into disrepute, and is but little practised.' He goes on to explain: 'When the exercise becomes exceeding violent, the players kick each other's shins without the least ceremony, and some of them are overthrows at the hazard of their limbs.' Phillip Stubbes, in his *Anatomy of Abuses* (1583), called football: 'Rather a friendly kind of fight than a play or recreation, a bloody and murthering practise than a felowly sporte or pastime.'

Despite this, the expression 'football hooligan' did not enter the language until 1967, exactly 78 years after they first began calling it socca, socker or socker. While the expression 'over the moon' dates back to the 1850s, its companion 'sick as a parrot' seems first to have been used in a footballing context in 1978. According to Nigel Rees's *Dictionary of Catchphrases*, it may be connected with a psittacosis outbreak in West Africa around 1973, or possibly with an earlier expression 'as sick as a parrot with a rubber beak'.

The health risks of football are also well documented. According to research published in the *British Medical Journal* in 2001, 50 per cent more men died from heart attack or stroke in the Netherlands on the day their country was knocked out of the 1996 European Championship than on a normal day. No corresponding increase occurred in women. The Dutch lost to France in a dramatic penalty shoot-out.

There are only two mentions of football in Shakespeare, both rather derogatory. In *The Comedy of*

Errors, Dromio accuses Adriana: 'Am I so round with you, as you with me, That like a football you do spurn me thus?' While in *King Lear*, Kent calls Oswald a 'base football player' before tripping him up.

Notable dates in football include the following:

1857: In Sheffield, old boys of Cambridge University formed the first football club.

1890: The first football nets (invented by J.A. Brodie of Liverpool) were used in goal.

1891: The first penalty kick in English league football.

1932: Gillespie Road station on London's Piccadilly Line changed its name to Arsenal after lobbying from Herbert Chapman, Arsenal's manager.

1944: William Hill produced the first fixed-odds football coupon (and, when Ladbrokes went into football in 1960, he sued them for £1 damages for infringement of copyright).

1951: The white ball was officially sanctioned.

1994: A Colombian footballer, Andres Escobar, was shot dead by fans for scoring the own goal that led to their elimination from the World Cup.

2006: The Nigerian Football Association advised referees that they may accept bribes from teams, but should not let it affect their impartiality.

Among the unsung heroes of the football field, we should mention:

James Law (1560–1632), archbishop of Glasgow, who was censured by the synod of Lothian for playing football on a Sunday.

William Whiteley (1881–1955), chief whip of the Labour Party, who had played football for Sunderland and might have become professional, according to the *Dictionary of National Biography*, 'had not his father, a strong teetotaller, finding that the team changed in public houses, burnt his son's football clothes and boots'.

John Rutherford Gordon (1890–1974), newspaper editor, who was the first reporter to take carrier pigeons to football matches to ensure that his paper received the results quickly.

★ On 20 July 1885, the British Parliament legalised professional football.

☞ BASKETBALL, COW, DIVORCE, HULL, RUGBY, SUPER-STITION, TELEVISION

FORD, Gerald (b. 1913)

Gerald Ford is the only man to have become both Vice-President and President of the USA without ever being elected to either post. When he was President, so many requests were received for autographs of his dog Patsy that a rubber stamp was made of its pawprint.

FORGERY

In October 1997, Czech Police announced that they had found a 1,000-crown note, which they described as 'exceptionally well forged', in the town of Jablonec. The only thing that gave it away was the fact that the words 'Forging of notes will be prosecuted in accordance with the law' had been replaced by a message saying 'This note is a fake'.

☞ ALCHEMY, CAPITAL PUNISHMENT

FORTUNE-TELLING

The *Oxford English Dictionary* lists over a hundred different words for ways of foretelling the future. Among them are the following:

alectryomancy: divination by means of a cock with grains of corn.

ambulomancy: divination by means of walking.

anthracomancy: divination by the inspection of burning coals.

anthropomancy: divination by the entrails of men.

armomancy: divination by the shoulders of beasts.

astragalomancy: divination by dice or knuckle bones.

belomancy: divination by arrows.

catoptromancy: divination by a mirror.

ceromancy: divination by dropping wax into water.

gastromancy: divination by noises in the belly.

gyromancy: divination by walking in a circle until the subject falls over from dizziness.

ichthyomancy: divination by using the heads or entrails of fish.

molybdomancy: divination by molten lead.

myomancy: divination by movements of mice.

omphalomancy: divination by knots on the umbilical cord.

onychomancy: divination by inspection of fingernails.

ophiomancy: divination by serpents.

rhapsodomancy: divination by random selection of a line of poetry.

sycomancy: divination by figs or fig-leaves.

tyromancy: divination by cheese.

☞ BREAST

FORTY

Forty is the only number which, when spelled out in English, has its letters in alphabetical order.

☞ St SWITHUN

FORTY-SEVEN

There are 47 regional prefectures in Japan. Also in Japan, the 47 Ronin were masterless Samurai from Naganeri Asano, who dramatically avenged their master's death at the end of 1702.

- Forty-seven bullets killed the Mexican revolutionary Pancho Villa (1878–1923).
- Forty-seven piglets were used in making the film *Babe*.
- Forty-seven members of the royal family were present at the funeral of Diana, Princess of Wales.
- There are 47 degrees of latitude between the tropics of Cancer and Capricorn.
- There are 47 strings on a concert harp.
- Osama bin Laden was his father's 47th child.
- Pythagoras's Theorem is Proposition 47 in Euclid's Elements.
- The pedestal of the Statue of Liberty is 47m high.
- 'Hamlet' is the 47th most frequently used word in Shakespeare's *Hamlet*.
- The AK47 assault rifle takes its name from the year in which it was designed: 1947. Its successor was the AK74. The letters stand for Avtomat Kalashnikova – the Kalashnikov Automatic, after its designer Mikhail Timofeyevich Kalashnikov.

☞ AFGHANISTAN, BILLIARDS, CHAMPAGNE, SANTA CLAUS

FOSSIL
☞ AMMONIA, BUCKLAND, PEANUT

FOX

Foxes have long featured in medical applications. The ancient Romans believed that a headache could be cured by binding the genitals of a fox to the sufferer's forehead, while, in the year 2000, a Scottish company began trials of a device in the form of a copper collar that was designed to cure arthritis in wild foxes.

People named Fox have also made their mark. In 1901, a pair of twin criminals called Fox, who lived in Hertfordshire, were partly responsible for the introduction of fingerprinting in Britain. Other forms of identification could never tell them apart. More recently, according to a 'Magnificent Mammaries' poll in a US film magazine in 1998, the model Samanatha Fox was judged to have had the 43rd most beautiful breasts of all time.

Less successfully, the 1941 film *The Little Foxes* gained nine Oscar nominations but did not win any. The collective noun for a group of foxes is a 'leash'.

The Japanese for 'foxtrot' is *fokkusutorotto*.

☞ FOXTROT, ICELAND

FOXTROT
The dance known as the foxtrot was invented by Harry Fox in 1914.

☞ FOX

FRANCE
In the ninth century, France was ruled by kings known

as Charles the Bald, Charles the Fat and Charles the Simple. Charles the Simple was the son of Louis the Stammerer. Charles VIII of France (1470–98) had six toes on one foot. He is said to have popularised square-toed shoes in order to hide this deformity. Charles VIII was born only 17 years after the end of The Hundred Years War between Britain and France, which lasted 116 years, from 1337 to 1453.

The rules of the Miss France contest specify that the winner must be at least 1.70m tall.

In July 1984 the Court of Cassation held that a French couple might not lawfully register their daughter under the name Manhattan. Under a law of 11 Germinal, year XI (1 April 1803) only saints' names or names of well-known figures of ancient history are permissible.

Despite the existence of such a law as this, there are more judges in Los Angeles than in the whole of France.

☞ AA, ADDRESS, BAR CODES, BEAUTY, BILLIARDS, BLYTON, BOOKS, BRAIN, BUCKLAND, CHAMPAGNE, CHANNEL, COLOMBIA, COMPUTATION, CORK, CRICKET, DWARF, EURO, FASHION, FOOTBALL, FROGS, GUILLOTINE, HENRY III, INCOME TAX, LAVATORIES, LAWYERS, LIECHTENSTEIN, LOUIS XIV, METRIC SYSTEM, MICKEY MOUSE, MUSHROOM, OLYMPIC GAMES, POMPADOUR, RUGBY, SHOES, St SWITHUN, TENNIS, THIRTEEN, TRANSPLANTATION, TRANSPORT, TROUSERS, WHISKY

FRANKLIN, Benjamin (1706–90)

Benjamin Franklin rose early every day and sat naked for half an hour or an hour either reading or writing, a practice he described as 'agreeable'. Sometimes he would then return to bed for 'one or two hours of the most pleasing sleep that can be imagined'.

He was strongly against the use of the words 'notice', 'advocate' and 'progress' as verbs.

☞ GUNS, RHUBARB, TAX

FREDERICK I BARBAROSSA, Holy Roman Emperor (c.1123–1190)

☞ UNIVERSITIES

FRECKLES

According to Galen the physician, crocodile dung is good for freckles.

FRENCH

☞ ALCHEMY, BAUDELAIRE, BILLIARDS, BIRMINGHAM, BISCUITS, BRASSIERE, BURNS, CHAMOIS, CHANNEL, CHIPS, CINDERELLA, COSMETICS, CRISPS, DANDELION, DENIM, D'EON, DOG, FRANCE, GARLIC, GOLF, HALIFAX, KISSING, LAVATORIES, PANAMA, PENGUIN, PIG, PORTER, POTATO, SEAL, SHOES, SNAIL, SWIMMING, TENNIS, THIRTEEN, TOILET, TUESDAY, VANUATU, VOLTAIRE, WELLINGTON, WEREWOLVES

FRIDAY

Friday takes its name from the Norse goddess of love, Freyja or Frigga. Fear of Fridays is known as Friggaphobia.

Crucifixions in ancient Rome, hangings in England, moving house in the UK, airline price rises and bank robberies in the USA are all events that happen or happened more often on Fridays that any other day of the week. Friday is also the working day on which companies are least likely to hold board meetings and is also the day on which an American is most likely to die.

If you arrange the days of the week in alphabetical order, Friday comes first.

☞ CALENDAR, MONDAY, THIRTEEN

FRISBEE
The Frisbee gets its name from the Frisbie Baking Co. of Bridgeport, Connecticut. A representative of the Wham-O Co. had the idea for the invention when he saw delivery men from Mother Frisbie's pies showing Yale students how to throw empty pie pans through the air. The Wham-O Co. adopted the name Frisbee in 1958.

☞ SEX

FROG
The town of Vittel in France is headquarters to the Brotherhood of Frog Thigh Tasters and holds an annual Frog Eating Festival. The EU annually imports more than 6,000 tonnes of frogs' legs from Asia. The French eat 42 per cent of them, while Belgium and Luxembourg consume another 44 per cent. The great French chef Auguste Escoffier introduced frogs' legs to the British in 1908 when he served them to the Prince of Wales under the name Les Cuisses de Nymphes Aurore, or 'Thighs of the Dawn Nymphs'. Depending on their size, it takes between 10.8kg and 18kg of frogs to produce 450g of frogs' legs.

Frogs never eat with their eyes open. They use their

eyeballs to push against the roof of the mouth to force food down into the stomach.

Most frogs have four fingers (or toes) on each limb. The Carpenter frog has a croak that sounds like a hammer. If a human could jump as far as a Cricket frog, the world long-jump record would be around 70m.

Fear of frogs is called ranidaphobia. This should not be confused with bufonophobia, which is fear of toads, or batrachophobia, which is fear of amphibians.

The mating position adopted by frogs and toads is called 'amplexus'.

☞ COLOMBIA, IRELAND, ZAMBIA

FRUITCAKE

Assumption Abbey in Ava, Missouri, in the Ozark mountains, is the only Trappist monastery in the world that sells fruitcakes on the Internet. When the monastery set up its bakery, which is its main source of income, it sought advice from Jean-Pierre Augé, who at one time served as chef to the Duke and Duchess of Windsor. His generous help and donation of a recipe have established Assumption Abbey Fruitcakes as a leader in the Trappist Fruitcake field.

In 1992, pollsters in America asked respondents what they thought was the most appropriate use of fruitcake. Thirty-eight per cent said 'a gift for someone else'; 13 per cent said 'a good doorstop'; and 4 per cent said 'landfill'.

FUNERALS

A new range of pendants was launched at the National Funeral Directors Convention in Cincinnati in 1996.

Called the Heirloom Pendant Collection, it was designed to enable people to wear their loved one's ashes round their necks. The pendant came in three designs: Teardrop, Infinity and Love.

The top ten songs requested at funerals in the UK in 1999 were:

1. My Heart will Go On – Celine Dion
2. Candle in the Wind – Elton John
3. Wind Beneath my Wings – Bette Midler
4. Search for the Hero – M People
5. My Way – Frank Sinatra
6. You'll Never Walk Alone – Gerry and the Pacemakers
7. Please Release Me – Engelbert Humperdinck
8. Memories – Elaine Paige
9. Strangers in the Night – Frank Sinatra
10. Bright Eyes – Art Garfunkel

A poll conducted throughout Europe by Music Choice in 2005, reported the following top five among songs people wanted at their funerals:

1. The Show Must Go On - Queen
2. Stairway to Heaven - Led Zeppelin
3. Highway to Hell - AC/DC
4. My Way - Frank Sinatra
5. Requiem - Mozart

The British number one was Angels by Robbie Williams.

☞ BUFFALO, BULGARIA, FERRARI, FORTY-SEVEN, GOLF, HOMEWORK, PHOENIX, SHOES, TELEVISION, VICTORIA

GALILEI, Galileo (1564–1642)

Galileo enrolled at the University of Pisa to read medicine but lost interest in the subject and left without obtaining a degree.

★ On 22 June 1633, Galileo was forced by the Inquisition to sign a statement recanting his view that the Earth moved around the Sun. The Vatican finally admitted that he had been right in 1992.

'To assert that the earth revolves around the sun is as erroneous as to claim that Jesus was not born of a virgin' – Cardinal Bellarmine (1615, during the trial of Galileo).

☞ HAWKING

GARDENING

The first recorded conviction for drunken driving while in charge of a lawnmower was in Norway in 1995. A 54-year-old man had been cutting grass for the southwestern town of Haugesund when police caught him driving a small lawnmower from one garden to another. Police just stopped him as part of a spot check and found that his blood alcohol level was well over the limit for motorised vehicles. He was fined and sentenced to 24 days in jail, but the sentence was suspended on the grounds that the lawnmower's top speed of about 10mph was too slow to do any damage.

☞ KARLOFF

GARLIC

Garlic is one of the world's oldest cultivated crops. It was fed to the builders of the Great Pyramid of Cheops in Egypt in the belief that it gave them strength.

'Garlics, tho' used by the French, are better adapted to the uses of medicine than cookery' – Amelia Simmons (*American Cookery*, 1796). It sounds from this as though Ms Simmons was an alliumphobe – the term for a garlic-hater.

Garlic may repel vampires but it attracts leeches. Experiments show leeches take 14.9 seconds to attach themselves to a hand covered with garlic, but 44.9 seconds to suck blood from a clean one. In view of this, it may be wise to know that a recommended way to get the smell of garlic out of your hands is to rub them with salt and lemon juice and rinse; to banish garlic breath, chew on fresh parsley or a coffee bean.

The average American eats over 3lb of garlic a year and the habit is clearly an old one. The city of Chicago is named after garlic: 'chicagaoua' was the Indian word for wild garlic.

➥ The word 'garlic' occurs 21 times in Bram Stoker's *Dracula*, and only four times in the entire works of Shakespeare.

➦ The longest continuous string of garlic contained 1,600 garlic bulbs and was 36.5m long.
☞ TAIWAN, VAMPIRES

GATES, William Henry (b. 1955)

William Henry ('Bill') Gates III was the son of William Henry Gates II. The total value of his shares in Microsoft is approximately equal to that of all British banknotes currently in circulation. If that were changed into dollar bills and put in a line, it would go to the moon and back seven times.

GENETICS

According to current knowledge, there are about 21,600 distinct human genes, which combine in different ways to form every human being. This is roughly the same number of distinct components as are needed to make a top-of-the-range Mercedes car with air conditioning.

GEORGE I, King of Great Britain and Ireland (1660–1727)

George I was the last King of England who could not speak English. He spent most of his reign in Hanover and when he needed to communicate with his prime minister, Robert Walpole, they spoke Latin.

GEORGE II, King of Great Britain and Ireland (1683–1760)

The victory of George II at the Battle of Dettingen in 1743 in the War of the Austrian Succession was the last battle commanded by a British king. He died of a heart attack brought on by chronic constipation.

☞ ASH WEDNESDAY, CRICKET

GEORGE III, King of Great Britain and Ireland (1738–1820)

When the film *The Madness of King George III* was released in the US, the title was amended to *The Madness of King George* to avoid deterring people who might think it was the third part of a series of which they had missed the first two.

☞ BUTE, D'EON, DWARF, INDEPENDENCE DAY, WIG

GEORGE IV, King of Great Britain (1762–1830)

☞ EDWARD VIII, SHOES, WILLIAM IV

GEORGE V, King of Great Britain (1865–1936)

King George V had a pet parrot called Charlotte. The King always made a point of falling asleep at ten past eleven. His last words before dying were either 'How is the Empire?' or 'Bugger Bognor'.

☞ EDWARD VIII, QUEEN MARY

GEORGE VI, King of Great Britain (1895–1952)

King George VI was naturally left-handed but was forced to learn to write with his right. He played tennis left-handed. His first name was not George but Albert.

☞ EDWARD VIII

St GEORGE

St George replaced Edward the Confessor as patron saint of England in the 14th century. He is also patron saint of

Catalonia, the Greek army, knights, archers, boy scouts and sufferers from syphilis, though nobody is sure whether he ever existed. Although some say he was martyred in the fourth century, no connection was made between St George and the feat of slaying a dragon until the 12th or 13th century. In any case, the 'dragon' may not have been a dragon at all, but a nickname for the tyrant Emperor Diocletian, who persecuted the Christians.

Because of the uncertainty surrounding his existence, St George was demoted to 'optional worship' by Pope Paul VI in 1969, but Pope John Paul II reinstated him to full membership of the calendar of saints in 2000.

Shakespeare, Wordsworth and Rupert Brooke all died on St George's Day, 23 April.

GEORGIA, republic of

The area of the republic of Georgia is less than half the area of the US state of Georgia. Its capital, Tbilisi, takes its name from the word for 'warm' in the Georgian language. The Russians call Georgia 'Gruziya'; the Georgians call Georgia 'Sak'art'velo'. The Georgian language seems to be unrelated to any other and uses a 38-letter alphabet, called Mxedruli.

Georgia includes the ancient land of Colchis from where, according to legend, Jason and the Argonauts brought back the golden fleece.

From 1184 to 1213, Georgia was ruled by a queen known as the 'King-Woman Tamar', who was later made a saint in the Georgian Orthodox Church.

GEORGIA, state of

☞ PEANUT, SODOMY, WATERMELON

GERMANY

In 2001, the Advertising Standards Agency in Britain ruled that referring to Germans as 'krauts' is not offensive but is 'a lighthearted reference to a national stereotype unlikely to cause serious or widespread offence'. A German Embassy spokesman, however, disagreed saying, 'It is offensive. If you were called cabbage, you would not like it. It is the same for us.'

☞ AA, ANAGRAMS, ANIMAL NOISES, BEER, BLYTON, DRUNKEN DRIVING, DUCK, EURO, EUROVISION SONG CONTEST, GOLDFISH, HAIR, KNEE, LAVATORIES, ORANGE, PANCAKE, POLAR BEAR, POSTMEN, STAMPS, St SWITHUN

GHOSTS

Former Swaziland Prime Minister Prince Bhemkimpi was reported in 1995 to have complained about ghosts terrorising his subjects in the mountainous Enkhaba region. A family had taken refuge with the Prince's household after ghosts had invaded their own house, beaten them, ordered them to cook food and stolen their blankets. The Prince himself had also been verbally abused by the ghosts. Fortunately the ghosts had not invaded the royal household because they were afraid of the dogs.

Having banned celebrations, political groups, love affairs with women under 21 and all alcohol except traditional beer, the Prince was reported to have said that he was determined to ban ghosts as well.

In October 1995, a woman on the Isle of Wight complained of a ghost that turned on lights and electrical equipment. A spokesman for Southern Electricity said it was the first time they had had a high bill blamed on a ghost.

The Chinese in Singapore celebrate a month-long 'Hungry Ghost' festival in August and September. In 1996, a power failure in Singapore was caused by too many people cooking for the Hungry Ghosts.

In 1998, three workers resigned after seeing Ernest Hemingway's ghost in a Havana museum.

The sixth-century Irish saint St Kevin was canonised for putting up with the ghost of a woman he had murdered.
☞ PARAPSYCHOLOGY, QUEEN MARY

GIRAFFE
Giraffes cannot cough or swim.
☞ DINOSAUR, HIPPOPOTAMUS, OKAPI

GLADSTONE, William Ewart (1809–98)
William Gladstone is one of only two people to have had his coffin transported on the London tube. The other one was Dr Barnardo.

GOATS
According to official figures, there were 157,361,699 goats in China in 2001.
★ On 15 September 1996, police in Brazil were reported to be investigating allegations of a political assassination of a goat. The animal had been found dead after it had been registered to stand as a protest candidate for the post of mayor in a small town. The goat's owner suspected it had been poisoned.
☞ BIBLE, ITALY, MARQUESAS ISLANDS, NARWHAL, QUEENSLAND, TEETH, THOR, St VALENTINE

GODIVA

Lady Godiva – or Godgifu – was a real person. She was the wife of Leofric, Earl of Mercia, and is said to have ridden naked through the town of Coventry in exchange for her husband promising to cut taxes. She is mentioned in the Domesday Book of 1086 as having inherited various estates from her husband, who died in 1057. The story about the naked riding first appeared about a century after her death, and is almost certainly a myth. The horse is supposed to have been named Aethenoth, which means Noble Audacity.

GOLD

All the gold in Fort Knox is worth about £30 billion.

One-third of all the gold ever mined on earth comes from the Witwatersrand Basin in South Africa.

☞ ALCHEMY, BURIAL, CALIFORNIA, CAT, CHOCOLATE, St CLARE, SNORING, TOMATO

GOLDFISH

The Polish-born film director Sam Goldwyn was originally called Schmuel Gelbfisz. He anglicised his name to Samuel Goldfish after he came to England aged 15 and became Samuel Goldwyn at the age of 39.

Contrary to popular belief, goldfish do not have short memory spans. Their learning ability is at its best between January and March. Artificial waves, whether cold or warm, can make a goldfish seasick.

Goldfish have fine hearing: they can distinguish between sounds one 150-millionth of a second apart.

In 1976, researchers showed that, if you bung up a

goldfish's nose so that it cannot smell, its sexual behaviour decreases significantly. In the same year, it was also reported that one-eyed goldfish swim as fast as two-eyed goldfish, but blind goldfish are slower.

Goldfish have been taught to swim on their tails, as if standing up in the water.

An RSPCA inspector was commended in the 1970s for saving a goldfish from drowning. 'There are not many people who know that a fish could drown if it swallows too much water,' he said.

In their natural state, goldfish are olive green. Domestic varieties result from breeding for colour.

The domesticated goldfish was first documented in China in the 10th century. They were popular among the privileged classes and eating them was forbidden. The first book about goldfish was *Essay About the Goldfish*, written in China in 1596. The earliest use of the word 'goldfish' in English dates back to 1698.

Guests at the Russischer Hof Grand Hotel in Weimar, Germany, are offered a pair of goldfish as companions in their rooms.

☛ There are 14,700,000 pet goldfish in the UK. Despite this, a survey in September 2002 reported that the word 'goldfish' is only the 3,782nd most popular keyword entered into search engines.

☞ ALCOHOL, FISH, JAPAN, LIVERPOOL, PARAPSYCHOLOGY, POMPADOUR

GOLF

In 1456, King James II of Scotland decreed that 'futeball and the golfe be utterly cryit down' because they interfered with yeomen's archery practice. The ban lasted until 1502, when King James IV signed the Treaty of Glasgow, making peace with England and giving archers more spare time. The first officially documented golf match was between James IV himself and the Earl of Bothwell on 4 February 1504.

A golf hole is 4.25in in diameter because that was the size of a piece of drain pipe used to repair a hole at St Andrew's many years ago. The 18-hole course also originated at St Andrews. Until 1764, there were 12 holes, with a round teeing off from hole one, then 11 holes out and retracing the path with 11 back. The over-short first four, which became the last four on the way back, were then combined into two holes each way. Result: 18 holes.

A golfer's caddie takes his name from the French word *cadet*, meaning a boy, or youngest son: he was the one who carried the bags. The French, however, have contributed more to the game of golf than just this word. On 7 February 1928, French golfers voted to sentence a blackbird to death for stealing 30 golf balls from the Saint-Germain course near Paris.

In Ohio, statistics show that 6 per cent of all deaths by lightning occur when the victim is playing golf.

The worst ever round in a US Masters tournament was the 23 over-par 95 hit by Charles Kunkle in 1956. The title of worst golfer, however, goes elsewhere: in the Bob Hope Desert Golf Classic in 1971, Vice-President Spiro Agnew hit three spectators with his first two shots.

Putts missed through nervous tension formed the subject of a paper in the journal *Sports Medicine* in 2002 entitled: 'A Multidisciplinary Study of the "Yips" Phenomenon in Golf'.

Best golfing funeral:

Mr Thomas J. Caradonia, 70, from Houston, was buried in August 1984 wearing full golfing regalia and holding a putter in his right hand.

Golfing quotations:

'Excessive golfing dwarfs the intellect' – Sir Walter Simpson, *The Art of Golf* (1887).

'Golf is a good walk spoiled' – Mark Twain.

'I'm sure Jimmy would have wanted us to do that. He would have done the same.' Spoken at a golf club in Fife in September 1996 by a golfer who played on with three regular partners after a fourth – Jimmy Hogg, 77 – had dropped dead at the first tee.

☛ About one in 12,000 tee shots ends in a hole-in-one.

★ On 6 February 1971, Alan Shepard became the first person to hit a golf ball on the Moon. He took two swipes with a 6-iron. He mis-hit the first, which went only about 100ft, but the second stayed in the air for 30 seconds and travelled a distance of 200yd.

☞ ARCHERY, KIPLING, TREVINO

GOOSEBERRY
Chinese gooseberries come from New Zealand.

GORILLA
The correct scientific name of the subspecies Western Lowland gorilla is *Gorilla gorilla gorilla*. The Eastern Lowland gorilla is *Gorilla gorilla graueri*, and the Mountain gorilla is *Gorilla gorilla beringei*. In all cases the first name

(*Gorilla*) is its Genus, the second (*gorilla*) is its species and the third is its sub-species. Gorillas never snore.

★ The first gorilla in Britain arrived on 21 June 1876.

☞ HAIR

GOSSIP

Researchers in Michigan in 1995 reported that American children aged nine to 12 gossip on average 18 times an hour.

☞ CHILE

GRAFFITI

The first major auction of work by graffiti artists was held in New York in June 2000. Many of the items were withdrawn on failing to reach their reserve price, but one item, a door from an apartment space above an art gallery, was sold for over $25,000 to a telephone bidder. It was said to feature work from several leading graffiti artists such as Jean-Michel Basquiat, Keith Haring, Fab Five Freddie, Futura, Zephyr and LSD OM. Another door from the same gallery failed to sell when it brought no bids at $10,000.

GRAPE

There are more than 60 species and 8,000 varieties of grapes, and they can all be used to make juice or wine. The wine business has made grape-growing the largest food industry in the world, with 25 million acres of grapes worldwide producing 72 million tons of grapes.

The average person eats 8lb of grapes a year. Botanically, grapes are not fruit but berries.

☞ APPLE, BANANA

GRAPEFRUIT
In 1995 medical researchers announced that grapefruit juice may boost anti-rejection drugs for transplants.

GRAVITY
☞ APPLE, EARTH, SPIDER, TROUSERS

GREECE
The average Greek adult smokes 11 cigarettes a day.
☞ ADULTERY, St ANDREW, ANIMAL NOISES, LEPROSY, TUESDAY

GREENGAGE
The greengage was introduced into Britain in 1725 by Sir William Gage.

GREENLAND
The area of the European Economic Community (formerly known as the Common Market) was halved in 1981 when Greenland (until then part of Denmark) was granted full independence. The population of Greenland is 55,361 (July 2006 estimate).
☞ BUTTOCKS, MANDELA, SNOW

GROUSE
There are 17 known species of grouse in the world.
☞ KANSAS

GUATEMALA
Between five and 10 people are killed or injured in Guatemala by falling bullets every Christmas. In

December 2001, Police called on revellers not to fire pistols into the air to celebrate. 'Lots of people die when bullets fall on their heads,' a police spokesman said. 'This tradition of shooting in the air is a very dangerous practice.'
☞ BAR CODES

GUILLOTINE

The last people to be executed by guillotine in Britain were the Marquis of Argyll in 1661 and his son the Earl of Argyll in 1685.

The use of the guillotine in France began with a proposal submitted on 10 October 1789 by Dr Joseph Guillotin in an Assembly debate about the Penal Code. This included a recommendation that death, by means of decapitation, without the accompaniment of torture, should become the sole and standard form of capital punishment in France.

The first guillotine execution in France was in 1792. The last public guillotining was in June 1939, and the last use of all was for the execution of convicted murderer Hamida Djandoubi on 10 September 1977.

One of the more gruesome incidents associated with the guillotine occurred in 1905 when Dr Beaurieux experimented with the head of Henri Languille, who was guillotined at 5.30am on 28 June. 'Chance served me well for the observation, which I wished to make,' Beaurieux reported, describing how 'the head fell on the severed surface of the neck and I did not therefore have to take it up in my hands. I was not obliged even to touch it in order to set it upright.' After waiting for the spasmodic twitching to cease, the doctor loudly and clearly called out Languille's name. He reports that the eyelids lifted and 'Languille's eyes very definitely fixed themselves on mine and the pupils focused themselves.' When they had settled shut again, he repeated the name, with the same effect. A third call, however, elicited no movement. 'I have just recounted to you with rigorous exactness what I was able to observe. The whole thing had lasted twenty-five to thirty seconds.'

☞ HALIFAX, OYSTER

GUITAR

An inflammation referred to as 'guitar nipple' was mentioned in the *British Medical Journal* in 1974. It is caused by rubbing from the guitar soundbox. Guitar-string dermatitis is another occupational hazard for guitarists.

In 1999 a Pennsylvania man tried to sue God for not granting him the skills to play the guitar. Presidents Reagan and Bush, as God's earthly representatives, were named as co-defendants along with a number of religious leaders and other politicians. The case was thrown out.

The smallest guitar in the world is made of silicon and its length is one-twentieth the thickness of a human hair. It is strummed by a laser, played in a vacuum chamber at Cornell University, and emits a sound too high to hear.

The guitar's sixth string was added in the late 18th century. A five-string guitar was known in the 16th century and a guitar with four double-strings existed in the 15th century.

➡ The European Patent Office lists 2,388 guitar-related inventions.

GUNS

In February 1776, Benjamin Franklin wrote to a US major-general to advise him that guns could never be as efficient as bows and arrows:

'1. Because a man may shoot as truly with a bow as with a common musket.

2. He can discharge four arrows in the time of charging and discharging one bullet.

3. His object is not taken from his view by the smoke of his own side.

4. A flight of arrows seen coming upon them terrifies and disturbs the enemy's attention to his business.

5. An arrow sticking in any part of a man puts him *hors de combat* until it is extracted.

6. Bows and arrows are more easily provided everywhere than muskets and ammunition.'

The first machine gun was patented in 1718 by James Puckle, a London lawyer. Even two centuries later, improvements were being sought in the design of ordinary guns. In 1913, John Steinocher patented a gun-firing scarecrow; and in 1916, Albert Pratt patented a gun that was part of a soldier's helmet. It also doubled as a cooking utensil. Fortunately it was never used as a gun. The recoil could have been fatal to the wearer.

Since July 1998, it has been legal for ministers and church officers in Kentucky to carry a gun in church, as long as they have a permit for concealed weapons.

☞ BRASSIERE, CRIME, DIVORCE, FIREWORKS, FISHING, SCARECROW, SEX

HACKER

★ On 9 September 1997, a Cincinnati woman was put on probation for child neglect after she was found to have been been letting her children live in squalor while she spent 12 hours a day on the Internet. The woman's name was Hacker.

HAIR

Hairiness, said Aristotle, is a sign of 'abundance of residual matter', which, he went on to explain, is why hairy men are given to sexual intercourse and produce more semen than smooth men. Aristotle was also the first to point out that all hairy animals have eyelashes, that the Libyan ostrich is the only bird with eyelashes, that man is the only animal with lashes on both upper and lower lids, and that castrated men never go bald. 'Women do not go bald,' he said, 'because their nature is like that of children.'

Religion:

In Judaeo-Christian and Muslim tradition, gods tend to

appear bearded to emphasise their manliness. On ceremonial occasions in Egypt, Queen Hatshepsut often wore a beard for similar reasons.

Science:
Hairs are composed mainly of the protein keratin and are the result of cell- proliferation in the Malpighian layer of the epidermis. Each hair has a root, called the bulb, embedded in a socket called the follicle. Prenatal hair, soft and silky, is called 'lanugo', and gives way to 'vellus' and finally to 'terminal hair'. There are around 100,000 hairs on the average head, with about 50 lost each day. The empty follicle then rests for a few months before growing another hair. Each individual hair lives for about two years before falling out.

Hair grows at a rate of 1cm a month (beard hair slightly faster). A lifetime's growth of hair is about 25ft, but a single hair is unlikely to grow longer than 3ft.

Misconceptions:
That apes are hairier than men – humans have as many follicles as chimpanzees and gorillas.

That men are hairier than women – they have the same number of follicles, though the hairs are less conspicuous in women.

That shaving cream softens a beard – it's the water that softens it, though soap may help maintain the softness longer. Einstein knew this and therefore never used shaving soap.

Superstitions:

If a person's hair burns long and brightly when thrown on to a fire, it is a sign that the person will live long, but a dull flame or smouldering means a short life (Lancashire, 1850s).

A woman with friends or relatives at sea must not comb her hair after nightfall or it will bring disaster upon them (Aberdeen, 1880s).

Never throw your hairs away. If a bird uses them to make a nest, you will always have a headache (Co. Tyrone, date uncertain).

Legal aspects:

King Francis I of France (1494–1547) introduced the death penalty for anyone wearing a beard or moustache. Peter the Great of Russia imposed a beard tax in 1698, later adding a penalty that involved shaving with a blunt razor or being plucked with pincers, one hair at a time.

In 2005, a British court ruled that it is not sexual discrimination to sack a man for having long hair.

The correct term for fear of beards, incidentally, is 'pogonophobia'.

Geography:

The Scottish Highlands have the highest proportion of redheads in the world – around one in nine.

Records:

Fastest haircut: six seconds (to a US marine in World War II).

Greatest moustache span: 3.39m (11.1ft).

In 1996, at an auction in London a lock of Napoleon's

hair was sold for £3,680. The same buyer paid £598 for a lock of the Duke of Wellington's hair. A lock of Nelson's hair fetched £5,575 in 1988.

Historical footnote:
In the ninth century, Charles the Bald was King of Germany and Wilfred the Hairy ruled Catalonia. The two men did not get on well, and fought a brief war in 878.

On 22 May 1996, a court in Kassel, Germany, ruled that policemen may wear their hair in a plait if they wish, and a superior does not have the right to order them to remove it.

☞ ALPACA, ANAESTHETICS, ANDERSEN, AUGUSTUS, BUTTOCKS, BYRON, DICKENS, GUITAR, HAIRCUT, HAMSTER, HAT, LIFETIME, LION, LOUIS XIV, MERKIN, MUSIC, NAVEL, OPERA, POLAR BEAR, POTATO, SEA LION, SHAKESPEARE, VOICE, WEATHER, YETI

HAIRCUT
A person who has never had a haircut is correctly referred to as asercecomic.
☞ HAIR

HALIFAX
The Halifax Gibbet was an early type of guillotine that pre-dated the French version by well over a century. Used for summary executions for theft, it featured an iron axe blade, lifted up by cord and pulley. Under the Gibbet Law, the axe was kept by the Bailiff of the Lord of the Manor. Execution was the punishment for crimes involving the theft of goods worth 13.5 pence or more. A jury of 16

men was employed to judge the accused and assess the value of the stolen goods. If a guilty verdict was returned, execution was carried out immediately if it was a market day, otherwise saved until the next time they could be sure of a good crowd. If an ox, sheep, horse or other animal was among the items stolen, it was customary for the rope holding the axe to be attached to the beast. Freeing the animal would then cause the axe to fall.

An old vagabonds' prayer of the 16th or early 17th century ran: 'From Hell, Hull and Halifax, Good Lord deliver us.' The mention of Halifax referred to the gibbet; Hull was included because it was too strictly governed for beggars to make a decent living there.

HALITOSIS
Mr White's Halitosis Detector was patented in 1925 and consisted of a device that trapped the human breath while exhaling. A small pair of bellows was attached to let the trapped air be expelled, enabling the user to sniff it.

★ On 20 October 1997, the University of British Columbia, Canada, announced a bad-breath-testing service including both scientific analysis for halitosis and assessment by a human nose.

HALLOWE'EN
Hallowe'en seems to have begun as the Celtic festival of Samhain, when the spirits of the dead were meant to return to haunt the living. Fear of Hallowe'en is thus called Samhainophobia.

Bobbing for apples at Hallowe'en has its origins in the

late-October Roman feast of Pomona, the goddess of fruit and trees whose symbol was the apple.

☞ PUMPKIN

HAMBURGER

In 1989 the world's biggest hamburger was made in Wisconsin – it was a 5,520-pounder.

☞ CARS

HAMSTER

Experiments at the University of Massachusetts show that, if an adolescent golden hamster is left in a cage with an aggressive adult hamster for an hour each day, it will grow up to become a bully: it will pick on animals smaller than itself, but will cower in fear around hamsters its own size. As far as these experiments were concerned, a hamster's adolescence starts around 25 days of age.

The Golden (or Syrian) hamster was discovered in Aleppo, Syria, in 1930 by Professor Aharoni and the first group of their descendants was smuggled into the UK in 1932 in the pocket of a zoologist. It is by no means certain that all domestic hamsters are descendants of this original group, since several other groups of Syrian hamsters were brought into the UK later.

Originally, all Syrian hamsters were short haired, but breeding techniques have led to the recognition of four types of fur today: short haired, long haired, satin and rex (curly, frizzy). Long-haired male hamsters have longer fur than long-haired female hamsters.

Hamsters are the third most common animals to be used in experiments after mice and rats.

★ On 12 July 1992, the pet hamster in a South Glamorgan school died of a heart attack, apparently caused by the shock of a teacher firing a starting pistol in a school sports day rehearsal.

☞ PREGNANCY

HANDKERCHIEF

In 1785 Marie Antoinette decreed that the length of a handkerchief should equal its breadth. In 15th-century England, it was illegal for all but the nobility to carry a handkerchief. Queen Victoria had a mourning handkerchief with teardrop motifs sewn on to it.

☞ BRASSIERE

HANGING

Hanging is the second most common method of capital punishment in the world after shooting. In 2001, a total of 111 men and nine women are known to have been hanged in 11 countries. Hanging originated in Persia around 500BC and was only for men. Women were strangled at the stake instead.

The first long-drop execution in England with a calculated length of drop was performed in 1871 by William Marwood. According to Charles Duff in the *Handbook on Hanging* (1929), you need an 8ft drop for a 14st person, adding 2in per half-stone less. James 'Hangman' Barry noted, in his book *The Business Side of Hanging*, that he reduced drops by nearly half in the case of persons who had attempted suicide by slitting their throat.

In 1785, 90 per cent of people hanged in Britain were under 20 years of age.

In the 1940s and 1950s, the Home Office issued instructions for the proper preparations for a hanging. These began: 'Obtain a rope from Execution Box B making sure that the guttapercha covering the splice at each end is un-cracked by previous use.'

➡ From 1800 to 1964, some 5,508 people are known to have suffered death by hanging in Britain.

☞ CAPITAL PUNISHMENT, FRIDAY, MATISSE

HANGOVER

In Mongolia, a traditional hangover cure is to eat a pickled sheep's eye in a glass of tomato juice. A simpler Puerto Rican alternative is to rub lemon under your arms.

HAT

The hat band has no functional purpose. It is a relic of ancient Egyptian head bands worn to keep hair in place while travelling. According to a law at the time of Elizabeth I, everyone over the age of seven had to wear a flat cap on Sundays and holidays. The only exceptions were lords, ladies and knights with an income of over 20 marks a year.

When John Hetherington donned a top hat in 1797, he was arrested for wearing 'a tall structure having a shining luster calculated to frighten timid people'. Hat tax was abolished in Britain in 1851. Other items to have attracted specific taxes in Britain include bricks, candles, chimneys, wig powder and windows. The window tax ran from 1696 until 1851. It was calculated from the number of windows in a house. All houses were charged at 2 shillings, properties with 10 to 20 windows paid 4 shillings and those with more than 20 windows paid 8 shillings. Frugal house owners would block up their windows so they would qualify for a smaller fee.

The Trilby is named after the eponymous heroine Trilby O'Ferral of a George du Maurier novel.

★ The bowler hat was first tested and bought on 17 December 1849 by William Coke for 10 shillings. It was made by Thomas Bowler.

☞ ETIQUETTE, FASHION, OSCAR, PANAMA, SWAT

HAWAII

Mount Waialeale in Hawaii is the rainiest place on earth, with up to 350 rainy days a year.

☞ DARWIN, ICE CREAM

HAWKING, Stephen William (b. 1942)

★ The physicist Stephen Hawking was born on 8 January 1942, exactly 300 years to the day after the death of Galileo.

HEALTH

The UK National Health Service is the third largest employer in the world after the Russian army and Indian Railways.

☞ CHOCOLATE, CROCODILE, EGYPT, ELEPHANT, FOOTBALL, LAVATORIES, PENGUIN, SOAP OPERAS, SOUTH KOREA

HEDGEHOG

The hedgehog was a common symbol on ancient Egyptian amulets. Its hibernation and ability to survive outside fertile lands were taken as connotations of rebirth and triumph over death itself. Pliny the Elder, in the first century, wrote of hedgehogs climbing apple trees, knocking the fruit down, then impaling apples on their spines to carry to their burrows. This is nonsense. Hedgehogs can't climb trees.

One hedgehog, however, has been known to eat 63 caterpillars, 22 earwigs, 75 beetles and numerous slugs, snails, millipedes and larvae in one sitting. Hedgehogs have 36 teeth and up to 5,000 spines.

The fleas on hedgehogs are 'hedgehog fleas' and cannot live on other animals or in houses.

Baby hedgehogs are known as hoglets or piglets. 'Erinaceous' means 'pertaining to the hedgehog'.

In January 2002, eight policemen in New Zealand swooped on a house in Christchurch in response to a call about a burglary. The noise that disturbed the residents was found to be not burglars but two hedgehogs mating. They snuffle very loudly when mating.

HELICOPTER
☞ ISRAEL, PENGUIN, SOUTH KOREA

HELL
☞ HALIFAX, NORWAY, PUMPKIN

HEMINGWAY, Ernest (1899–1961)
☞ GHOSTS

HENRY II, King of England (1133–89)
☞ UNIVERSITIES

HENRY III, King of England (1207–72)
☞ UNIVERSITIES

HENRY III, King of France (1551–89)
King Henry III of France liked to walk the streets with a basket of puppies round his neck.

HENRY V, King of England (1387–1422)
☞ SAUSAGES

HENRY VI, King of England (1421–71)
☞ ALCHEMY, St APOLLONIA

HENRY VII, King of England (1457–1509)
The first recorded use of fireworks in Britain was at the wedding of Henry VII in 1486.

HENRY VIII, King of England (1491–1547)
The armour of Henry VIII has the largest codpiece in the Tower of London.
☞ BEER, BOLEYN, TWELFTH NIGHT

HERON
If stalked and surprised at close quarters, a heron will fall down in a kind of fit.
☞ PHOENIX

HESITATION

According to research published in 2002, English speakers say 'um' before a long pause and 'uh' before a short one. No US president between 1940 and 1996 uttered a single 'uh' or 'um' in his inaugural address.

HIPPOCRATES (c.460–c.377BC)
☞ SEX

HIPPOPOTAMUS

Britain's first hippopotamus arrived at London Zoo on 25 May 1850. Named Obaysch, after the island in the Nile where it was found, it was said to be the first hippo seen in Europe since Roman times.

Regent's Park Zoo had been opened in 1828. The first elephant arrived in 1831, a rhinoceros in 1834 and the first giraffes in 1836, but none of these attained the superstar status of Obaysch the hippo. Its popularity may have been boosted by the supposed identification of the hippopotamus with the biblical monster Behemoth mentioned in the Book of Job.

The number of visitors to the zoo doubled, and they rushed to buy hippo merchandise, including silver models of Obaysch. *Punch* magazine ran regular updates on the life of London's hippo, whom they elevated to the status of HRH ('His Rolling Hulk') and you could even buy sheet music for 'The Hippopotamus Polka'. Obaysch remained a celebrity until his death in 1878, when *Punch* published a long memorial poem, including this couplet:

'Old Hippo's mighty yet melodious bass
Sinks to a raucous whisper, short, not sweet!'

According to Sclater's *Mammals of South Africa*, all authors are agreed that the flesh of the hippopotamus is excellent eating, closely resembling succulent pork or veal.

★ The saddest day in the history of hippos may be 12 July 1995, when the youngest and oldest hippos in captivity died on the same day: Tanga, aged 61, passed quietly away in a zoo in Munich, while in Belgium, at Olmense Zoo in Balen, a baby hippo was killed when its mother rolled over on to it when frightened by a thunderstorm.

☞ NIGERIA, TEETH

HITLER, Adolf (1889–1945)

In the Navajo language, the nickname for Hitler was *Daghailchiih*, meaning 'he smells his moustache'.

If Adolf Hitler were still alive, he would be the oldest man on earth: he was born on 20 April 1889; the last surviving man to have been born before him was the Japanese Yukichi Chuganji who was born on 23 March 1889 and died aged 114 on 28 September 2003.

HOLES

The US Nobel Prize-winning astronomer John Wheeler coined the term 'black hole' in 1967. The first black hole was discovered two years later.

The only living things Louis Sachar, author of *Holes*, allows in his office are his dogs Lucky and Tippy.

In 2001, the USA reduced the minimum size for holes in Emmental cheese from 11/16in to 3/8in.
☞ BILLIARDS, BREAD, DOUGHNUTS, FASHION, GOLF, NETHERLANDS, SEAL

HOMES

According to a survey in 1999, the top ten reasons people hated their homes were as follows:

1. Too small
2. Undesirable neighbourhood and area
3. Too far from place
4. Noisy neighbours
5. In need of costly repairs
6. Traffic noise
7. No good for entertaining
8. Garden too small for work
9. Facing the wrong way
10. No garage

☞ ALEXANDER III, BEER, MISTLETOE, OCTOPUS, SWIMMING, TUNISIA, UGANDA

HOMEWORK

The ten reasons most commonly given by children for not doing their homework are as follows:

1. Not enough time – 19%
2. I can't be bothered – 14%
3. Lost my coursework – 12%
4. Family funeral/sickness – 10%
5. The pet ate my coursework – 9%
6. Forgot about my exams – 8%

7. Faked illness – 5%
8. Watched TV – 4%
9. Going out with friends – 4%
10. House burned down – 2%

HONG KONG
☞ BEAUTY, CHEWING GUM, LAVATORIES,
MICHELANGELO, NAVEL

HORSE
In 1875, road accidents, mostly involving horses, led to the death of 1,589 people in the UK. From 1921 to 1923 mortality among horse-riders in England and Wales was more than 60 per cent higher than among motor-vehicle drivers.

Horsemeat consumption worldwide declined from a 1979 peak of 628,300 tons to 567,400 tons in 1982 according to exporters at a 1984 international horsemeat forum in Tokyo. A horseflesh dinner was served at the Langham Hotel in London on Leap Day, 29 February 1868. One diner, Frank Buckland, said that he 'gave it a fair trial, tasting every dish from soup to jelly' but he did not approve of any of it.

Useful horse word: jumentous, which means 'resembling horse urine'.
☞ AFGHANISTAN, ANIMAL NOISES, ASCOT, BIBLE,
BURMA, CALIGULA, CAPITAL PUNISHMENT, CENTAUR,
CHRISTMAS, DIAGRAM, FISH, GODIVA, HALIFAX,
HUDSON, MARS, MOLE, ODIN, PAKISTAN, PHOENIX,
REINDEER, RHYME, STALLION, TAXI, TRANSPORT,
UNITED STATES, WASHINGTON

HORSERADISH
Bottled horseradish was the first product produced by Henry J. Heinz. He began selling it in 1869. The slogan '57 Varieties' was introduced in 1892, by which time Heinz were already producing over 60 different products.

HOT DOGS
The World Hot Dog Eating Contest is traditionally held on 4 July at Nathan's in Coney Island, New York.

★ On 4 July 2001, Takeru Kobayashi of Japan ate 50 hot dogs in 12 minutes, nearly doubling the previous world record to win the contest. In competition, Kobayashi favours the 'Solomon method', which involves breaking each hot dog in half, then stuffing both halves simultaneously into his mouth. Others prefer the 'Tokyo style', which is to eat sausage and roll separately.

HOUDINI, Harry (1874–1926)
The great escapologist's real name was Erich Weiss.
☞ AUSTRALIA

HOUSEWIVES
The patron saint of housewives is Martha, the sister of Lazarus and Mary of Bethany and a friend of Jesus. She is also a patron saint of butlers, cooks, dietitians, domestic servants, homemakers, hotel-keepers, housemaids, housewives, innkeepers, laundry workers, maids, manservants, servants, servers, single laywomen and travellers.

In 1832, Joseph Thompson, a Carlisle farmer, sold his wife for twenty shillings and a Newfoundland dog. This was not as unusual as you may think. Between 1840 and 1880, 55 cases of wife-sale were recorded in Britain.

The word 'hussy', meaning a promiscuous or immoral girl or woman, was originally a contraction of 'housewife'.

☛ According to the UN Human Development Report 1995, the annual value of women's unwaged work worldwide is about $11 trillion.

☛ According to the latest available official figures, 13 per cent of British women between 16 and 59 are housewives. The average housewife has been calculated to walk 594 miles a year in the course of her duties.

☞ ARGENTINA

HUDSON, Jeffrey (1619–82)

Also known by the name Lord Minimus, Jeffrey Hudson quite literally sprang to fame at the age of seven when he jumped out of a pie on the dining room table of his boss, George Villiers, the first Duke of Buckingham. Hudson, who was dressed in full armour and waving a flag, then saluted Villiers's guests, King Charles I and his Queen, Henrietta Maria, who adopted him as court dwarf. Hudson was 18in tall at the time, a height he maintained until the age of 30 (though he later shot up to 3ft 9in).

He was born to parents of ordinary stature in 1619 in Oakham, the county town of Rutland – which appropriately enough is England's smallest county.

Hudson went on to lead an extraordinary life,

including twice being captured by pirates, sold into slavery in North Africa, and taking part in the English Civil War. He survived two duels, one against a turkey cock and the other with a man named Mr Crofts. In the latter, his opponent tried to make light of the matter and turned up for the duel with a water pistol, but Hudson insisted that the duel go ahead. He was put on a horse to get him level with Crofts, whom he promptly shot dead.

Hudson was imprisoned as a papist plotter in London in 1678 and died penniless not long after his release in 1680.

At the height of his fame, he appeared as a character in a novel by Sir Walter Scott and was also painted by Sir Anthony van Dyck.

HULL
Hull City is the only team in the Football League whose name does not include any letters (such as a, b, d, e, o, etc.) that include an enclosed space that can be filled in by a doodler.

☞ HALIFAX, OBESITY, VALENTINO

HUMMINGBIRD
Research has shown that the earliest training given to hummingbird chicks by their mother birds is to elevate their posteriors above the nest edge when defecating. Hummingbird nests are thus cleaner than those of other birds.

Hummingbirds cannot walk but are the only birds that can fly backwards.

HUNGARY

The word 'coach' derives from the name of the Hungarian town Kocs, where multi-passenger wheeled vehicles first appeared around 1500.

☞ BODYGUARD, CONDOM

HUNTING

A hunting-lodge operator who shot his common-law wife because he mistook her for a bear was acquitted of second-degree murder in Quebec Superior Court in June 1984. The jury deliberated for nearly 10 hours.

☞ POLAR BEAR, SEAL, SNAIL, TAX

HUTTON, Sir Leonard (1916–90)

Len Hutton was the first professional cricketer to captain England regularly and scored 129 centuries in his first-class career, which is the same as the number of mystery novels written by Earl Stanley Gardner. In 82 of those novels, Perry Mason solves a case.

☞ CRICKET

HYDROGEN

☞ BODY, FART, SUN

HYENA

The hyena was excluded from Noah's ark in Raleigh's *History of the World* (1614) in the belief that it was a cat-dog hybrid.

☞ PENIS

HYGIENE

★ On 6 April 1928, the authorities in Rome decided to ban handshaking on the grounds that it was unhygienic.

☞ LAVATORIES

IBSEN, Henrik (1828–1906)

The Norwegian dramatist Ibsen had a pet scorpion that he kept in a jar on his desk to remind him that his task was not to entertain but to sting his audience into thinking. When the scorpion was ill, he dropped soft fruit into its jar, which it would attack and sting. After expelling its venom into the fruit, the scorpion recovered.

After a stroke, Ibsen became an invalid. When his nurse suggested that his condition was improving, Ibsen snapped, 'Tvärtemot!' ('On the contrary!') and promptly died.

☞ TROUSERS

ICEBERG

An iceberg reaching a height of more than 75m above the sea is officially classified as 'Very large'. An iceberg less than 1m above the sea is called a 'growler'.

ICE CREAM

At a rate of over 31 pints every year, the average Australian eats more ice cream than any other nation.

This is almost four times as much ice cream as the

average Briton consumes, despite the fact that the British spend £12 million on ice cream and sorbets every week.

When Ben Cohen and Jerry Greenfield went into business together, they opted for ice cream because bagel-making equipment was too expensive. Lovers of Ben & Jerry's ice cream have never regretted that decision.

In the USA, 25 per cent of Baskin Robbins '31 flavours' ice cream sales are for plain vanilla. In the State of Kansas, it used to be illegal to serve ice cream with cherry pie. Hawaii and Wisconsin are the only states with laws governing ice-cream container size.

The last thing Elvis Presley ate was four scoops of ice cream and six chocolate chip cookies.

★ On 13 June 1789, George Washington became the first US president to eat ice cream.

★ On 15 December 1903, Italo Marchiony of New York received Patent No. 746,971 for his 'new and useful Improvements in Moulds' including 'apparatus for forming ice cream cups and the like' – and the age of the ice-cream cone was upon us.

☞ ASTRONAUTS, SARDINE, TELEVISION

ICELAND

The first armed robbery in Iceland's history took place in Reykjavik in 1984 when 2 million crowns (£48,500) was taken from two messengers in the National Bank of Iceland.

When man first settled in Iceland in the ninth century, the arctic fox was the only native mammal. There are now around 150 mammalian species including the

Icelandic field mouse, which is the largest field mouse in the world. Lake Myvatn in northern Iceland also boasts 16 different species of nesting ducks, which is more than any other lake in the world.

There are no reptiles, amphibians or poisonous animals in Iceland.

The average Icelander goes to the cinema more often than any other nationality.

☛ Ninety-seven per cent of the plant species found in Iceland can also be found in Norway.

☞ AMERICA, BLYTON, PENIS

INCEST

Mrs Mary Ann Bass, 43, was charged with incest in Charlotte, Tennessee, in 1984, when it was discovered she had been married for six years to her son, given up for adoption 23 years before.

INCOME TAX

On 9 January 1799, William Pitt introduced Britain's first income tax. The rate was two shillings in the pound (10 per cent) and it was collected in order to finance the Napoleonic Wars with France. It was brought in as a temporary measure and ran from 1799 to 1801, then again from 1803 to 1816. It returned in 1842 and has been with us ever since. An earlier income tax had been levied in 1404, but was so unpopular, it was not only abolished but also all records of it were ordered to be destroyed.

There are 12 countries without income tax: Andorra, Bahamas, Brunei, Bahrain, Kuwait, Maldives, Monaco,

Nauru, Oman, Qatar, United Arab Emirates and Vanuatu.

In New Zealand, condoms, lubricants, gels, oils, lingerie, costumes, whipped cream and bubble bath all constitute deductible expenses for sex workers.

In the 1970s top rates of income tax were so high in Norway that some 2,000 people were listed as paying more than 100 per cent of their total income in tax.

'The hardest thing in the world to understand is the income tax' – Albert Einstein.

INDEPENDENCE DAY
King Taufa'ahau IV of Tonga was born on 4 July (in 1918).

On 4 July 1776, the date celebrated as US Independence Day, King George III of England wrote in his diary: 'Nothing of importance happened today.'

Dogs also gained their independence on 4 July: that was the day in 1984 when the UK abolished dog licences.

☞ COMMUNISM, HOT DOGS

INDIA
India has 8,407 universities, which is more than any other country. The USA comes second with 5,758. Over 45 per cent of the world's individual visits to cinemas take place in India.

★ On 6 September 1987, military scientists in India announced the development of the world's first long-life chapati.

☞ ADULTERY, BANANA, BRAZIL, BUFFALO, HEALTH, LIECHTENSTEIN, MOUSTACHE, OBESITY, YETI

INDONESIA
A £700 prize was offered in 1985 for a song extolling the joys of planting soya beans. The director-general of food crops said he hoped the song would encourage farmers to plant more beans, thereby slashing imports.
☞ CANADA, COCONUT, COFFEE, KOMODO

IN-FLIGHT CATERING
In-flight meals are almost as old as flying itself. The first regular air services began in March 1919, and, by October of the same year, passengers from London to Paris were offered packed lunches for an extra three shillings. It took another eight years before passengers were offered hot meals, with the first in-flight cooking carried out on 1 May 1927 on Imperial Airways 'Silver Wing' first-class flights between London and Paris. Meals were cooked in a galley at the rear of the plane, though restrictions of time and space allowed them to offer hot meals to only 18 passengers on each flight.

INSURANCE
☞ ASTROLOGY, BRAZIL, FLYING SAUCERS, LEGS, VAMPIRES, WIFE-CARRYING

INTERNET
☞ FRUITCAKE, IRELAND, PENIS, PRAYER, SOUTH AFRICA

IPSWICH
☞ LIGHT BULB, SARDINE

IRAN

At weddings in Iran, it is traditional for the bride and groom to lick honey off each other's fingers to ensure their life together starts sweetly. This did not have the desired effect at a wedding in the city of Qazvin in December 2001 when a 28-year-old bridegroom was reported to have choked to death on one of his new wife's false fingernails.

☞ ALCOHOL

IRELAND

Ireland used to be known as Greater Scotia and Scotland is believed to take its name from the Scotti tribe of Ireland, who colonised it. There are no snakes in Ireland, the only reptile is the common lizard and the only amphibians are one species each of frog, newt and toad. St Patrick is credited with banishing all the snakes from Ireland; he was born in either Wales or Scotland. Ireland has won the Eurovision Song Contest more often than any other country.

In 18th-century Ireland, duelling was so common that innkeepers kept pistols behind the bar for the use of their customers.

Recent history:

The first 'Virtual Irish Pub' on the Internet was launched in June 1995. Those who log on can hear the chat of a genuine Irish barman and his customers.

In 1996, a San Francisco bar and restaurant called The Bank of Ireland changed its name to The Irish Bank after being sued by the Bank of Ireland.

In March 2002, the Australian Quarantine Inspection

Service used sniffer dogs to seize more than 60 four-leafed clovers sent from Ireland for St Patrick's Day.

☞ BEER, DRACULA, SKIING, TOURISM, UNIVERSITIES

ISLAM

The colour blue is believed to protect against the evil eye in the Islamic religion.

☞ TOURISM

ISOCRATES (436–388BC)

☞ UNIVERSITIES

ISRAEL

In 1989, a hotel in the holiday resort of Tiberias, Israel, lost its kosher food licence for permitting a couple to have sex in a helicopter above its swimming pool.

☞ CEMETERIES, CROCODILE, EUROVISION SONG CONTEST, ROBBERY

ITALY

Mussolini's government imposed a tax on bachelors in December 1927 to raise the growth rate of the population and encourage the young to work harder. He imposed a tax on goats in January 1927.

In 1996, an Italian court ruled that government workers have a statutory right to a morning coffee break.

According to a survey in 1997, 70 per cent of Italians tell between five and 10 lies a day.

☞ ALBANIA, St ANDREW, EUROVISION SONG CONTEST, DA VINCI, LOVE, MICKEY MOUSE, OCTOBER, PIZZA, PREGNANCY, SANDWICHES

IVORY COAST
☞ FIREWORKS

JACKSON, Thomas Jonathan 'Stonewall' (1824–63)

The US Confederate General Stonewall Jackson is buried in two different places. His left arm was shattered during the Battle of Chancellorsville by fire from his own side and was amputated the next day. He died a week later. His arm is buried at Fredericksburg, Virginia, and the rest of his body is interred at Lexington, Virginia.

JAPAN

In Japanese, the verb *tsujigiri* means 'trying out a sword on a chance passer-by'.

Lost property on public transport in Tokyo in 1979 included 17 goldfish bowls, complete with fish.

☞ BOOKS, BRASSIERE, CHOPSTICKS, COMPUTATION, COSMETICS, ETIQUETTE, FART, FORTY-SEVEN, FOX, HITLER, HOT DOG, LAVATORIES, LEADERSHIP, MICKEY MOUSE, NAVEL, NORTH POLE, PAPER, PIGEON, PINEAPPLE, POETRY, SMOKING, TEA, TOURISM, TUNA, WELLINGTON BOOTS

JERUSALEM
☞ PRAYER

JIFFY

How long a jiffy is seems to depend on the area in which you are working. In computer engineering, a jiffy is the length of one cycle, or tick, of the computer's system clock. Originally this was most frequently equal to one period of the alternating current powering the computer: 1/60 second in the USA and Canada, but 1/50 second elsewhere. More recently the jiffy became standardised as 1/100 second.

In chemistry and physics, however, a jiffy was defined by Gilbert N. Lewis (1875–1946) as equal to a 'light centimetre', the time required for light to travel one centimetre. This is about 33.3564 picoseconds. As there are a trillion picoseconds in a second, this means there are about 300 million chemists' jiffies in a computer engineer's jiffy.

JOHN PAUL II, Pope (1920-2005)

Pope John Paul II has created nearly 500 new saints – far more than were created altogether in the 500 years before he became Pope.

He is the fourth longest-serving pope in history, outlasted only by St Peter and Pius IX.

In the 27 years of his papacy he has conducted 100 foreign tours, on which he has visited 129 countries. When he visited the Philippines in 1995, an estimated four million people attended the Mass he celebrated in Manila, which is probably the largest crowd in history.
☞ AZERBAIJAN, St GEORGE, POPES

JOHNSON, Lyndon Baines (1908–73)

Lyndon Johnson, 36th President of the United States, was the first president to wear contact lenses.

JOHNSON, Samuel (1709–84)

☞ ALCOHOL, BOSWELL, CELIBACY, CUCUMBER, TRANSPORT, WEATHER

JONSON, Ben (c.1573–1637)

When the poet and playwright Ben Jonson killed an actor in 1598, he was put on trial but escaped the death penalty by claiming Benefit of Clergy, a handy loophole available to almost anyone who could read. When Jonson died, the plot made available for his body in Poets' Corner in Westminster Abbey was too small and he had to be buried in a sitting position. His heel bone was later stolen by William Buckland when the grave was disturbed in 1849, but turned up again in a furniture shop in 1938.

☞ DINOSAUR

KANGAROO

A fully grown kangaroo can jump 13m. Its means of locomotion is more efficient than running for speeds over 18mph. Kangaroos and emus cannot walk backwards, which is why they were selected to appear on the Australian coat of arms.

☞ DINOSAUR

KANSAS

Kansas has the largest population of wild grouse (or prairie chicken as the Americans call it) of any state in America.

☞ ICE CREAM, STRING

KARLOFF, Boris (1887–1969)

The real name of horror film star Boris Karloff was William Henry Pratt. According to his daughter Sara, speaking in 1995: 'He loved playing cricket and gardening, and had a pet pig called Violet.'

KEATS, John (1795–1821)

Thomas Carlyle described Keats's poetry as 'fricassee of dead dog'.

KENNEDY, John Fitzgerald (1917–63)

According to research published in 2001 in *Science and Justice*, the journal of the Forensic Science Society, there is a 93.6 per cent chance that John F. Kennedy's assassination was not the work of a lone gunman.

☛ In a speech made in 1961, John F. Kennedy was recorded as speaking at 327 words per minute, the fastest rate of public speaking in history.

☞ DOG

KIPLING, Rudyard (1865–1936)

The youngest winner of a Nobel Prize for Literature was Rudyard Kipling, in 1907 when he was 42. Kipling wrote in violet ink, which he mixed himself. He also invented the game of snow golf, played in the snow with red balls.

KISSING

During World War I, it was reported that: 'To kiss a girl in Hyde Park is an offence against the law for which a soldier is often fined the whole of the money he has in his pocket.'

According to anthropologists, kissing is based on cultural rather than biological conditioning. The inhabitants of the South Pacific island of Mangia had never heard of kissing until the English arrived in the 1700s. We know from Sanskrit texts that the Indians have been kissing since 1500BC. The Greeks seem to have been the first Europeans to do it, while the Romans added finesse to the art of kissing. They even had words for three different types of kiss: *osculum* was a peck-on-the-cheek; *basium* a more amorous kiss; and *saviolum* was a full-blooded snog.

The English language is now far richer in kissing words:

baisemain: a kiss on the hand

cataglottism: a lascivious kiss

deosculate: to kiss affectionately

exosculate: to give a big and hearty kiss

suaviate: to kiss

★ On 5 April 1910, kissing was banned on French railway platforms because it caused delays.

☞ ARCHERY, BRAZIL, CHRISTMAS, ELIZABETH I, CINEMA, MISTLETOE, POPES, RUSEDSKI

St KITTS and NEVIS

The Federation of St Kitts and Nevis (formerly the Federation of St Christopher and Nevis) comprises two islands in the eastern Caribbean: St Kitts and Nevis. St Kitts is shaped like a baseball bat and Nevis has the shape of a ball. The inhabitants are known as Kittitian or Nevisian, depending on which island they come from. The population of the islands is 38,736, including one World Athletics Championship gold medallist, Kim Collins, who is a Kittitian.

KNEES

Police in the Philippines in 1995 were reported to be

seeking a gang who specialised in stealing kneecaps from graves. The thieves were believed to be members of a sect who believed that spiritual energy could be gained by grinding up kneecaps and scattering them around a house. The spiritual power of the dead was believed to be concentrated in the knees because people kneel to pray.

In April 1996, surgeons in southern Germany performed the world's first knee transplant on a 17-year-old who had smashed his leg in a motorcycle accident.

☞ ALEXANDER I, BODY, BRAZIL, MOLE, SKIING, YETI

KOALA

The koala gets its name from an Aborigine word meaning 'no drink', because it gets all the moisture it needs from Eucalyptus leaves. Koalas communicate with each other by making a noise like a snore and then a belch, known as a 'bellow'. Koalas have two thumbs on their front paws and sleep more than sloths.

In 1996, Maciej Henneberg, a forensic scientist and biological anthropologist at Adelaide University, announced his discovery that koala fingerprints are very similar to human ones. 'Although it is extremely unlikely that koala prints would be found at the scene of a crime, police should at least be aware of the possibility,' he advised.

★ On 24 April 1997, Australia launched its first birth-control programme for koalas.

KOMODO

The island of Komodo, Indonesia, contains more

poisonous snakes per square metre than any equivalent area on Earth.

KOREA
☞ ARCHERY, PAPER, SOUTH KOREA, TENNIS

KUWAIT
After Saddam Hussein occupied Kuwait in 1990 and declared it to be the '19th Province of Iraq', some dissidents started referring to it as 'Wimbledon' which, as SW19, could perhaps be considered the 19th province of south-west London.

★ On 31 July 1995, the *Al-Watan* newspaper in Kuwait carried a report about a Kuwaiti man who had been rushed to hospital suffering from exhaustion and back pain. His condition was put down to his having made love to his 17-year-old wife six times a day in the week following their wedding. 'He was pale and without energy and could not speak,' a neighbour was quoted as saying.

☞ INCOME TAX

LADYBIRD
There are 140,000 ladybirds to the gallon.

LAOS
According to the CIA, Laos is the world's third largest illicit opium producer. Its currency is the kip.
☞ RICE

LATVIA
The currency unit in Latvia is the lat. The 500-lat note, worth about £550, is one of the world's most valuable banknotes in current circulation.

The highest point in Latvia is only 312m above sea level, which is about 70m lower than the top of the Empire State Building.

Latvia's first ever Olympic gold medal was won by Igors Vihrovs in the men's floor gymnastics event in Sydney 2000. At those Olympics, Latvia ended with a complete set of medals: one gold, one silver, one bronze.

In 1997, a team of doctors in the Latvian capital,

Riga, wrote to *Guinness World Records* staking their claim for an entry on the grounds that they had sewn back four severed hands in five days.

☞ ESTONIA

LAVATORIES

'Toilet' is currently the most popular word for the little boys' (or girls') room, being used by over half the population. 'Loo', on 33 per cent, comes second, though its derivation is obscure. Some claim a French connection, from *l'eau*, and the chambermaid's cry of '*Gardez l'eau!*' to warn that a chamber pot was about to be emptied from a window. Others maintain a link via water closet and Waterloo, or derive it simply from *lieu*, the place.

The *OED* lists 39 euphemisms for lavatory (from the Latin: lavatorium, a place for washing). Neither Shakespeare nor Jane Austen used the word at all, and the entire *Dictionary of National Biography* mentions not a single 'lavatory', though two plural 'lavatories'. Longfellow, in his 'Hyperion', produced the memorable line: 'On a lavatory below sat a cherub.'

The earliest known lavatory – a hut built above a pig pen – dates back to around 3000BC and was unearthed in the ancient city of Xian in China. The water closet, however, dates back only to 1589, when it was devised by Sir John Harrington. The flush, overflow pipe and cistern all form part of his design as described in his lavatorial treatise 'The Metamorphosis of Ajax', published in 1596.

The invention, however, fell into disuse, largely because there were no sewers yet built to carry away the waste. The real toilet revolution had to wait for the estimable Sir Thomas Crapper (1837–1910) to improve Harrington's design in the 1880s with the invention of the boxed flush lavatory. He did not, however, give his name to a common expletive, which had already been around for four centuries by the time he was born.

Among other less-celebrated lavatory pioneers, we should mention the following:

William Henry Cornfield (1843–1903), professor of hygiene and public health, whose 'Disease and Defective House Sanitation' (1896) was translated into French, Italian and Hungarian.

John Nevil Maskelyne (1839–1917), stage magician, plate-spinner and escapologist, whose patented inventions included a cash register, a typewriter and, in 1892, a coin-operated lock for public lavatories that was used in England until the 1950s.

A. Ashwell of Herne Hill in south London, who, on 17 February 1883, patented the Vacant/Engaged sign for public lavatories. This must have come as a considerable relief, since the first public conveniences had been opened in London in 1852, on 2 February, in Fleet Street, for men, and on 10 February, in Bedford Street, for women.

The Custer Battlefield monument in Montana boasts the world's first solar- powered toilet.

'Public Toilets should be the concern of every civilisation,' said Professor Wang Gung, at the opening of the 1995 International Symposium of Public Toilets in Hong Kong, 'because the cleanliness and standards of hygiene they do or do not set are truly a measure whereby the standards of a society can be gauged.'

Recent inventions registered with the European Patent Office include a large number of designs for lavatories for cats and dogs, mostly from France, as well as the following:

'Explosion-proof electrical incinerator toilet' (Germany, 1981); 'Personal weighing device on toilet seat' (France, 1987); 'Hot water spraying lavatory seat' (Taiwan, 1988); 'Toilet chute for railway carriages' (Germany, 1988); 'Apparatus for detecting a person seated on a toilet seat' (Japan, 1992); and finally 'Coreless toilet paper' (Japan, 1992).

☞ CHINA, RAILWAY, RECRUITMENT, SCRABBLE

LAWYERS

Two-thirds of the world's lawyers live in the USA.

☞ DWARF, GUNS, DA VINCI, MOTHER TERESA, SWAT

LEADERSHIP

Honcho is a Japanese word meaning 'leader', so the phrase 'head honcho' is tautological.

LEGS

There is a memorial at Waterloo in Belgium to the leg of Lord Uxbridge, blown off in the eponymous battle. When Uxbridge died 39 years later, the leg was exhumed and buried with the rest of him. It is not known whether this leg was the same length as Lord Uxbridge's surviving one, but research has shown that 23 per cent of people have legs that differ in length by a centimetre or more. In 1942, the actress

Betty Grable insured her legs for half a million dollars.

Police in Winchester once received a 999 call from a man whose wife had hidden his wooden leg.

It is a general rule among warm-blooded animals that those from cold climates have shorter legs than those from hot climates.

The millipede *Illacme plenipes* has 750 legs, more than any other insect.

☞ ABORIGINE, ADMIRALTY ISLANDS, ALCHEMY, ASCOT, ATHLETICS, AUGUSTUS, CHANNEL, CRICKET, DINOSAUR, DONKEY, DUELLING, FLAMINGO, FROGS, KNEES, LONDON, MOLE, NAPOLEON BONAPARTE, ODIN, OYSTER, PLATYPUS, PORTER, SANTA ANNA, SPIDER, STEPHENSON, STOCKINGS, SWIMMING, TROUSERS

LEPROSY

Since 1983, leprosy has no longer been grounds for divorce in Greece.

☞ ARMADILLO, POTATO

LETTUCE

★ On 28 August 1988, the Yantlee Polyclinic in Bangkok published a claim that you can get rid of hunger by pressing lettuce seeds into your ears 10 times before meals.

LEWINSKY, Monica Samille (b. 1973)

Monica Lewinsky is an anagram of 'Yes, I lick man now'.

'President Clinton of the USA' is an anagram of 'To copulate, he finds interns'.

☞ MACKEREL

LIBYA

The Libyan flag is plain green, the only country with a plain flag. In 1997, the Libyan leader Colonel Gaddafi warned his people to fear the West. Among the possible reasons he listed for the West wanting to invade Libya were its camels, sand and watermelons.

☞ AMMONIA, ATLANTIC, HAIR, TEMPERATURE

LICENCE PLATES

In October 2001, a Federal Appeals Court in the USA ruled that a Vermont car owner did not have the right to a car licence plate reading 'SHTHPNS'. Paula Perry had sued the Motor Vehicles Department saying she was a victim of 'viewpoint discrimination' when it revoked her specially requested plates that bore the shorthand version of the phrase 'shit happens'. Arguing that plates saying POOPER had not been objected to, she said the refusal for her plates was a denial of free speech. However, the court ruled that 'shit' is a profanity and 'pooper' is not.

LIECHTENSTEIN

Liechtenstein is the last survivor of the 343 states that once made up the Holy Roman Empire of German Nations. The national anthem is sung to the same tune as 'God Save the Queen'.

Liechtenstein is the world's major exporter of false teeth. Thanks largely to this domination of the denture market, Liechtenstein tops the world trade league for per capita exports with around £50,000 worth of goods per person each year. There are even two false-teeth factories specialising in making dark-brown teeth, for export to countries such as India where people chew tooth-blackening betel nut.

Johannes the Good, Prince of Liechtenstein from 1858 until 1929, was Europe's second longest-reigning monarch, exceeded only by Louis XIV of France.

Liechtenstein won its first ever Olympic gold medal when Hanni Weizel won the giant slalom in 1980. With nine Olympic medals in total since 1948 (all from the Winter Games) and a population slightly above 30,000, Liechtenstein is well ahead of any other nation in the league table of Olympic medals per capita.

If the entire population of Liechtenstein went to the Millennium Stadium in Cardiff, there would be 39,500 empty seats.

☛ Liechtenstein has no army and only 22 policemen.

☞ UZBEKISTAN

LIFETIME

In an average lifetime, a person will walk a distance equivalent to three times round the equator, produce over 6,000 gallons of saliva, grow 2m of nose hair from each follicle, catch 140 colds, shed 40lb of skin, create over 100,000lb of rubbish and spend about five years dreaming. The average American will also visit McDonald's 1,811 times and spend six months waiting at red traffic lights.

☞ DOG, HAIR, SKIN, TELEVISION, VAN GOGH

LIGHT BULB

The first street in the world to be lit by electric light

bulbs was Mosley Street in Newcastle, England, in 1879. The light bulbs were invented by Joseph Wilson Swan. Unfortunately, Swan was rather slow in filing for a patent and Edison got in first with a rather inferior version of the light bulb in January 1880.

In January 2001, a light bulb in the men's toilet in a shop in Ipswich, England, finally failed after giving nearly 70 years' good service. The shape of the bulb at the Martin and Newby electrical shop dated it back to the 1930s. This is believed to be a world record for a light bulb in constant use.

LIGHTNING
★ On 22 July 1918, in the Wasatch National Park in Utah, 504 sheep were killed by lightning.
☞ AUGUSTUS, CAMEL, DEATH, GOLF, THOR, TREVINO

LINCOLN, Abraham (1809–65)
Lincoln's celebrated Gettysburg Address was dismissed by the *Chicago Times* as 'silly, flat and dishwatery utterances'. The play Lincoln was watching when he was assassinated was Tom Taylor's *Our American Cousin*.
☞ DARWIN, UNITED STATES

LINDBERGH, Charles Augustus (1902–74)
When Charles Lindbergh made the first solo, non-stop flight across the Atlantic in 1927, he took with him five sandwiches, two canteens of water and 451 gallons of petrol as well as some maps. He took only a bite from one of the sandwiches. When his grandson Erik Lindbergh commemorated the 75th anniversary of this feat in 2002

by making the same flight himself, he brought six sandwiches along and ate one and a half. 'I did it in half the time and ate twice as much,' he commented.

LINNAEUS, Carolus (1707–78)
☞ CHOCOLATE

LION
Experiments in 2002 showed that lionesses prefer their men to be dark and hairy. Researchers at Serengeti National Park in Tanzania used four custom-built model male lions with clip-on manes made with tawny and dark brown, and with clipped or bouffant hair. Analysing the reaction of females to these dummies, and taking infra-red measurements of their body temperature, the researchers were able to conclude that females prefer dark, hairy males. Reference: West, P.M. & Packer, C., 'Sexual Selection, Temperature and the Lion's Mane', *Science*, 297, 1339–1343 (2002).
➤ According to a report in the *National Geographic Magazine*, in 1982 a pair of lions were observed to copulate 23 times in 5hr 20min. The lioness instigated all but one of the encounters.
☞ ALEXANDER III, BIBLE, DANDELION, DAVIDSON, PREGNANCY, SWAHILI

LITHUANIA
Lithuanian is the modern language most closely resembling ancient Sanskrit.

LIVER
In the film *The Silence Of The Lambs*, Hannibal Lecter spoke of eating a census-taker's liver with 'fava beans and a nice Chianti'. In Thomas Harris's book, however, he drank not Chianti but Amarone, which goes far better with liver.

The philosopher Pythagoras, active in the sixth century BC, would not let his followers eat fava beans: he believed they contained the souls of the dead.
☞ AUSTRIA, POLAR BEAR

LIVERPOOL
In 2003, Liverpool Council banned stallholders at fairs from giving goldfish as prizes.
☞ CAPITAL PUNISHMENT, CAT, FOOTBALL, OBESITY, STEPHENSON, TRANSPORT, TUG-OF-WAR

LLAMA
☞ ALPACA, CAMEL

LLOYD GEORGE, David (1863–1945)
Lloyd George was the first prime minister to have a bathroom at 10 Downing Street.

LOBSTER
Lobsters urinate most when other lobsters behave aggressively towards them.

LOCH NESS
★ The first sighting of the Loch Ness monster is supposed to have been on 22 August 565 by St Columba.
☞ SCOTLAND, TOURISM

LONDON

The first escalator on the London Underground was installed at Earls Court station in 1911. Initially, several members of the public were afraid of the new moving staircases, so the authorities employed a one-legged man known as 'Bumper' Harris to ride up and down all day to show how easy they were to use. This was not a total success because some people became concerned that the escalator had been the cause of his losing his leg in the first place. Harris subsequently retired to Gloucester to make cider and violins.

☞ ADDRESS, ASHES, BALLET, BENTHAM, BEQUESTS, BISCUITS, BUCKLAND, BUTCHELL, CAPITAL PUNISHMENT, CHILE, CHOCOLATE, DAVIDSON, DOG, ELEPHANT, EPONYM, FASHION, FLIGHT, FOOTBALL, GLADSTONE, GUN, HAIR, HENRY VIII, HIPPOPOTAMUS, HORSE, HUDSON, IN-FLIGHT CATERING, KUWAIT, LAVATORIES, LUNACY, MACKEREL, MOTORING, OLYMPIC GAMES, OSTRICH, PIGEON, POLAR BEAR, QUAGGA, REINDEER, RHUBARB, RUBBER BANDS, SCENT, SKATES, TAXI, THAMES, TOURISM, TRAFFIC LIGHTS, TUG-OF-WAR, UMBRELLA, UNDERGROUND, WELLINGTON, WELLS

LOUIS XIV, King of France (1638–1715)

The Sun King, Louis XIV, was born with two teeth. He permitted only his hairdresser to see him without his wig on. Louis XIV was great-grandfather of Louis XV, great-great-great-grandfather of Louis XVI and great-great-great-great-grandfather of Louis XVII. He reigned for 72 years, outlived his son and grandsons, and was succeeded by his great-grandson.

☛ King Louis XIV of France only took three baths in his life but owned 413 beds and changed his linen three times a day.

☞ BUCKLAND, LIECHTENSTEIN, SHOES, TABLE MANNERS, TEETH

LOVE

According to the organisers of the First International Conference on Love and Attraction in Cardiff in 1990, love is 'the cognitive-affective state characterised by intrusive and obsessive fantasising concerning reciprocity of amorant feeling by the object of the amorance'.

More recently, academics in England and Italy have delved even more deeply into the meaning of true love. The British, using sophisticated brain scanning techniques, found in 1999 that the sites in the brain that are most active when a person falls in love are generally the same as those stimulated by cocaine. The Italians added to this by looking at the changes in the brain chemicals of people in love. Their conclusion was that love is a form of obsessive–compulsive behaviour.

☛ According to a recent survey, when a man says 'I love you' the odds are four to one he's just saying it to get the person he's speaking to into bed. Other survey results include the following:

2% of people have fallen in love in a supermarket
12% of business travellers say they think about sex while travelling
13% of women have said 'I love you' just to have sex

15% of people said they would accept an e-mailed proposal of marriage

34% of men say they have faked an orgasm

35% of 18-to 24-year-olds say they have had oral sex while driving

38% of Canadian women would prefer to eat chocolate than make love

49% of men are dissatisfied with their sex lives

50% of women say the experience of losing their virginity was 'disappointing' or 'awful'

52% of British couples have made love in a car

53% of people believe in love at first sight

55% of men say they would not have sex with a female boss in order to gain promotion

61% of men claim to have had an affair with a work colleague

70% of divorce petitions are filed by women

71% of American men are satisfied with the size of their partner's breasts

84% of pet owners would rather have their toes licked by their dog than by their partner

The average British male learned about sex at school, lost his virginity just before he was 18, makes love 105 times a year, marries for the first time when he is 29.8 to a woman 2.1 years younger than himself and divorces at 31.5.

The average Brazilian, by contrast, learned from friends, started at 16.5, makes love 107 times a year and wishes his partner was Demi Moore.

☞ ALCOHOL, ANDERSEN, BALI, BIRMINGHAM,

CALIFORNIA, CHARLES II, CHOCOLATE, DIVORCE,
EUROPE, FRIDAY, FUNERALS, GHOSTS, KUWAIT, LUTHER,
MISTLETOE, SEX, SHOES, SHOPPING TROLLEYS, TURKEY
(country), VALENTINE, WELLINGTON

LUCRETIUS (c.99–55BC)
☞ CENTAUR

LUGOSI, Bela (1882–1956)
☞ BURIAL

LUNACY
★ On 11 September 1905, scientists blamed a rise in
lunacy in Britain on the tedium of country life. On 17
September 1910, a London doctor warned that, if lunacy
continued to increase at the same rate, the insane would
outnumber the sane by 1950.
☞ ASH WEDNESDAY

LUNCHEON
The word 'luncheon' originally meant a thick slice or
a hunk.
☞ ALCHEMY, ASCOT, CRISPS, IN-FLIGHT CATERING,
SANDWICHES

LUTHER, Martin (1483–1546)
The church reformer Martin Luther recommended
making love twice a week. More was lustful; less gave
insufficient chance of conception.

LUXEMBOURG

With 79.68 telephone lines per 100 people, Luxembourg has the highest ratio of telephone lines to people in the world.

☞ FROGS

McENROE, John (b. 1959)
☞ CUBA

MACKEREL
The only station on the London Underground system whose name has no letters in common with the word 'mackerel' is St John's Wood. The only two tube stations which have all five vowels in them are Mansion House and South Ealing.

The only American state with no letters in common with the word 'mackerel' is Ohio. The only state with no letters in common with the name Lewinsky is Utah. Durham is the only English county with no letters in common with the name Lewinsky.

MADONNA (b. 1958)
Stage name of Madonna Louise Veronica Ciccone.
☞ BARCELONA

MADRID

Short-sighted Sanchez Fabres, 41, took off his glasses as a disguise when robbing a bank in Madrid in 1999. He then tripped over furniture and subsequently surrendered to police.

☞ CHIMPANZEE, MARIJUANA

MAINE

Maine is the only state in America whose name has only one syllable.

☞ CHEWING GUM, DOUGHNUTS, MOOSE, OKLAHOMA, TOOTHPICK, UMBRELLA

MALARIA

More soldiers died from malaria in World War I than were killed by weapons.

☞ MEDICINE, PANAMA

MALAYSIA

In 1984 in Malaysia, a 16-year-old boy was beheaded and offered as a human sacrifice by a Chinese medium looking for the lucky number in a weekly lottery. The medium and three other men were arrested.

★ On 26 August 1997, a model of the Malaysian flag was completed, made out of 10,430 floppy disks. The country's deputy education minister described this as 'an event Malaysia can be proud of'.

☞ CINEMA, CRIME, SCRABBLE

MALDIVES

There are no political parties in the Maldives.

☞ INCOME TAX

MAMMOTH

☞ ALCOHOL

MANDELA, Nelson (b. 1918)

★ On Nelson Mandela's 70th birthday on 18 July 1988, Margaret Thatcher was the only Western leader not to send him a card.

Mandela was voted 'Santa Claus of the Year' in December 1995 – the first recipient of that title awarded by the Santa Claus Foundation of Greenland.

MANILOW, Barry (b. 1946)

Barry Manilow was born Barry Alan Pincus.

★ On 14 August 1995, the Independent Television Commission in Britain reported as follows in response to a viewer's complaint: 'One viewer who complained about a man wearing an artificial penis on his nose in the *Big Breakfast* was informed that this was not the case and the man was in fact doing an impression of Barry Manilow.'

MARCO POLO (1254–1324)

☞ TOURISM

MARIE ANTOINETTE (1755–93)

☞ HANDKERCHIEF, POTATO, WHISTLING

MARIJUANA
The first Madrid Marijuana Cup competition for cannabis growers was held in the Spanish capital in 1997. It attracted 51 entrants, one of the organisers was arrested and one woman passed out from the fumes and had to be helped out of the building.

☞ MEDICINE

MARQUESAS ISLANDS
The only word for a domestic animal in the language of the Marquesas Islanders in the Pacific is the word for pig. Goats are called 'pigs with teeth on their heads'.

MARRIAGE
Wedding rings are worn on the third finger of the left hand because the Romans believed that a nerve led directly from there to the heart.

The Priestess of Demeter was the only married woman allowed to watch the ancient Olympic Games. Any other married woman spectator was liable to be sentenced to death by being thrown from a cliff.

Another curious marriage law in ancient Rome specified that senators were forbidden to marry the daughter of an actor or actress.

In ancient Sparta, men who remained unmarried by the time they were 30 forfeited the right to vote.

Research in the USA has shown that more than 10,000 marriages a year now begin with romances started during coffee breaks. Research has also shown that bachelors are three times more likely to go mad than married men.

Until 1912, it was legally impossible for a British

woman to commit a crime in her husband's presence without him being considered to have coerced her into doing it.

According to research published in the *British Medical Journal* in 2001, men who had a low birthweight and were smaller at birth are significantly less likely to get married. Even in old age, men who had stayed bachelors were 2.1cm shorter than their married peers. Research on men born in England and Finland around 1930 showed that, for every extra kilogram they weighed at birth, they were 1.42 times more likely to marry. Every extra centimetre in length at birth meant they had a 1.13 greater chance of walking down the aisle.

Even after social factors such as class and income were taken into account, shorter, lighter, thinner men were still significantly less likely to marry.

'There is not one in a hundred of either sex who is not taken in when they marry' – Jane Austen, *Mansfield Park* (1814).

☞ AGE OF CONSENT, AIR HOSTESSES, CELIBACY, DICKENS, LOVE, CENTRAL AFRICAN REPUBLIC, DIVORCE, MOLE, OBEDIENCE, THIRTEEN, ZAMBIA

MARS

The red appearance of the planet Mars is caused by oxidised iron on its surface – basically rust. The ancient Egyptians were the first to name it after its colour. They called it 'Har Decher', the Red One. The Assyrians called it the 'Shredder of Blood'. The Greeks called it Ares and the Romans called it Mars – in both cases the names of their gods of war.

The two moons of Mars were discovered by American astronomer Asaph Hall in 1877 and named Phobos (fear) and Deimos (panic), after the horses that pulled the chariot of the Greek god of war.

The average temperature on Mars is –63°C.

Belief in intelligent life on Mars was fuelled by the mistaken claim in 1877 of Italian astronomer Giovanni Schiaparelli that he had discovered canals on its surface.

The temperatures on Mars vary between –130°C and +20°C. The atmospheric pressure is less than 1 per cent of that on Earth, so, even at those low temperatures, water would instantly boil into vapour.

A day on Mars lasts 24hr 37min – almost the same as an Earth day – but a year is 686.7 Earth days.

In a controlled experiment performed by psychologists in Cambridge in 1982, only one rat out of eight preferred a Mars bar to cheddar cheese.

☛ If you weigh 150lb on Earth, you will weigh 57lb on Mars.

☞ ASTRONOMY, TUESDAY

MARSTON, William Moulton (1893–1947)

William Moulton Marston's two greatest achievements were both connected with the pursuit of justice: he was the inventor of the polygraph (or lie detector) and was also the creator of the first superheroine, Wonder Woman. With a law degree and a doctorate in psychology, he was a tireless advocate of the use of lie detectors in courts. He even appeared in a 1938 Gillette razor blade advertisement that used a lie detector test to reveal men's 'true' feelings about various shaving methods. (The tests, incidentally, overwhelmingly confirmed that Gillette blades minimised the emotional disturbances caused by rival products.)

In 1941, under the pseudonym Charles Moulton, Marston created Wonder Woman. Unlike most of his fellow academics, he encouraged parents to let their children read comics. 'It's too bad for us "literary" enthusiasts, but it's the truth nevertheless,' he said, 'pictures tell any story more effectively than words... If children will read comics... why isn't it advisable to give them some constructive comics to read?'

MARY, QUEEN OF SCOTS (1542–87)

Mary, Queen of Scots used to test her food for poison with something that was supposed to be a piece of unicorn's horn. When she was beheaded at Fotheringay Castle in 1587, it took the executioner three blows of the axe (or two blows and one small cut) to sever the head completely. She left an embroidered bedcover to her son, James I.

☞ BILLIARDS

MATISSE, Henri (1869–1954)

★ On 3 December 1961, Henri Matisse's painting *Le Bateau* was finally put the right way up at New York's Museum of Modern Art after it had been hanging upside down for 46 days apparently without anyone noticing.

St MATTHEW

In 2001, the Russian Orthodox Church named the apostle Matthew patron saint of Russia's tax police.

St Matthew himself was a tax collector, before giving up the profession to follow Jesus. A spokesman for the tax police said, 'We are not planning to make our heavenly protection into a cult. It simply means that tax police will have another holiday, 29 November, St Matthew's Day.'

☞ St ANDREW

MAY

In Old English the month of May was called Thrimilce (three milks) – the season when you could milk cows three times between sunrise and evening. The Emperor Charlemagne, however, called May 'wunnimanoth' or 'joy-month'.

According to old Cornish superstition, it is unlucky to buy a broom during the month of May, while, according to a Greek superstition, May is an unlucky month altogether, especially if it begins on a Saturday. The Romans thought it unlucky to get married in May. According to the poet Ovid: 'Bad girls wed in May.'

Anthony Trollope advised: 'Let no man boast himself that he has got through the perils of winter till at least the seventh of May.'

The proverbial saying 'Cast ne'er a clout till May be out' means 'Don't give up your winter clothes', though some say this refers not to the end of the month of May but to the appearance of blossom on the hawthorn, or may-tree.

MAYDAY

In 1644 Maypoles were banned by Parliament in England as a 'heathenish vanity'.

☞ ARGENTINA

MEDICINE

Marijuana was prescribed by the Chinese as a remedy for gout, rheumatism, malaria, beri-beri and forgetfulness.

In ancient Rome, barbers dressed cuts with spiders' webs soaked in vinegar.

In modern Britain, doctors spend an average of 9.4 minutes seeing each patient in their surgeries. The European average is 10.7 minutes.

☞ ALCOHOL, BASEBALL, GALILEI, GARLIC, GOLF, TABLOID, St VALENTINE

MELON

According to research by the supermarket chain Tesco, male shoppers buy melons most similar in size to the way they want their women's breasts to be. Female buyers tend to pick varieties that match most closely their own bust shape and size. Experts also found that small is beautiful for most shoppers – one branch swapped 2lb 2oz melons (DD cup size) for 1lb 2oz melons (C cup size) and sold a million more melons.

☞ CELIBACY

MEMORY

Researchers at the University of Wisconsin in 2002 showed that people who perform a memory task (remembering a list of words) then watch a video of a tooth extraction or a rabbit-processing factory will perform better at the task than people who watch an emotionally neutral video or no video at all. The experiment was part of a study designed to show that emotion helps us remember, even if it is of no personal

relevance. A practical conclusion of the research was a recommendation that, immediately after a swotting session, students should watch a thriller or work out. 'Do something that'll get you excited,' a researcher said.
☞ DUCK, GOLDFISH, SEA LION, WORM

MENSTRUATION
➤ According to a survey at Holloway prison in 1945: 'Ninety-three per cent of female crimes are committed during the pre-menstrual phase.' There is also evidence that accidents in the home and on the road are more likely to happen to women before menstruation.
☞ PREGNANCY

MERKIN
The Oxford Companion to the Body dates the origins of the merkin, or pubic wig, back to 1450. As a measure against lice, some women shaved off their pubic hair and covered the area with an artificial hairpiece. Prostitutes also wore them, though their motivation seems more likely to have been a desire to cover up signs of disease. The *Oxford Companion* also mentions a tale of one gentleman who acquired the diseased merkin of a prostitute, dried it, combed it well and then presented it to a cardinal, telling him he had brought him St Peter's beard.

METEOROLOGY
★ An extremely rare event in the history of weather forecasting took place on 10 July 1997: a group of weather forecasters apologised for getting it wrong. It happened in Belgium, where the forecasters issued an

apology 'to the inhabitants of the centre of the country who could not enjoy the bright spells we forecast'.
☞ St SWITHUN, UGANDA

METHANE

The flatulence of a single sheep could power a small lorry for 25 miles a day, according to New Zealand scientist Dr David Lowe. Harnessing the methane output of 72 million sheep could solve the nation's fuel problems. The belches of 10 cows are enough to heat a small house. Bovine flatulence adds 85 million tons of methane to the atmosphere each year. Termites' eating habits add an estimated 150 million tons.
☞ FART

METRIC SYSTEM

The metric system of measurements was devised in France in the period immediately following the Revolution as the country was changing from monarchy to republic. In 1790, a group of scientists met Louis XVI, who gave approval to their ideas. The following day, the King tried to flee the country but was arrested and jailed. From jail he directed two engineers to determine the length of a metre, the first metric measure. The length that had been agreed on was one ten-millionth of the distance along the meridian from the North Pole to Paris. The system was finally adopted in 1795, two years after Louis XVI was beheaded. The motto for the new egalitarian metric system was 'For all people, for all time.'

More recently, the metre was redefined as equal to 1,650,763.73 wavelengths in vacuum of the radiation corresponding to the transition between the levels 2p10 and 5d5 of the krypton-86 atom.

The kilogram is the only SI unit that is still linked to a real object: a cylinder deposited in the International Bureau of Weights and Measures at Sèvres, France.

MEXICO
Ten times as many people are killed from scorpion stings in Mexico as die from snakebite.
☞ AGE OF CONSENT, MICKEY MOUSE, SANTA ANNA, St VALENTINE

MIAMI
☞ AARDVARK, PANAMA

MICHELANGELO (1475–1564)
Despite spending four years painting the ceiling of the Sistine Chapel, Michelangelo always thought of himself primarily as a sculptor and was irritated whenever he was described as a painter.

On 1 August 1995, the High Court in Hong Kong ruled that Michelangelo's sculpture David is not obscene.
☞ VATICAN

MICKEY MOUSE (b. 1928)
Mickey, Minnie and Donald Duck are the only Disney characters with official birthdays. Mickey and Minnie are said to have been born on 18 November 1928, which was the release date of the cartoon *Steamboat Willie*, the first Disney cartoon with sound. That was in fact Mickey's third appearance. He had previously been in

two silent cartoons called *Plane Crazy* and *Gallopin' Gaucho*.

Walt Disney originally called him Mortimer Mouse, but his wife Lillian thought Mortimer sounded pompous and suggested Mickey instead. The actor Mickey Rooney, however, always maintained that the character was named after him, following a visit he made as a five-year-old child star to Walt Disney.

In France, Mickey Mouse is known as Michal Souris. He is Topolino in Italy, Mikki Ma-u-su in Japan, Raton Mickey in Mexico, Mikki Hirri in Finland and Miguel Rantoncito in Spain.

His ears are always perfect circles whatever angle they are viewed from.

Italian dictator Benito Mussolini was a great Mickey Mouse fan. He met Disney in Rome in 1935.

According to Swiss law professor Karl-Ludwig Kunz, Mickey Mouse committed seven criminal acts in his comics in 1952. His conduct since then does not appear to have been monitored so rigorously but Mickey did go on strike at EuroDisney in 1998.

MILK
Swedish cows were fitted with plastic discs impregnated with insecticide in 1984 to keep their heads fly-free in summer. Scientists say this improved milk yield.
☞ BEER, BUFFALO, CAMEL, MAY, NERO, SARDINE, SLOANE, TEETH

MISOGYNY
By the age of 63, in 1984, Indian Hindu leader Pramukh Swami had not seen a woman for 46 years. Women were

kept away from his route for a papal audience at the Vatican. He was accompanied by nine other monks and a group of laymen with the task of warning him of approaching women and guiding him with his eyes shut.

MISTLETOE

Mistletoe (of which there are around 2,000 species) has no roots but lives as a parasite off the tree to which it attaches itself. Its seeds are spread through the droppings of birds that eat the berries. The parasitic nature of mistletoe is reflected in the botanical name of the common American variety Phoradendron, which means 'thief of the tree'.

The practice of kissing beneath the mistletoe goes back to a Norse myth in which Balder, god of the summer son, was killed by Loki, god of evil, and restored to life by his mother Frigga, goddess of love. Her tears became the white berries on mistletoe and in her joy she kissed all who passed beneath. Traditionally a berry should be plucked for each kiss beneath the mistletoe; when the berries run out, no more kisses may be claimed.

A 'kissing ball' of decorated mistletoe was a popular decoration in 18th-century British homes. Any girl standing under it could not refuse to be kissed, but, if she stood under it and remained unkissed, it meant she would not be married in the next year.

The Druids called mistletoe 'Allheal', believing it to be sacred and an antidote to poisons.

MOLE

The post of Mole Controller to Queen Elizabeth II at

Sandringham is held by Victor Williamson. As Royal molecatcher he is on record as saying that he does not use poison but prefers traps.

The old name for a mole was mouldwarp or moldiwarp, literally meaning 'earth-thrower'.

The average human being has 25 moles on his or her body.

Moles' feet carried in a pocket are said to be a charm against cramp; moles' forefeet are said to cure aching arms, while the hind feet are supposed to be good for relieving pain in the legs.

The collective noun for moles is a 'labour' or 'company'. Moles do not hibernate.

★ On 8 March 1702, King William III died of complications following his breaking his collarbone after falling when his horse was startled by a mole. Jacobite opponents of the King promptly instituted a new toast: 'To the little gentleman in black velvet' in honour of the mole.

☞ BUCKLAND, ELEPHANT, MOLEOSOPHY

MOLEOSOPHY

Fortune-telling by the position of moles on the body is called moleosophy. Predictions include the following:

- A mole on the right-hand side of the forehead is said to be predictive of talent and success; on the left it indicates stubbornness and an extravagant personality.
- A mole on the right knee predicts a happy marriage; on the left knee it means a bad temper.

- Moles on the buttocks indicate a lack of ambition; moles on the elbows indicate a desire to travel.
- Generally a round mole signifies goodness, an oblong mole means a modest share of acquired wealth, and an angular mole suggests both positive and negative characteristics.

MONACO
☞ INCOME TAX

MONDAY
Monday is the only day of the week that is an anagram of a single word: dynamo. The Russian for Monday is 'ponedyelnik', which means 'after do-nothing'.

Research has also show that Monday is:

- The most common day for sudden deaths from psychological stress.
- The most common day for heart attacks.
- The least rainy day of the week on the east coast of America. This is thought to be due to daily changes in the pattern of man-made pollution.
- The most common day for teenage suicide attempts in Oregon, especially in the spring.

'The Monday Effect' is the name given by stock market investors to a theory that share prices on Monday will continue in the same direction they moved on the Friday before.

MONET, Claude-Oscar (1840–1926)

Monet's 1872 painting *Impression, Sunrise* is the one that gave rise to the term 'Impressionism'. In 1866, plagued by debt, he burned 200 of his own paintings to prevent them being seized by creditors.

☞ PIGEON

MONEY

The word 'money' comes from Moneta, one of the names of the goddess Juno. The Roman mint was in her temple. In the USA, calling a dollar a 'buck' comes from a time when buckskin was used as currency. Piggy banks get their name from a clay called pygg. Money was saved in pygg jars, which were then made in the shape of pigs and called piggy banks.

The total value of all Bank of England banknotes in circulation at the start of 2005 was £35,416,000,000. The coins in circulation added about another £3.3 billion to the total.

The estimated numbers of each coin in circulation at the end of 2004 according to the Royal Mint were as follows:

Coin	Number (millions)	Value (£million)
£2	249	498
£1	1,410	1,410
50p	738	369
20p	2,128	426
10p	1,557	156
5p	3,578	179
2p	6,339	127
1p	10,360	104

If all those coins were divided equally among the population of the UK, each person would end up with four £2 coins, 23 £1 coins, 12 50p coins, 35 20p coins, 26 10p coins, 60 5p coins. 106 2p coins and 173 penny coins.

A £2 coin weighs exactly 12g; a £1 coin weighs 9.5g; a 50p coin weighs 8g; a 20p coin weighs 5g; a 10p coin weighs 6.5g; a 5p coin weighs 3.25g; a 2p coin weighs 7.12g; and a 1p coin weighs 3.56g. So, if all the national coinage were divided equally among the entire population, every Briton would be weighed down with over 2.1kg of loose change.

'Money is better than poverty, if only for financial reasons' – Woody Allen.

☛ In the United States, a dime has 118 ridges around its edge but a quarter has 119 ridges.

☞ ATHLETICS, BHUTAN, GATES, MONOPOLY, NAURU, NETHERLANDS, ROBBERY, TRISTAN DA CUNHA

MONGOLIA
☞ BAR CODES, HANGOVER

MONKEY
There is a simple rule to tell an ape from a monkey: monkeys have tails; apes don't. There are, however, two important differences between New World monkeys (from Central and South America) and Old World monkeys (from Africa and Asia): if a monkey is swinging by its tail, it is probably from Central or South America. Monkeys from Africa and Asia do not generally have prehensile tails.

Also, New World monkeys have 36 teeth; Old World monkeys have 32 teeth.

The Howler monkey of America is the loudest land animal. Its call can be heard three miles away.

Significant moments in recent monkey history:

In October 1997, a monkey was arrested in the African state of Benin for stealing a television aerial. The street juggler who trained it was also arrested and jailed. The monkey was sent to a zoo.

In May 1998, the world's first overhead monkey crossing was built across a busy road in Taiwan. The result: 'fewer dead monkeys and damaged cars'.

Finally, also in 1998, researchers in Washington established that monkeys can count up to nine. The monkeys in the experiment were called Rosencrantz and Macduff.

The marmoset and the tamarin are the only monkey species that are truly monogamous.

☞ CARUSO, DONKEY, PEANUT

MONOPOLY

According to a statistical analysis of the game of Monopoly, the property most often landed on is Trafalgar Square (Illinois Avenue in the US version). In 1975, twice as much monopoly money as real money was printed in the USA.

World records for Monopoly include the following:

Longest game ever played: 1,680 hours (70 days)
Longest game played in a treehouse: 240 hours (10 days)
Longest game in a moving elevator: 384 hours (16 days)
Longest game played underground: 100 hours (4 days 4 hours)

Longest game in a bathtub: 99 hours (4 days 3 hours)

Longest game on a balance beam: 200 hours (8 days 8 hours)

Longest game under water: 1,200 hours (50 days)

Longest game on the back of a fire truck: 101 hours (4 days 5 hours)

Longest smallest game: (played on a board measuring one square inch) 30 hours

MONTEZUMA II (1466–1520)
Emperor of the Aztecs.

☞ CHOCOLATE

MOON
Neil Armstrong's 'One small step…' speech is often quoted as the first words broadcast from the Moon, but the first words were, in fact, 'Houston, Tranquility Base here. The Eagle has landed.'

The first words spoken (rather than broadcast) from the Moon were Buzz Aldrin's: 'Contact light. OK, engine stop. ACA out of detent. Modes control both auto, descent engine command override, off. Engine arm, off. Four thirteen is in.' The last words spoken on the Moon to date were: 'America's challenge of today has forged man's destiny of tomorrow' (Eugene Cernan, 11 December 1972).

Pliny the Elder (AD23–79) believed that the Moon was larger than the Earth. In fact, it has a diameter of 2,159 miles and weighs about 73,500,000,000,000,000,000 tonnes.

According to a paper in *Science* journal in 1970,

seismological studies reveal that the structure of the Moon is closer to that of cheese than to rocks on Earth.

Research shows that people in the UK are most likely to be bitten by dogs when there is a full moon.

Buzz Aldrin, the second man on the Moon, recorded the 37th best pole vault in the USA in 1951.

☞ EASTER, FEBRUARY, FOOTBALL, GATES, GOLF, MARS, PREGNANCY, SONGS, WIMBLEDON

MOOSE

The species know as a moose in North America is referred to as an elk in Europe. What the Americans call an elk is known as a wapiti in Europe.

Here are 25 more useful facts about moose:

1. The correct scientific name for the moose is *Alces alces*.

2. Moose are even-toed herbivorous mammals and live from 15 to 25 years.

3. The correct term for a spike on a moose's antlers is 'tine'. Only the male moose has ntlers.

4. The gestation period of a moose is approximately eight months.

5. Moose can run at up to 35mph and swim at 6mph.

6. The European elk and North American moose are different versions of the same pecies of animal.

7. Although European elk can be found in North America, American moose do not exist in Europe.

8. After the mating season, males knock their antlers off against trees every November or

December. After shedding its antlers a moose grows back a bigger pair the following year.

9. A fully grown moose weighs between 1,000lb and 1,600lb.

10. The world record biggest moose weighed in at 1,800lb.

11. The span of a moose's antlers may be almost six feet.

12. The correct term for the antler spread of a moose is 'rack'.

13. An adult moose eats between 40lb and 60lb of food a day, but does not eat much grass.

14. Moose especially like aquatic plants, which provide them with much-needed salt.

15. Before mating, a bull moose often digs a shallow pit with his paws, fills it with urine, then rolls around in it. The smell apparently attracts females.

16. Male moose may get very bad-tempered during the mating season.

17. When a car hits a moose in America, the damage to the car usually exceeds $500.

18. On one 50km stretch of railway in Alaska, 68 moose were once killed in a single night in collisions with trains.

19. There are more moose per mile in Maine than any other US state.

20. The word 'moose' comes from an Algonquin Indian language and means 'twig-eater'.

21. Although the general word for a moose in the Alaskan Inuit language Inupiaq is *tuttuvaq*, some dialects favour *tiniika* or *tiniikaq*.

22. Female moose usually give birth to twins and often triplets.
23. The moose is believed to be a descendant of the Megaceros, which was around in one million BC.
24. The Irish elk became extinct around 10,000BC.
25. Moose hoofprints have pointed ends pointing in the direction of travel.

☞ ALASKA, CANADA

MOSCOW

Moscow was founded in 1147 by Prince Yuri Dolgoruky; his name means 'Yuri the long-armed'.

Moscow includes the world's busiest McDonald's (in Pushkin Square, where 40,000 people are served every day), the world's biggest bell (the Tsar Kolokol in the Kremlin, which has never been rung because it was cracked before its installation) and the start of the world's longest train journey (170 hours from Moscow to Vladivostok).

Since 1800, 49 populated places in the United States have been named Moscow. Today, there are 27, though only five are large enough to be included in the *Times Atlas of the World*.

☞ ALCOHOL, COW

MOSQUITO

Research based at the University of Durham in 2000 found that pregnant women attract twice as many mosquitoes as non-pregnant ones.

☞ DINOSAUR, UMBRELLA

MOTH

According to research published in 2002, female moths prefer to mate with larger males. In a paper entitled 'Paternal inheritance of a female moth's mating preference' (*Nature*, vol. 419) the mating preferences of female arctiid moths were analysed. The results showed that females with larger fathers showed the strongest preference for large mates, thus confirming that the female's mating preference is inherited from the male parent.

☞ VIRGINITY

MOTHER TERESA (Agnes Gonxha Bojaxhiu, 1910–97)

In 1997, Bob Bernstein, owner of the Bongo Java coffee shop in Nashville, was asked by Mother Teresa's lawyers to stop selling a cinnamon bun bearing her likeness. Mr Bernstein immediately dropped Mother Teresa's name from his 'nun bun' and offered 15 per cent of the profits to her Sisters of Mercy charities.

MOTORING

The Locomotive Act of 1865 specified that a person carrying a red flag must walk at least 60yd ahead of any car. In 1878, the red flag became optional, but the speed limit stayed at 2mph in towns and 4mph in the country. When this was increased to 14mph in 1896, it was celebrated by an 'Emancipation Run' from London to Brighton, which began with Lord Winchilsea tearing up a symbolic red flag.

Drunken driving became illegal in 1872.

In 2000, there were 3,409 fatal injuries on British roads, together with 38,155 serious injuries and

278,719 slight injuries needing hospital treatment. These accidents happened despite the fact that in the same year the 4,500 speed cameras in England and Wales caught 656,000 motorists.

In 2000, a Hertfordshire man was jailed for six weeks for speeding at 175mph on his Honda Fireblade motorcycle. This is Britain's fastest speeding conviction.

In August 2003, the Bureau of Transportation Statistics revealed that for the first time there were more vehicles than drivers in the USA.

The average Briton makes 645 car journeys a year.
☞ CARS, HORSE

MOUNTAINEERING
Noteworthy events in the history of mountaineering include the following:

1950: A four-month-old kitten followed a party of climbers in Switzerland and reached the top of the Matterhorn.
1974: A German team that had set out to climb Annapurna 4 reached the top of Annapurna 2 by mistake.
2000: An expedition that set out to clean up Mount Everest of previous climbers' garbage counted 632 discarded oxygen bottles among the debris they removed.

★ On 27 June 1988, Dave Hurst and Alan Matthews of Britain became the first blind climbers to scale Mont Blanc.
☞ St BERNARD, EVEREST, YETI

MOUSE

When Douglas Engelbart invented the computer mouse in 1968, he called it an 'X-Y Position Indicator for a Display System'.

☞ BREAD, CRESS, DICKENS, HAMSTER, ICELAND, MICKEY MOUSE

MOUSTACHE

In 2004, it was announced that police in northern India would be paid an extra 30 rupees (40p) a month to grow a moustache. A spokesman for the Madhya Pradesh state police said that research showed police with moustaches were taken more seriously. However, he added, the shape and style of police moustaches would be monitored to ensure they did not start to look too mean.

Researchers at Tel Aviv University have shown that men with thin moustaches have a greater propensity to suffering from ulcers.

☞ HAIR, HITLER, OPERA, PLAYING CARDS, WOODPECKER

MOUTH ORGAN
☞ ELEPHANT

MOZART, Wolfgang Amadeus (1756–91)

★ Mozart was born on 27 January 1756; Lewis Carroll was born on 27 January 1832; Verdi died on 27 January 1901; Kaiser Wilhelm II was born on 27 January 1859; Thomas Edison took out a patent for the electric lamp on 27 January 1879; and John Logie Baird first demonstrated television on 27 January 1926.

☞ WIG

MUGGING

The first Muggers Conference was held in Bangladesh in 1996. It ended with the title of Master Hijacker being conferred on Mohammed Rippon for his record 21 muggings in two hours.

MUSHROOM

A person who studies mushrooms and fungi is a mycologist. If you eat them, you are a mycophagist; if you like them, you're a mycophile. The Italian mycologist Bruno Cetti published descriptions and pictures of 2,147 types of mushroom.

- Mushrooms differ from other plants in that they contain no chlorophyl. Because of this, some would argue that they are not plants at all.
- Most fatal cases of mushroom poisoning are caused by a variety called *Amanita phalloides* or Death Cap. Roman Emperors Tiberius and Claudius, Tsar Alexander I of Russia, Pope Clement II and King Charles V of France all died of mushroom poisoning.
- The official state mushroom of Minnesota is the morel. The official state mushroom of Oregon is the Pacific golden chanterelle.
- There is a mushroom museum in Kennett Square, Pennsylvania. It is open daily from 10am to 6pm.
- China is the world's biggest mushroom producer, with an annual yield of about four million tonnes. According to the UN Food and Agriculture

Organisation, UK mushroom production was 67,626 tonnes in 2002, which is only half the 1994 figure.

☞ PHOBIAS, RHYME, SLUG

MUSIC

Beethoven had thick black hairs on the backs of his hands.

In 2006, an RSPCA rescue centre in Somerset reported that stressed dogs are calmed by the music of Mozart and Beethoven, but do not respond well to pop or dance music.

☞ CALIFORNIA, CHINA, CONDOM, FLIES, HIPPO POTAMUS, OLYMPIC GAMES, SINGAPORE, SUICIDE, TOURISM, VENICE, WAGNER

NABOKOV, Vladimir (1899–1977)

Besides writing novels such as *Lolita*, Nabokov was a keen lepidopterist and discovered several species of butterfly that now have his name, including Nabokov's pug (*Eupithecia nabokovi*) in Utah 1943.

NAMES

★ On 12 June 1996, a Swedish woman won a nine-year-long battle to be allowed to name her son Christophpher rather than Christopher or Christoffer.

☞ ALDRIN, AMERICA, ANAGRAMS, BARRIE, BIBLE, BOSWELL, BOUNTY, BOWIE, BUNKER, BURNS, CAT, CLINTON, COLORADO, DOG, DUCK, ELECTRIC CHAIR, EPONYM, EVEREST, FRANCE, GEORGE VI, GOLDFISH, HACKER, HOUDINI, KARLOFF, MADONNA, NEWTON, NORWAY, PARKER, PHOENIX, PICASSO, POPEYE, PRESLEY, QUEEN MARY, RALEIGH, REAGAN, ROMANIA, ROOSEVELT, SEAL, STEWART, TENNIS, TRUMAN, WALES, WELLINGTON, WESSEX

NAPOLEON BONAPARTE (1769–1821)
Napoleon's surgeon, Baron Dominique Larrey, could reputedly amputate a man's leg in 14 seconds.

☞ BRUMMELL, EPONYM, HAIR, TEETH, TINS, WELLINGTON

NARWHAL
When a two-tusked narwhal is found, the tusks always spiral in the same direction. Those of goats and all other two-tusked animals always spiral in opposite directions.

NAURU
With an area of 21sq km and a population of 12,570, the Republic of Nauru in the South Pacific (formerly Pleasant Island) is the world's smallest independent state. Its economy is mainly based on phosphate mining, but the CIA lists it as a 'broad-based money-laundering centre' too.

☞ INCOME TAX

NAVEL
In 1944 a sub-committee of the House Military Affairs Committee of US Congress opposed the distribution of the book *The Races of Mankind* to US soldiers, partly on the grounds that Adam and Eve are depicted with navels.

- In 2002, Berlin psychologist Gerhard Reibmann published a book called *Centred: Understanding Yourself Through Your Navel*. In it, he identifies six different navel types, each associated with a personality type and life:
- A horizontal navel, spreading sideways across the stomach, means you are highly emotional and will live for only 68 years.

- A vertical navel, running up and down the stomach, signifies generosity, self-confidence and emotional stability. Life expectancy: 75 years.
- A protruding navel, or 'outie', indicates optimism, enthusiasm and 72 years of life.
- An owner of a concave navel, on the other hand, will be gentle, loving, cautious, delicate, sensitive and prone to worrying. This type has the lowest life expectancy: only 65 years.
- An off-centre navel is a sign of being fun-loving with wide emotional swings. Life expectancy: 70 years.
- The best navel to have is evenly shaped and circular. This means modesty and an even temper with a quiet, retiring personality and 81 years of life.
- Concave navels are, of course, better containers for fluff, as Australian research Karl Kruszelnicki pointed out when he studied bellybutton fluff through samples sent to him by 4,799 people. His main conclusion was that the fluff is a combination of clothing fibres and skin cells that are led to the navel, via body hair, 'as all roads lead to Rome'. His research also identified that: 'Your typical generator of bellybutton lint or fluff is a slightly overweight, middle-aged male with a hairy abdomen.' Specifically, he found that 66 per cent of respondents had bellybutton fluff. Far more fluff-carriers were male than female, and about 97 per cent of fluff-carriers were either 'not very hairy', 'moderately hairy' or 'very hairy'. Only 3 per cent had 'no hair' or 'very little hair'.

- For people troubled by bellybutton fluff, the Japanese have developed the Stick-on Bellybutton Cleaner. It is an adhesive pad which you apply 'over and into the offending area, and then remove it after 10 minutes (making sure you dispose of the evidence discreetly)'. They are available from the Lung Shing Dispensary Company in Hong Kong at a cost of HK$48 for six adhesive strips.

NEEDLE
The novel *The Eye of the Needle* was written by Ken Follett, and should not be confused with *The Needle's Eye*, which is by Margaret Drabble. To add to the potential confusion, both Follett and Drabble have a birthday on 5 June.
☞ St CLARE

NEPAL
The Himalayan kingdom of Nepal is the only country that does not have a rectangular flag. Its flag is shaped like two slightly overlapping triangles.
☞ YETI

NERO, Emperor of Rome (AD37–68)
Nero's second wife, Poppaea, kept 500 asses to provide milk for her bath. Nero had had his first wife, Octavia, and his mother, Agrippina, put to death in AD59.

NETHERLANDS
The hole in the centre of a CD is the size of a Dutch 10-cent coin – the smallest coin in Europe – which

was abolished when the Netherlands adopted the euro. The entire population of the Netherlands were sentenced to death by the Spanish Inquisition in 1568.
☞ FOOTBALL, ROBBERY

NEWCASTLE

The name of Newcastle-upon-Tyne dates back to Norman times when Robert Curthose, eldest son of William the Conqueror, built a castle there on his return from a raid into Scotland. He called it his 'New Castle' and the name stuck.
☞ LIGHT BULB

NEWFOUNDLAND

☞ AMERICA, St ANDREW, CANADA, DOG, HOUSEWIVES, SEAL, SWIMMING

NEW GUINEA
☞ COCONUT, SEX

NEWTON, Isaac (1642–1727)

Isaac Newton has been credited with the invention of the cat-flap. He is said to have devised it as a means of allowing cats to enter his study without spoiling his optics experiments.

Prof. Philipp Lenard (1862–1947) had a phobia of the name of Newton. When he lectured at Heidelberg and Kiel, he had to turn his back and have the name written on the board for him when necessary. Lenard won the Nobel Prize for Physics in 1905.
☞ ALCHEMY, APPLE, SLOANE

NEWTON-JOHN, Olivia (b. 1948)
☞ QUANTUM MECHANICS

NEW YORK
☞ BRUSSELS SPROUTS, CARUSO, CHICKEN, CHOCOLATE,
CHRISTMAS, DOUGHNUTS, FLIRTING, GRAFFITI, HOT
DOGS, ICE CREAM, MATISSE, OYSTER, PENGUIN,
PLATYPUS, POLAR BEAR, SANTA CLAUS, SNOW, SUICIDE,
TRAFFIC LIGHTS

NEW ZEALAND
New Zealand was the first country to give votes
to women.
★ Brewers in New Zealand decided to abolish barmaids
on 18 January 1909.
☞ GOOSEBERRY, HEDGEHOG, INCOME TAX, METHANE,
OBESITY, SANTA CLAUS, SHEEP, TATTOO

NIGER
☞ FIREWORKS

NIGERIA
With 134 million people, Nigeria is the most populous
country in Africa and has the ninth highest population
in the world. It does, however, come fourth in the world
league of Aids sufferers, and life expectancy at birth is
only 50 for both men and women. The women,
however, give birth to an average of 5.5 children. A
Nigerian has a greater than one-in-three chance of not
reaching the age of 40.

The serendipity berry, which was discovered in

Nigeria in the 1960s, is 1,500 times sweeter than sugar.

In the 1980s, it was reported that Nigeria's navy included 20 ships whose names all meant 'hippopotamus' in various languages and dialects spoken in the country.

It is illegal to import green cars into Nigeria.

☞ EXAMINATIONS, PALINDROME

NIXON, Richard Milhous (1913–94)
☞ CLINTON, PRESLEY

NOAH
According to the Book of Enoch in the Apocrypha, Noah was an albino.

☞ HYENA, RAIN

NOBEL PRIZE
Alfred Nobel, who founded the prizes that bear his name, was the inventor of dynamite. His father, Immanuel Nobel, invented plywood.

Up to the end of 2003, only 30 women have ever been awarded a Nobel Prize. The first was Marie Curie in 1903. This was one fewer than the total number won by men from Trinity College, Cambridge. Three more female Nobel Laureates in 2004 enabled women to overtake Trinity in the Nobel race.

Linus Pauling (Chemistry and Peace) and Marie Curie (Chemistry and Physics) are the only people to have won two Nobel Prizes in different disciplines. John Bardeen (Physics) and Frederick Sanger (Chemistry) each won two Nobels in the same discipline.

In 1964, Jean-Paul Sartre turned down the Nobel Prize for Literature on the grounds that such honours could interfere with a writer's responsibilities to his readers. ★ 21 May and 6 June have each been the birthdays of seven Nobel Prize winners. No other dates have as many.

☞ BOOKS, BRAIN, ECONOMICS, HOLES, KIPLING, NEWTON, QUANTUM MECHANICS, St LUCIA, UNIVERSITIES

NORTH POLE
★ On 20 April 1987, Fukashi Kazami of Japan became the first person to reach the North Pole on a motorcycle.

☞ ANTARCTICA, EARTH, METRIC SYSTEM, SANTA CLAUS

NORWAY
There is a town called Hell in Norway. Statistics show that 22 per cent of Norwegians named August were born in August.

☞ AA, BERGMAN, BOOKS, EUROVISION SONG CONTEST, GARDENING, ICELAND, INCOME TAX, POLAR BEAR, SKIING, VICTORIA

NOSE
According to a survey conducted by Waitrose in 2004, the women with the top ten most beautiful noses are:

1. Halle Berry
2. Kylie Minogue
3. Nicole Kidman
4. Gwyneth Paltrow
5. Cameron Diaz
6. Julia Roberts
7. Britney Spears
8. Liv Tyler
9. Catherine Zeta Jones
10. Jennifer Aniston

The ten most beautiful men's noses are those of:

1. Orlando Bloom	6. Robbie Williams
2. Brad Pitt	7. Hugh Grant
3. David Beckham	8. Johnny Depp
4. George Clooney	9. Justin Timberlake
5. Tom Cruise	10. Jude Law

☞ ADULTERY, ANDERSEN, BILLIARDS, BODY, CAPITAL PUNISHMENT, COW, GOLDFISH, HALITOSIS, LIFETIME, MANILOW, PIZZA, SNORING, VOLTAIRE, WASP

NOSTRIL

Research in 2002 showed that, if a person is taught to recognise a particular smell through one nostril, he or she will recognise it through the other one as well.
☞ BODY

NOVA SCOTIA
☞ St ANDREW

NUDISM

Nudist Tomas Cameselle was fined a total of £65 in July 1982 in Pontevedra, Spain. The sum of £60 was for appearing naked in a public place (the beach) and £5 for failing to carry identity papers.

NUMBERS

None of the numbers from one to 99 contains the letter A.

The highest number that can be spelled out without using any letter more than once is five thousand. The next highest is eighty-four.

The only sum that can be spelled out without repeating a letter is FOUR + SIX = TEN.

☞ ADDRESS, BENFORD'S LAW, BOOKS, COMPUTATION, DARTS, FORTY, FORTY-SEVEN, PARAPSYCHOLOGY, RHYME, ROULETTE

OBEDIENCE

☞ On 12 September 1922, the House of Bishops of the US Episcopal Church voted to delete the word 'obey' from the marriage vows.

OBESITY

According to a recent study, the ten most overweight cities in the UK are: Glasgow, Sunderland, Durham, Belfast, Leeds, Bradford, Wolverhampton, Hull, Sheffield and Liverpool in that order. The people of the United States are overweight by a total of about 3.9 billion pounds.

★ On 6 August 1996, a 'pot-bellies seminar' was held in India to which 110 fat policemen were ordered to attend. A police chief commented, 'Photographs in the press of pot-bellied policemen have given the police a bad name.'

On 5 November 1997 in Wellington, New Zealand, William Dickie, 43, was sentenced to 12 months' house arrest because he was too big for prison clothing or a prison bed. Mr Dickie's weight was given as 305kg.

☞ BUTTOCKS, CALIFORNIA, FRANCE

OCTOBER

The Welsh for October is Hydref (originally Hyddfref), a word signifying the lowing of cattle. The Anglo-Saxons, however, called October Winterfylleth (or Winterfilth as Tolkien's hobbits preferred it) meaning the 'fullness' (rather than 'dirtiness') of winter.

According to a recent study in Italy, October is the best month for conceiving a boy. This would not have applied in Catholic Europe in 1582, when October had only 21 days. Because of the change to the Gregorian calendar, the days from 5 to 14 October were omitted.

The 'October Revolution' in Russia in 1917 took place in November, but at the time Russians had not yet changed from the Julian calendar. Even when its anniversary had moved into November, they continued celebrating the October Revolution.

☞ BOUNTY

OCTOPUS

In July 1996, the Sealife Centre in Blackpool, England, issued an urgent appeal for two unwanted Castlemaine XXXX beer bottles to serve as homes for their Australian blue-ringed octopuses. In the wild, they choose such bottles for their nests: the neck is just wide enough for them to get in while keeping predators out.

☞ BEER, QUEENSLAND

ODIN

The Norse god Odin had an eight-legged horse called Sleipnir, which could convey its rider to Valhalla or the

Underworld. In modern times, the Bell Sleipnir™ Lift Device is a stretcher specially designed to be used by undertakers.

☞ THOR

OKAPI

The okapi, *Okapia johnstoni*, is the only known relative of the giraffe. It was discovered by British colonial administrator Sir Harry Johnston in 1901 after having been mentioned in the writings of Henry Morton Stanley a decade earlier. It lives in the Democratic Republic of the Congo and the People's Republic of the Congo and can lick its eyes with its tongue. The first postage stamp to depict an okapi was issued by the Belgian Congo (now the Democratic Republic of the Congo) in 1932.

OKLAHOMA

In May 2000, the state of Oklahoma announced plans to eliminate the word 'squaw' from its place names. 'Squaw' originated as a term used by trappers and is defined in many dictionaries as an American Indian woman, but critics say it is a slur meaning a prostitute or a woman's genitalia.

The Oklahoma legislature agreed unanimously to join a national movement to remove the word from all geographic place names. Montana, Maine and Minnesota had already passed similar legislation.

The town of Red Rock started the movement in Oklahoma, when a bridge over Squaw Creek was being replaced. After hearing appeals by members of the Otoe-Missouria tribe, Red Rock Mayor Geary Watson supported their viewpoint. 'If this creek's name was in its English equivalent,' he said, 'it would be considered an unprintable word.'

☞ SHOPPING TROLLEYS

OLIVE

'Light that shines on olive leaves is like a diamond and makes the painter lose focus' – Pierre Auguste Renoir.

☛ There are about 800 million olive trees in the world, of which about 20 million are in China. Olive oil is mentioned 140 times in the Bible.

☞ OLYMPIC GAMES, PENGUIN, POPEYE

OLYMPIC GAMES

Nobody knows when the first Olympic Games took place. There was certainly such a festival at Olympia in 776BC, after which it became a regular four-yearly event, but there is a good deal of evidence that the Games had been going on for some time before that, if sporadically.

The Greeks even calculated their calendar in 'Olympiads' – periods of four years between successive celebrations of the Games and, for that purpose, 776BC was taken as the first year of the first Olympiad. (The use of the word 'Olympiad' to describe the competition itself is an error that dates back at least to the 16th century.) The 293rd Olympiad ended in AD393, when the Roman emperor Theodosius banned the Games because they were becoming too pagan.

The earliest known Olympic gold medallist (in fact, winners received an olive wreath at the time, not a gold medal) was Coroibus of Elis, a cook who won a 200yd race. This sprint down the length of the stadium was apparently the only athletics event in the early Games, though a second race, over twice that distance, was added at the 14th Olympics. There were, however, also competitions in music, oratory and theatre. The accent shifted to physical prowess only when the Spartans joined in during the 18th Olympics, bringing a pentathlon of running, jumping, wrestling, the javelin and discus-throwing to the event.

The earliest Games had been held to honour Zeus, and, because of the intense religious connotations, included a ceasefire in all wars in the region. It was the growth of competition for personal gain and glory, particularly in the chariot races, that led Theodosius to call a halt.

Baron Pierre de Coubertin (1863–1937) brought the Games back in 1896, when 13 countries competed in Athens. The United States won nine of the 12 track-and-field gold medals. The Olympics have since been held every four years, except for the war years of 1916, 1940 and 1944, though not without considerable teething troubles. In 1900, the Olympics was merely a sideshow at the World Exhibition in Paris and dragged on over five months. In 1904, the Americans squabbled so much over whether they should be held in Chicago or St Louis that most European nations stayed at home. The event was revived with the 'Intercalated Games' of 1906 in Athens, which set the Olympic movement back on track for the highly successful London Olympics of 1908 (at which the English protested about the Irish flag, the Russians complained about the Finnish Flag and everybody complained about the British judges and referees).

Other events of which little has been seen in recent Olympics include cricket, at which Britain beat France – the only other team that entered – in Paris 1900; and croquet, at which France won all the medals in 1900.

Although there had been women's archery events in the 1904 Olympics, and women's swimming in 1912, there were no track-and-field events for women until 1928. Women had been banned completely from the ancient Olympics, even as spectators.

Most unlikely quote: 'The Americans are such good losers' – David Cecil, Baron Burghley, after winning the 400m hurdles in 1928.

Greatest Olympian of all: Aladar Gerevich, the Hungarian fencer who won gold medals in six consecutive Olympic Games between 1932 and 1960.

☞ ARCHERY, CHINA, CRICKET, LATVIA, LIECHTENSTEIN, MARRIAGE, RUGBY, SEX TEST, SKIING, TUG-OF-WAR

OMAN
☞ INCOME TAX

ONION
☞ BAUDELAIRE, CRISPS, SARDINE

OPERA
While singing in Act II of Boito's *Mefistofele* at the Casino Theatre, Vichy, in 1955, the Belgian tenor Jan Verbeek swallowed a false moustache. He was able to continue, but high notes were clearly more difficult for

him, owing to irritation from hairs sticking to the back of his throat. A similar accident had happened to Walter Midgeley in *Rigoletto* at Covent Garden in 1953.

☞ BALLET, BALLOON, BUFFALO, CARUSO

OPINION POLLS

★ The first opinion poll was carried out in Delaware on 24 July 1824 and was designed to predict the result of the US presidential election contest between Andrew Jackson and John Quincy Adams. It predicted a win for Jackson. It was wrong.

OPOSSUM

☞ PREGNANCY

ORANG-UTAN

The orang-utan gives a loud belch as a warning signal.

ORANGE

Research published in Germany in 2001 showed that the smell of oranges reduces fear and stress in women who are waiting to see a dentist but has no effect on men.

In Spanish, the verb *anaranjear* means 'to kill a cock by throwing oranges at it'.

☞ BANANA, PENGUIN, PERU, RHYME

ORGAN-GRINDERS

☞ COMPUTATION

OSCAR

The Academy Award statuette commonly known as an

Oscar is 13.5in high and weighs 8.5lb. The nickname 'Oscar' has been used since 1934, five years after the Awards were instituted, and allegedly comes from a remark by Academy secretary Margret Herrick, who said the statue looked like her uncle Oscar.

If there were an Oscar for Greatest Disappointment, it would probably be shared by the films *The Turning Point* (1977) and *The Color Purple* (1985), each of which received 11 Oscar nominations without winning a single award.

The only men to win two Best Actor Oscars in a row are Spencer Tracy (1938–9) and Tom Hanks (1994–5). Jason Robards was Best Supporting Actor in 1977–8. Katherine Hepburn won the Best Actress Oscar in 1968 and shared it with Barbra Streisand in 1969. Jack Nicholson (who has received more nominations and won more Oscars than any other actor) is said to use one of his Oscar trophies as a hat stand.

☞ ARCHERY, FOX

OSTRICH

The ostrich is the largest living bird. In the UK, ostriches are zero-rated for VAT under the terms of 'VAT Notice 701/37/94: Live animal', which does, however, exclude 'ostrich feathers, ostrich skin, leather and other parts of the bird not used for human consumption or animal feed', which are taxed at the standard rate.

Early history:

Ostrich eggs were much admired by the ancient Persians, who sent them as tributes to the emperors of China. The

Spartans displayed the ostrich egg from which Castor and Pollux were supposed to have hatched. A cup made from an ostrich eggshell was found in a grave in Mesopotamia dating back to about 3000BC. However, Diodorus of Sicily, a historian of the first century BC, believed the ostrich was the missing link between birds and camels.

According to Seneca (c.4BC–AD65), Cornelius Fido, a son-in-law of the poet Naso, burst into tears when Corbulo called him a plucked ostrich (*struthocamelum depilatum*).

Behaviour:

'God hath deprived her of wisdom, neither hath He imparted to her understanding' (Job, xxxix, 17). Pliny also commented on the stupidity of the ostrich, for believing that it could not be seen by a pursuer when it thrust its head into a bush. Diodorus praised the same behaviour as a sign of intelligence in realising that its head was its most vulnerable part.

According to F.J. Haskin, writing in about 1920, 'the ostrich is abnormally finicky about mating. Some birds remain determined bachelors all their lives, and every one chooses his mate only with great delay and caution.' Once he has chosen, however, 'he is her devoted slave for life', and if she dies 'he remains a melancholy widower to the end of his days.'

Culinary:

The Romans liked roast ostrich, particularly the wings. The emperor Heliogabalus (reigned AD218–222) once served 600 ostrich heads at a banquet. The usurper

Firmus, who rebelled against Aurelianus in Egypt, once ate a whole ostrich in a day.

To boil an ostrich egg, cook it for between 40 minutes and one-and-a-half hours, according to taste. An ostrich egg omelette will feed eight hungry persons.

Unsung heroes:

Edward, the Black Prince (1330–76), whose badge was an ostrich feather – supposedly for peace.

Robert Hay Drummond (1711–76), Archbishop of York, who attracted the patronage of Queen Caroline through his intrepidity, while acting in *Julius Caesar* at Westminster School, in continuing with his part although his plume of ostrich feathers had caught fire.

Myer Salaman, a 19th-century ostrich-feather merchant of Redcliffe Gardens, London, whose son, Redcliffe Nathan Salaman (named after the street in which they lived) grew up to be a leading authority on the potato.

Ostrich statistics:
Height: up to 8ft
Weight: 300lb
Speed: 45mph
Life-span: up to 68 years
Pointless measure: an ostrich's eye is bigger than its brain
Value of South African ostrich feather exports in 1913: £2,750,000
Useful word: ratite (pertaining to a flightless bird)

Further reading: 'Lectures on the Anatomy of the Ostrich' (by Joshua Brookes, the *Lancet*, vol. xii, 1829); *Ostrich Egg-shell Cups of Mesopotamia and the Ostrich in Ancient and Modern Times* (by Berthold Laufer, Field Museum of Natural History, Chicago, 1926).

☞ HAIR

OWL

The horned owl does not have horns. The bits that look like horns are tufts of feather.

☞ TUESDAY

OXFORD

☞ CARROLL, CELIBACY, CHOCOLATE, DINOSAUR, RUGBY, UNIVERSITIES, DE VERE

OXYGEN

☞ BODY, FART, FIZZY DRINKS, MOUNTAINEERING

OYSTER

Oysters are generally ambisexual, starting life as males then changing back and forth between the two sexes as their life progresses.

In 1868, Maryland, USA instituted a State Oyster Police Force to enforce oyster laws. There is no such force in Jamaica, where one species of oyster lives in trees.

The close season for oysters in Britain is 15 June to 4 August. Oyster Day (also known as Old St James's Day) is 5 August.

The last words of the Duc de Lanzon de Biron before he was guillotined in 1793 were: 'I beg a thousand pardons, my friend, but permit me to finish this last dozen of oysters.'

Molly the Whistling Oyster was a great success at the Drury Lane Theatre in 1840. A baby oyster is called a spat.
➤ Sonya Thomas set a new world record at the Acme Oyster House World Oyster Eating Competition in March 2005 by consuming 46 dozen oysters in ten minutes. This shattered the old record of 18 dozen oysters set by Boyd Bulot in 2003. In 2006, Sonya Thomas also won the World Grilled Cheese Eating Championshipo by eating 26 grilled cheese sandwiches in ten minutes. The Acme Oyster House World Oyster Eating Championship, incidentally, is recognised as one of the majors on the International Federation of Competitive Eating circuit.

Unverified oyster-eating claims include that of the Roman emperor Vitellius, reputed to have eaten 1,000 oysters in a day. Casanova recommended eating 50 oysters for breakfast.
☞ TOOTHPASTE

PACIFIC
The point on earth farthest from land is in the South Pacific. At 48°30'S, 120°30'W, halfway between Pitcairn Island and Antarctica, you will be 1,660 miles from the nearest land of any sort.
☞ ADMIRALTY ISLANDS, ATLANTIC, EASTER, KISSING, MARQUESAS ISLANDS, NAURU

PAKISTAN
More than 120 people are bitten each day in Karachi by animals, mainly dogs but also horses, camels and donkeys.
☞ CRICKET, SWAT

PALINDROME
Illibilli in Sudan is the longest place-name in Africa that reads the same forwards as backwards. Uburubu in Nigeria takes second place.

PALMERSTON, Henry John Temple, 3rd Viscount (1784–1865)
Lord Palmerston must surely be the oldest British prime

minister to be cited as co-respondent in a divorce case. He was 78 when it happened.

Palmerston's last words are often quoted as: 'Die, my dear doctor? That's the last thing I shall do.' More reliable sources, however, give them as: 'That's article 98; now go on to the next.' It is believed he was re-living some incident during his time as Foreign Secretary at the time.

PANAMA

Panama is the only place on Earth where you can watch the sun rise over the Pacific Ocean and set over the Atlantic. The currency unit in Panama is the balboa, named after Spanish explore Vasco Núñez de Balboa who trekked across the isthmus of Panama in 1513.

The Panama Canal was built by the Americans between 1904 and 1914 and cost $352 million. Five thousand workers lost their lives during its construction. When the French had tried to build a canal in Panama in the 1880s, nearly 20,000 workers died through landslides, malaria and yellow fever.

A daily average of 34 transits of the Panama Canal are made, each of one large or several small ships. The canal and its locks are wide enough to cope with 93 per cent of all seagoing vessels.

General Manuel Noriega, former president of Panama, is prisoner number 38699-079 at the Federal Metropolitan Correctional Center in Miami.

Panama hats are made in Ecuador not Panama.

☞ CURTIS

PANCAKE

In 2003, Stephen Wilkinson, a physicist at Leeds University, announced the secret of pancake tossing:

$W = (g\sqrt{\pi})/4r$

where W = the angular velocity of the pancake, g = the acceleration due to gravity and r = the distance from the centre of pancake to the tosser's elbow.

In practical terms, according to Dr Garry Tungate this means that 'you should try to flip the pancake into the air at a speed of 10 miles an hour which will mean it will take less than half a second to reach the top of its trajectory. If you are lucky the pancake should now have rotated 90 degrees at a rate of .55 revs per second. If not you could be in trouble and have a sticky mass of flying batter spinning through the air. It should take 0.45 seconds on the downward journey – total airtime just nine tenths of a second – completing the perfect toss with a 90 degree flip on the way down.'

Ralf Laue of Leipzig, Germany, holds the record for the most tosses of a pancake in two minutes: 416.

Aunt Jemima pancake flour was the first ready-mix food to be sold commercially. It was invented in St Joseph, Missouri and introduced in 1889.

If you do not like pancakes, another traditional Shrove Tuesday amusement in Britain is 'cock-throwing' in which things were thrown at a cockerel that was tied to a stake. This practice died out in the 18th century. The word 'shrove' is the past tense of the verb to shrive, which means to confess or impose a penance.

PANDA

In 1985 it was finally established at the Smithsonian Institute in Washington and the National Cancer Institute in Maryland that the giant panda is a bear. The lesser panda, however, is more a racoon. The male genitalia of the giant panda are unlike those of bears. It has six fingers on each paw, one a grasping thumb. It does not hibernate and bleats rather than roars.

☞ CATARACT

PAPER

Paper was invented by a Chinese eunuch named Ts'ai Lun. He was an official at the Chinese Imperial Court and around the year AD105, he presented Emperor Han Ho Ti with samples of paper. He was promoted by the Emperor for his invention and became wealthy. Later he was arrested for matters unconnected with paper and killed himself in prison by taking poison.

For the next 500 years, the Chinese kept paper a secret, which the Koreans finally discovered early in the seventh century. Even then, it was another twelve and a half centuries before wrapping paper began to be made.

The earliest patent for corrugated cardboard for wrapping dates back to 1871, but it quickly became popular. The average European household now produces two tonnes of rubbish a year of which half is packaging, and Americans produce more than three times as much.

All the Christmas gift-wrap used in the UK in one year would cover an area equal to that of Guernsey.

America and Japan have a lot to offer anyone seriously interested in paper: the museum at the Research

Institute of Paper History and Technology in Brookline, Massachusetts, claims to have 'probably the largest collection of handmade toilet paper in the world', while the paper museum in Asukayama Park, Tokyo has 40,000 exhibits of historic items relating to paper. You will find wrapping paper in exhibit number 12 in Exhibition Gallery 2F.

☞ COW, CRISPS, LAVATORIES, NUDISM, SCISSORS, STRAW

PARACHUTE
☞ CHANNEL, SPORT

PARAGUAY
Paraguay is the only country with a national flag that is not the same on both sides. Both front and back have three horizontal stripes of, from top to bottom, red, white and blue, but the white stripe on the front bears the National seal, while the blue stripe on the back has the Treasury seal.

☞ BOLIVIA

PARAPSYCHOLOGY
Recent research by Rupert Sheldrake has produced evidence that dogs can sense when their owners are setting off for home, even when departure times are varied randomly. However, investigation of possible psychic links between animals and humans is nothing new.

In 1983, the journal *Research in Parapsychology* published a paper entitled 'Superposition of PK Effects by Man and Dog' by the well-known German parapsychologist Helmut Schmidt. The design for the experiment was simple: a man performed a standard test of extra-sensory perception (ESP), attempting to guess what symbols were illustrated on a series of concealed cards, and a dog (a 'supposedly non-psychic' miniature dachshund) was rewarded with a chocolate every time the man guessed correctly.

The dog was thus motivated to improve the man's performance by psycho-kinetic (PK) means. The results showed that the man's results did indeed improve, but the best results of all were obtained when the dog performed the ESP test on its own. The conclusion was that further research was needed.

Psychic phenomena, in both humans and animals, date back to the dawn of superstition, but research into such areas only gained a measure of scientific respectability with the founding of the Society for Psychical Research in 1882. Its stated purpose was 'to develop systematic, scientific investigation of certain phenomena which were attracting considerable public attention because, if genuine, they were apparently inexplicable on any generally accepted hypothesis'. Their founders and leading members included professors of physics and Fellows of the Royal Society, and their early work included valuable research on hypnosis, certain psychiatric disorders and the debunking of several spiritualists and clairvoyants. Ghosts and telepathy were on the agenda from the start; more modern phenomena such as spoon-bending and crop circles were added as they became parapsychologically fashionable.

The possible existence of life after death has also been a continuing concern, though recent research is somewhat discouraging. In 1989, the journal of the Society for Psychical Research published a paper entitled 'Two Tests of

Survival After Death: Report on Negative Results'. The research concerned the attempts of two scientists to prove survival after death. One had encrypted messages for which only he knew the key word to break the code. The other had set a padlock with a combination only he knew. Both promised that after they died they would do their best to communicate the secrets to the living. 'Since their deaths in 1979 and 1984, numerous trials have been made with key words and numbers, but none of these has enabled the passages to be decoded or the lock to be opened.' However, not all findings have been so negative.

- In 1967, research showed that goldfish can tell if they are about to be fished out of a tank. The evidence for their precognition is their increased movement when their numbers come up on dice thrown in another room.
- In 1968, experiments showed that the leaves of a phildendron plant react to the death of shrimps.
- In 1970, a cat was found to be able to influence a heat lamp that was supposedly going on and off at random. When the cat had access to the area it warmed, the lamp stayed on longer.
- In 1979, human willpower was shown to influence the activity levels of gerbils on a treadmill.
- In 1991, a healer demonstrated the ability to stimulate germination and growth of cress seeds that had been soaked in a saline solution.
- In 1992, Drosophila flies demonstrated telepathic abilities, but only in conditions of sustained light or darkness. With light and dark alternating every 25 minutes, all telepathic abilities seemed to vanish.

- But in 1979, holy water was found to have no significant effect on the growth of radishes, and in 1992, 'spirit entities' failed to rearrange the playing cards – as it had been claimed they would – in a sealed deck. The failure was, however, put down to the 'conspicuous officiousness' of the experimenters, which caused the responsible entity to withdraw its co-operation.

Further research is clearly needed.

PARIS

Dogs deposit 16 tonnes of excrement on Parisian streets and sidewalks every day.

☞ ADDRESS, ALCHEMY, BALLOON, COW, EPONYM, GOLF, IN-FLIGHT CATERING, DA VINCI, METRIC SYSTEM, OLYMPIC GAMES, ROBBERY, TOURISM, UMBRELLA, UNIVERSITIES, WHISTLING

PARKER, Dorothy (1893–1967)

Writer and wit Dorothy Parker had a pet dog called Cliché and a pet parrot called Onan. The parrot's name came from the fact that it spilled its seed on the ground (see Genesis 38: 7–10).

☞ COOLIDGE

PARLIAMENT

According to Erskine May's official handbook entitled *Parliamentary Procedure*, 'Good temper and moderation are the characteristics of parliamentary language.' It is the responsibility of the Speaker to rule whether a particular expression is or is not acceptable and more than a century of such decisions led to a glossary of unparliamentary language. Recent editions of Erskine May have abandoned the practice of listing banned words. The last such complete list was as follows:

Blackguard	Member returned by
Blether	refuse of a large
Cad or caddishness	constituency
Calumny, gross	Murderer
Cheeky young pup	Pecksniffian cant
Corrupt or corruption	Personal honour, not
Coward	consonant with
Criminal	Pharisees
Dishonest	Rat
Dog	Rude and vulgar
Guttersnipe	interruptions
Hooligan	Ruffianism
Hypocrites	Slanderer
Impertinence	Stool-pigeons
Impertinent puppy	Swine
Impudence	Traitor
Jackass, behaving like a	Treason, charges of
Malignant attack	Vicious and vulgar
Malignant slander	Villains

The most recent word to be added to the now purely notional list is 'git'. This happened when the Member for Bolsover, Dennis Skinner, objected to the Speaker about David Owen taking up too much of Prime Minister's Question Time. 'What I want to know, Mr Speaker,' Skinner began, 'is why you allow this 'ere pompous git…' The Speaker then interrupted him saying, 'That, sir, is unparliamentary language. I demand you withdraw it.'

Skinner thought it over, then replied, 'In deference to you, Mr Speaker, I withdraw "pompous".'

☞ ARMOUR, ASCOT, CAPITAL PUNISHMENT, CHRISTMAS, DAYLIGHT SAVING, FOOTBALL, MAYDAY, SPORT, STEPHENSON, TAIWAN, TRAFFIC LIGHTS

PARROT

The German explorer Humboldt reports meeting a talking bird in South America with the sole knowledge of a dead language of an extinct tribe of Indians, the Atures.

☛ There are 25 species of parrot fish in the seas around the Seychelles.

★ On 11 August 1995, Henry the parrot was banned from the Avenue and Victoria bowls club in Leamington Spa, Warwickshire because its repeated shrieks of 'You're a yard short, a yard short' were irritating contestants in the preliminary rounds of the English Women's Bowls Championship.

☞ FOOTBALL, GEORGE V, PARKER, TAXIDERMY

PASTA

According to purists, a perfect strip of tagliatelle should be 6mm wide.

☞ SHOPPING TROLLEYS

PASTEUR, Louis (1822–95)

☞ BEER

PATIENCE

'Patience: a minor form of despair disguised as virtue' –
Ambrose Bierce, *The Devil's Dictionary*.

Research shows that, when waiting for a lift, some
people begin to get impatient after 15 seconds; most get
impatient within 35 seconds.

PEACOCK

The peacock can only hold its train high when its head
is in the air; the tail drops if it looks down. Hence the
myth that it is ashamed of its feet.

☞ PHOENIX

PEANUT

The peanut (also known as groundnut, earthnut, goober,
goober pea, pinda, pinder, Manila nut or monkey nut) is
the edible seed of the plant *Arachis hypogaea*. It is a
member of the pea family and the fruit is not a nut, but a
legume or pod.

In 1981, a fossilised peanut more than 100,000 years
old was found in China. Quite what happened to
peanuts over the next 98,000 years is unknown, but it is
known that they arrived in Europe from South America
where they have been cultivated for over 2,000 years.

Peanuts are the official state crop of Georgia where, in
Turner County, you can see the 'World's Largest Peanut'.
It is a 20ft-tall monument erected in honour of the
importance of the peanut.

It takes about 550 peanuts to make a 12oz jar of
creamy peanut butter. Fear of peanut butter sticking to
the roof of your mouth is called 'arachibutyrophobia'.

The high protein content of peanut butter draws moisture from your mouth. That's why it sticks.

The average American eats seven pounds of peanuts and peanut butter a year.

The *Peanuts* strip cartoon first appeared on 2 October 1950. Its creator, Charles Schultz, retired in December 1999 and died on 12 February 2000, the night before the last of his 18,000-odd *Peanuts* cartoon strips was published.
☞ POLAR BEAR, SANDWICHES, SARDINE

PENCIL

In 1858, Hyman Lipman of Philadelphia was granted the first patent for a pencil with an eraser at one end. His invention, however, went on to become the subject of a series of celebrated battles in patent law. In 1862, Joseph Reckendorfer came up with what he saw as an improvement. Lipman's version was a pencil which could be sharpened at both ends, one end producing the usual lead, but the other revealing a piece of india rubber. Reckendorfer instead tapered and moulded the wood of the pencil in a way that formed a receptacle for the rubber. A series of court battles between the men followed, which were not finally resolved until 1875 when an Appeal Court ruled against both men.

The decision clarified the guidelines for what constitutes an invention. The crucial point is that taking two things that already exist and sticking them together cannot, in itself, be considered an invention.

'It may be more convenient,' the court ruled, 'to turn over the different ends of the same stick than to lay down one stick and take up another. This, however, is not invention within the patent law… We are of the opinion, that, for the reasons given, neither the patent of Lipman nor the improvement of Reckendorfer can be sustained.'

In other words, you can patent the widget that holds the rubber to the pencil, but you cannot patent the idea of a rubber at the end of a pencil.

★ The date of Hyman Lipman's patent was 30 March 1858.

PENGUIN

There are 17 species of penguin in the world (or 16 or 18, depending which source you consult).

Penguins are generally extremely short-sighted on land, though they can see very well under water.

Antarctic researchers have made several significant contributions in recent years to our knowledge of penguin behaviour. Two projects in particular have investigated reports that penguins fall over backwards when looking upwards at planes flying overhead. In 1999, researchers found that flying a helicopter over baby penguins makes them flap their flippers or run away. Two years later, a million-pound project proved that penguins do not fall over when aeroplanes fly overhead. In between these two important results, scientists finally confirmed in December 2000 that waddling is the most efficient way for Emperor penguins to walk.

The most striking recent discovery about penguins, however, dates back to research published in 1998, and concerns female Adélie penguins in Antarctica selling sex in exchange for gifts of rocks. In a paper entitled 'Female Adelie Penguins Acquire Nest Material from Extrapair

Males After Engaging in Extrapair Copulations' in the journal *Auk* (vol. 115, number 2, pages 526–8), F.M. Hunter and L.S. Davis report the first known case of prostitution among birds. Several female penguins were seen to mate with males who were not their usual partners in exchange for gifts of rocks which they then used as nesting material. Some birds even indulged in courtship behaviour, then took the rocks without mating. One particularly flirty example was seen to take 62 rocks from one male without ever delivering on her apparent sexual promises.

Further vital information about penguins was reported in the journal *Polar Biology* in December 2003 when Victor Benno Meyer-Rochow and Jozsef Gal published a brief note entitled 'Pressures Produced When Penguins Pooh – Calculations on Avian Defaecation'.

As the authors point out: 'Chinstrap and Adélie penguins generate considerable pressures to propel their faeces away from the edge of the nest.' To work out how much pressure, all you need to know is the density and viscosity of penguin pooh, the shape and height above the ground of the penguin's rear end, and how far away from the nest the penguin pooh lands. 'With all of these parameters measured, we calculated that fully grown penguins generate pressures of around 10kPa (77mm Hg) to expel watery material and 60kPa (450mm Hg) to expel material of higher viscosity similar to that of olive oil. The forces involved, lying well above those known for humans, are high, but do not lead to an energetically wasteful turbulent flow.'

Their concluding words point the direction for

further research: 'Whether a bird chooses the direction into which it decides to expel its faeces, and what role the wind plays in this, remain unknown.'

Further penguin facts:

- Penguins sleep more deeply in the afternoon than in the morning. This was discovered by a French researcher in 2002 who went round penguin colonies prodding sleeping penguins with a stick and seeing how many prods were necessary to wake them up at different times of day. His research showed that an average of five prods is enough in the morning, but nine are needed in the afternoon.
- In February 2001, a baby penguin was treated for depression after it was found wandering the streets of Melbourne, Australia.
- Adélie penguins have pink feet; Gentoo penguins' feet are orange; but Gentoo penguins have pink excrement.

☛ On 1 September 1988, the New York Health Department revealed that in the previous year they had treated 8,064 people for dog bites, 1,587 people bitten by other people, and one who'd been bitten by a penguin.

On 23 August 1997, Edinburgh Zoo reported that it had been using suncream on its penguins because the unusually hot weather had been causing the birds to moult. This left patches of bare skin that needed protection from the sun.

☞ ANTARCTICA

PENIS

The average size of an erect penis is only 5in (12.8cm), according to a 1995 survey, which is significantly smaller than most men believe. An Italian study in 2002 discovered that, of 67 men seeking enlargement operations, all had penises well within the normal size range.

The most common causes of injury to the penis are ritual circumcision, animal attacks, bicycle accidents and zipper injuries.

The world's only museum of penises is the Phallological Museum in Iceland. At the beginning of 2004, there were 208 penises of 84 different species of Icelandic mammals in the collection. No human penis is yet on view, although four have been promised on the death of their present owners. The Internet address of the Museum is www.phallus.is. Unfortunately, the even more appropriate address of www.pen.is is used by a Reykjavik erotica shop.

The human and the hyena are the only carnivorous mammals that do not have a penis bone.

☞ ARGENTINA, DONKEY, MANILOW, SINGAPORE, STALLION, WHALE

PEPYS, Samuel (1633–1703)

☞ CHARLES II, CHOCOLATE

PERCEVAL, Spencer (1762–1812)

★ Spencer Perceval was the only British prime minister to be assassinated – by John Bellingham on 11 May 1812.

PERU

Peru is the only country whose name can be typed on a single row of letters of a typewriter. It is also the only country on earth with place names that begin with a double-Q (Qquea, Qquecquerisca and Qquero are all places in Peru) and is the world's second greatest fishing nation – its annual catch is exceeded only by China.

The currency of Peru is the new sol, a modern relic of the sun worship of the ancient Incas.

The world's worst soccer riot occurred at a Peru–Argentina match in the Peruvian capital, Lima, in 1964 after an unpopular decision by the referee. It ended with 300 fans killed and more than 500 injured.

The Interior Ministry in Peru has banned chili sauce and hot spices from prison food because they might arouse sexual desires. The prisoners may prefer the camu-camu fruit, which grows in the Peruvian rain forest, and has the highest vitamin C content of any food, around 60 times that of oranges.

☞ ALPACA

PETRARCH, Francesco (1304–74)
☞ UNIVERSITIES

PETER the GREAT, Czar of Russia (1672–1725)
☞ ALCOHOL, CATHERINE I, HAIR

PHILIPPINES

In 1997 Marikina City, a suburb of the Philippine capital of Manila, passed a proposal to outlaw vomiting in public. Offenders would be asked to clean up their mess and to pay a fine. People who vomit because of sickness or from eating rotten food would be excluded from the ban.

In May 2006, a world record for simultaneous public breastfeeding was set by 3,738 mothers in Manila.

☞ COMPUTATION, CONDOM, JOHN PAUL II, KNEES, YO-YO

PHOBIAS

Among some of the lesser-known phobias, we should like to mention the following:

Atelophobia: fear of imperfection
Clinophobia: fear of beds
Dikephobia: fear of justice
Eosophobia: fear of dawn
Gamophobia: fear of marriage
Gymnophobia: fear of nudity
Hedonophobia: fear of pleasure
Helminophobia: fear of worms
Katagelophobia: fear of ridicule
Koniophobia: fear of dust
Laliophobia: fear of stuttering
Mycophobia: fear of mushrooms
Nelophobia: fear of glass
Octophobia: fear of vehicles
Selaphobia: fear of flesh
Uranophobia: fear of heaven
Zelotypophobia: fear of jealousy

☞ CHOPSTICKS, FRIDAY, FROG, GARLIC, HAIR, HALLOWE'EN, NEWTON, PEANUT, SLIME, STRING, THIRTEEN

PHOENIX

The legend of the phoenix is thousands of years old and occurs in several mythologies, beginning with ancient Egypt. While they all agree that the phoenix is a bird, the Egyptians described it as similar to a heron, but the Greeks and Romans said it was more like a peacock or eagle. They all agree that it is the only one of its kind, and lives for 350, 500, 1,461 or 12,954 years, according to which mythology you read. When it dies it is reborn from the ashes of its own funeral pyre. This made the phoenix popular in early Christian art as a symbol of resurrection.

The Greek historian Herodotus wrote about the phoenix in the fifth century BC, but noted: 'I myself have never seen it.' According to the third-century Roman philosopher Aelian, the dawn song of the phoenix was 'so ravishingly beautiful, the rising sun reined in his horses to listen'.

Project Phoenix is the name given to the world's most sensitive search for extraterrestrial intelligence.

The actor River Phoenix's real name was River Bottom. He died of a drug overdose at the age of 23.

In Phoenix, Arizona, it is illegal to bury a dead animal or place it in your garbage or recycling container.

PICASSO, Pablo (1881–1973)

The full name of Pablo Picasso was Pablo Diego Jose Francisco de Paula Juan Nepomuceno Maria de los Remedios Cipriano de la Santisima Trinidad Ruiz Picasso.
☞ PIGEON

PIG

★ On 17 July 1408, a sow was hanged in the French town of Pont de l'Arche having been convicted 'for the crime of having murdered and killed a young child'.

☞ AARDVARK, ANIMAL NOISES, CLOONEY, DICKENS, EURO, KARLOFF, LAVATORIES, MARQUESAS ISLANDS, MONEY, RICE, VALENTINO

PIGEON

A pigeon called G.I. Joe was awarded the Dickin Medal in 1946 for message-carrying services to the US army in World War II.

In 1995, Japanese psychologists reported that they had trained pigeons to tell the difference between paintings by Picasso and Monet, but they could not tell a Renoir from a Cézanne.

The first London Underground station to use kestrels and hawks to kill pigeons and stop them setting up homes in the stations was Northfields on the Piccadilly line.

Martha, the last known passenger pigeon in the world, died in Cincinnati Zoo on the first day of September in 1914.

☞ DARWIN

PINEAPPLE

In Japan, bathing in coffee grounds mixed with pineapple pulp is supposed to remove wrinkles.

'Anonaceous' means 'pertaining to pineapples'.

PIUS

The name of 12 popes, including the only two to have become saints in the last 500 years: Pius V and Pius X.
☞ JOHN PAUL II, POPES

PIZZA

The world's first real pizzeria was the Antica Pizzeria Port' Alba in Naples. It opened in 1830 and is still serving pizzas today. The true father of today's pizza was Rafaele Esposito of Naples who, in 1889, created the Pizza Margherita for King Umberto I and Queen Margherita of Italy. The colours of the tomato, mozzarella cheese and basil in Pizza Margherita were designed to mimic the red, white and green of the Italian flag. Pizza standards in Italy are maintained by the Associazione Verace Pizza Napoletana.

However, Europe's first pizza convention, Pizzatec, was held in January 1997 – not in Italy but Berlin.

The world's largest pizza was 122ft 8in in diameter, made in Norwood, South Africa, in 1990.

Inmates of the Dutra Ladeira Prison in Brazil run a pizza-delivery service both in and out of the jail.

The US Congress declared 4 June 1997 National Pizza Day to celebrate 100 years of American pizza.

Research in Britain shows that people with pierced noses, lips or eyebrows are 23 per cent more likely to ask for vegetarian toppings than meat toppings on pizzas.

☛ According to a survey in 2004, 6 per cent of people say pizza is the food they would most miss if they were stranded in an Australian jungle.

★ On 19 August 1998, US clothing manufacturers VF

Corporation ordered 13,386 pizzas for their 40,160 employees. *Guinness World Records* ranks it as the largest single order for pizza.

☞ ASTRONAUTS

PLATO (c.427–347BC)

Plato's given name was Aristocles, meaning 'the best' or 'most renowned'. He acquired the nickname of Plato, meaning 'wide', in his youth because of his wide shoulders.

☞ ALCHEMY, CELIBACY, UNIVERSITIES

PLATYPUS

The platypus has a muzzle like a duck's bill, a tail like a beaver, lays eggs and suckles its young. It does not have any teeth but grinds its food on grinding pads inside its mouth. It is mostly silent but has been reported to make a noise like a puppy growling, or a sound like a brooding hen. It spends about half the day eating and consumes about a quarter of its body weight daily. Only the male duck-billed platypus can sting – through spurs at the back of its hind legs.

When the Europeans first reached Australia, they called the platypus duckbill, watermole or duckmole. In 1799 it was given the name of *Platypus anatinus*, which simply means a flat-footed animal of the duck family. Then the *Platypus* part of this name was changed to *Ornithorhynchus*, which means birdlike snout. Aborigines called the platypus mallangong, boondaburra or tambreet.

The platypus and two forms of echidna form the Monotremata – mammals that have a single orifice for both excretion and reproduction.

★ The American public had their first sight of a duck-billed platypus on 15 July 1922 at New York Zoo.

PLAYING CARDS
The King of Hearts is the only playing card king without a moustache.
☞ MOUSTACHE, PARAPSYCHOLOGY, SEX

PLINY the Elder (c.AD23–79)
Scientific encyclopedist and historian Pliny the Elder was killed by the eruption of Mount Vesuvius.
☞ HEDGEHOG, MOON, OSTRICH, SEX, SHOES, UNICORN

POETRY
According to the Japanese, the optimum length of human speech in a single breath is 17 syllables, hence the Haiku, a poem of 17 syllables.
☞ COLOMBIA, FORTUNE-TELLING, HIPPOPOTAMUS, KEATS, SEXUAL HARASSMENT

POLAND
Augustus II (1670–1733) of Poland sold a regiment of dragoons for 50 pieces of Ming porcelain. He is said to have fathered over 500 illegitimate children.
☞ EURO, TAX, ZYWOCICE

POLAR BEAR
The first polar bear in Britain arrived during the reign of Henry III (1216–72) and was probably a gift from Haakon IV of Norway. There is evidence that Haakon IV made a practice of giving polar bears to fellow

monarchs whom he liked. He gave one to the Emperor of Germany and another to the Holy Roman Emperor Frederick II.

King Henry kept his polar bear at the Tower of London and let it swim on the end of a rope in the Thames. He issued a writ 'directing the sheriffs of London to furnish six pence a day to support our White Bear in our Tower of London; and to provide a muzzle and iron chain to hold him when out of the water; and a long strong rope to hold him when he was fishing in the Thames.'

Nomenclature:
The description 'white bear' sufficed until 1781, when the first recorded usage of 'polar bear' appeared in T. Pennant's *History of Quadrupeds*. The correct word to mean 'of or pertaining to the polar bear' is 'thalassarctine' (from the Greek *arktos*, 'bear', and *thalassa*, 'sea'). The scientific name for the polar bear is *Thalarctos maritimus*.

Literature:
The first reference to a polar bear in literature appears to be in Charles Dickens's *Sketches by Boz*, in which he describes some characters with the words: '... in their shaggy white coats they look just like Polar bears'.

Superstition:
In certain Inuit communities, the women never comb their hair on the day on which a polar bear is to be killed.

Psychology:

Most research into polar bear behaviour has concentrated on their major psychological problem of obsessive walking or swimming. Polar bears kept in zoos have frequently developed long rituals, known as 'stereotypic behaviour', which they perform incessantly in a trancelike state, pacing up and down their cages or swimming round and round the same path. One theory is that such behaviour is a sign of boredom and frustration; another is that such pacing develops as a formalised version of food-hunting behaviour.

In *Beasts in my Belfry* (1973), Gerald Durrell refers to such behaviour as 'a soothing and interesting habit to pass the time until the next meal'. An academic study in 1992 ('Stereotypes and Attentiveness to Novel Stimuli: A Test in Polar Bears', by B. Wechsler, *Applied Animal Behaviour Science*, vol. 33) showed that bears are still alert to unusual smells on their stereotyped paths.

Nevertheless, when Gus, a polar bear in Central Park Zoo, New York, developed stereotypic swimming behaviour in 1994, an animal psychiatrist was employed at a cost of $25,000 to devise a course of therapy. By delivering his food wrapped and at irregular times, and giving him playthings laced with peanuts and honey, the therapist managed to rekindle the bear's interest in life. After a year, his compulsive swimming behaviour was down by a third, he had stopped being mean to his female companions and was soon deemed fully recovered. A zoo spokesman said, 'He has done something that many New Yorkers find difficult to do. He has stopped seeing his therapist.'

Science:

In 1995, British scientists discovered that polar bears' hairs block infra-red radiation and seem to suck in ultraviolet light, which is used to heat their bodies. Possible applications of this discovery include better lasers for eye surgery, more efficient solar panels covered with polar bear fur and military camouflage undetectable by infra-red cameras.

Useful facts:

One pound of polar bear liver contains enough vitamin A to fulfil a human's requirements for 20 years. In the 19th century, a team of Arctic explorers all died from a vitamin A overdose after they had eaten a polar bear liver.

A polar bear's gestation period is 39 weeks and results in between one and four cubs. Full-grown, it may be up to 11ft long and weigh almost 1,500lb.

Polar bears do not slip on ice, due to the hair on the soles of their feet.

All polar bears are left-handed.

Further reading: *Polar Bears in the Middle Ages*, by T.J. Oleson (*Canadian Historical Review*, 1950).

POLYGRAPH
☞ MARSTON

POMPADOUR, Marquise de (1721–64)

Madame de Pompadour, mistress of Louis XV, was the first person in France to have a pet goldfish. Her original surname was Poisson, which means 'fish'.

POPCORN

The definitive science of popcorn can be found in the paper 'The Effects of Ingredients on Popcorn Popping Characteristics', by M. Ceylan and E. Karababa, in the *International Journal of Food Science and Technology*, 2004. According to the Turkish researchers, popcorn popped in a microwave oven needs 1.5g of salt, 2g of vegetable oil and 6g of butter for every 25g of corn to get both the most expansion and the fewest unpopped kernels. On a stove top, however, only 1.1g of salt and 4.2g of butter will achieve optimum results. Adding about 0.3g of sodium bicarbonate can also enhance the popping. Microwave popping, however, gives about 10 per cent less expansion than heating on top of the stove.

☞ ANCHOVY

POPES

Popes are always right-handed and tend to die in the job. The last pope to hand over the papacy while still alive was Pope Gregory XII, who retired in 1415. On the death of a pope, the Papal Chamberlain must call out his baptismal name three times and tap his head with a silver hammer before he is officially declared dead. Twenty-six popes are said to have been assassinated. Once the death of a pope is established, his successor is elected by the College of Cardinals. All cardinals have a vote, except those over the age of 80.

- In 897, Pope Steven VII had the body of Pope Formosus, who had died in 896, dug up, propped in a chair and put on trial for violating church laws.

- Because of an 11th-century miscount, there was a Pope John XIX and a Pope John XXI but no John XX.
- Adrian IV (born Nicholas Breakspear), who was pope from 1154 to 1159, was the only English pope.

All the above popes would have been accustomed to having their toes kissed. From the eighth century until the 18th century, this was the traditional way to greet a pope. This custom is said to date back to AD798 when 'a certain lewd woman' gave a pope's hand a squeeze when kissing it. The pope, seeing the moral danger inherent in this act, cut his hand off and instituted toe-kissing.

In 1978, John Paul II became the first non-Italian pope since the death of Adrian VI in 1523.

☞ AZERBAIJAN, CASANOVA, CHRISTIANITY, St GEORGE, JOHN PAUL II, MUSHROOM, PIUS, St VALENTINE

POPEYE

Popeye the Sailor was the first cartoon character to have a statue erected in his honour. It was put up in Crystal City, Texas, as a gesture of thanks from the people in the spinach capital of America.

In Spain, the name of Popeye's girlfriend Olive Oyl is seen as an insult to the olive tree and she has been renamed Rosario.

★ Popeye was born on 17 January 1929; his statue was unveiled on 26 March 1937.

POPULATION

Every 24 hours, some 237,000 people are born and 140,000 die. That is 2.74 births and 1.62 deaths every second.

In 1800, 2.8 per cent of the world population was in the Americas, and 67 per cent in Asia. By 2000, 14 per cent were in the Americas and 58 per cent in Asia. At the time of Christ, the world population was about 250 million. In 1600, it was about 500 million (including five million in Britain). The figure is estimated to have reached one billion in 1804, two billion in 1927, three billion in 1960, four billion in 1974, five billion in 1987 and six billion in 1999.

If the present population of over six billion were shrunk to 100 people, keeping all categories in the same proportion, they would look like this:

- One person would be near death and one would be near birth.
- There would be 57 Asians, 21 Europeans and eight Africans.
- 52 would be female, 48 would be male.
- Six people would possess 59 per cent of the entire world's wealth.
- 80 would live in substandard housing.
- 70 would be unable to read.
- 50 would suffer from malnutrition.
- Only one would have a college education and only one would own a computer.

★ According to American estimates, the world population

reached six billion at 6.33pm on Monday, 9 August 1999.
☞ BABBAGE, BEER, CHINA, CHOPSTICKS, CRIME,
EUROPE, GREENLAND, ITALY, KANSAS, St KITTS and NEVIS,
LIECHTENSTEIN, MONEY, NAURU, NETHERLANDS,
NIGERIA, RAT, St LUCIA, SOUTH AFRICA, TURKEY (country),
UGANDA, VANUATU, WALES

PORTER, Cole (1891–1964)

After his first show was a Broadway flop, Cole Porter
joined the French Foreign Legion and won the Croix de
Guerre in 1917. He had a leg amputated after a riding
accident in 1937 and had a piano built around his bed so
he could continue work.

PORTUGAL

In 1996, the Society for the Portuguese Language set up
a commission to halve the influx of English words.
Among those listed as particularly offensive were
'franchising', 'mall' and 'shopping centre'.

Of all Portugal's exports to Slovenia, rubber bands
account for 3.7 per cent of the total value. Half the
world's cork comes from Portugal.
☞ COLOMBIA, EUROPE

POSTMEN

In 2001, the German Postal Service instituted training
courses to teach dog psychology to postmen. This was in
response to figures showing that every year in Germany
over 3,000 postmen are bitten by dogs, resulting in 2,255
pairs of torn trousers, 12,720 lost working days, £8
million of medical bills and 755 hospital stays.
☞ UKRAINE

POTATO

Until the late 18th century, the French generally believed that potatoes caused leprosy. The vegetables became more popular thanks to Marie Antoinette's habit of wearing potato blossoms in her hair.

In 1952, Mr Potato Head was introduced and became the first toy to be advertised on television.

In October 1995, the potato became the first vegetable to be grown in space. This was part of a NASA and University of Wisconsin project to find ways to feed astronauts or space colonies.

Around the world, 727,000 tonnes of potatoes are harvested every day. In Britain in a year, the average person eats 820 potatoes, while slugs eat a total of 36,000 tonnes of potatoes.

The latest state-of-the-art technological improvement in the world of potatoes is an industrial peeler that uses three laser beams to peel a potato in one second. Less technologically, Clark, the 'potato capital of South Dakota' holds regular Mashed Potato Wrestling contests.

According to an old folk remedy, carrying potatoes in your pocket can cure or prevent rheumatism. It can also cure problems for film directors: in the film *Close Encounters Of The Third Kind*, dried potato flakes were used to look like snowflakes.

☛ The cultivated potato generally has 48 chromosomes in its genetic make-up. A human being has only 46.

★ On 15 June 1992, the US Vice President, Dan Quayle, misspelled 'potato' as 'potatoe'. It happened at a School in Trenton, New Jersey, when he was 'correcting' the already correct spelling of William Figueroa, 12, by adding an 'e' at the end.

☞ BALLET, CHIPS, CRISPS, OSTRICH, SHAKESPEARE, SLUG, TRISTAN DA CUNHA

PRAYER

The power of prayer was demonstrated in September 1996 to a Spaniard on a business trip to Sweden. While driving through the countryside, Edouardo Sierra stopped at a Catholic church, which he found empty except for a coffin with a body lying at rest inside it. He stopped to pray for the deceased, then signed a book of remembrance left by the coffin. Apart from his signature, the book was empty. Some weeks later he received a telephone call telling him he was a millionaire. The body was that of a Swedish businessman with no close relatives who had left his fortune 'to whoever prays for my soul first'.

In October 1996, the recently launched Internet company Virtual Jerusalem announced that it was receiving between 15 and 20 prayers each day by e-mail which it printed out and placed on the Wailing Wall.

☞ HALIFAX

PREGNANCY

Nobody knows who first discovered what causes pregnancy. Aristotle certainly understood how babies were made: 'When a young couple are married, they naturally desire children; and therefore adopt the means that nature has appointed to that end.' If the woman wants a daughter, he explained that she should lie on her left side at the time of conception and think strongly of a female. 'The best time to beget a female is when the moon is on the wane, in Libra or Aquarius.'

The sex of the unborn child may easily be determined by examining the mother, he says: 'If it is a male, the right breast swells first, the right eye is brighter than the left. The face is high-coloured, because the colour is such as the blood is, and the male is conceived of purer blood and of more perfect seed than the female.'

Despite a general understanding of the means of conception that dates back to prehistory, the details were confirmed only comparatively recently. The first person to see a sperm was the Dutch microscopist Anton van Leeuwenhoek in 1677; the first human egg had to wait until 1930. The two were not introduced to each other in a laboratory until 1944.

Whether 'adopting the means that nature has appointed', as Aristotle so delicately put it, is the only way to become pregnant is still a matter of debate in some quarters. Superstitions recorded in recent years include the following:

'If you are in the company of two pregnant women, slap your backside three times or you too will become pregnant' – County Tyrone (1972).

'If you sit in a chair recently occupied by a pregnant woman, you will soon get pregnant' – Bedfordshire (1982).

More scientific research has come to different conclusions. It is generally agreed that childbirth takes place between 250 and 285 days after ovulation, with the majority between 266 and 270 days. Since no woman can possibly know the precise time at which one of her eggs has become fertilised, the estimated delivery date is calculated as nine calendar months and one week after the last menstrual period.

In cases involving the legitimacy or otherwise of a child, an American court once accepted a 355-day pregnancy as legitimate, while British courts have accepted 331 and 346 days as within the bounds of possibility. There is only a 5 per cent chance that a baby will be born on its 'due' date, and only a 25 per cent chance that it will be born within four days of its scheduled arrival. Only 5 per cent are more than a fortnight early or late.

The human pregnancy period of about 268 days fits in between the fallow deer (250 days) and the buffalo (300 days) in the gestation league. Generally, larger animals take longer than smaller ones, though the piglet (113 days) is slower to emerge than a tiger or lion cub (107 days each). At the more extreme ends, we have the Virginia opossum (12 to 13 days), golden hamster (16 days) and elephant (700 days).

A pregnant woman in Britain has a one-in-84 chance of having twins. The Belgians, oddly enough, have a one-in-56 chance. According to Hellin's Law, your chance of having triplets is roughly the square of your chance of having twins, and for quadruplets, you must raise it to the third power. (Which would predict about one in 7,000 for triplets, one in 600,000 for quads, and about one in 20 billion for octuplets.) This 'Law' is only roughly supported by the figures.

Nonuplets have been reliably reported on three

occasions, but none of the 27 children survived. Maddalena Granata of Italy (born 1839) is said to have given birth to 15 separate sets of triplets. Other records include an 18th-century Russian woman who had 69 children in 27 confinements, a 17th-century Hertfordshire mother who had 39 children in a record 38 confinements, and a Dublin woman with a record 13 births by Caesarean section.

★The British Ministry of Defence placed its first order for maternity uniforms on 3 October 1995.

☞ CAMEL, FASHION, MOSQUITO, SEX, SEX EDUCATION, SEX TEST, STRAWBERRY, TOGO, St VALENTINE

PREMATURE EJACULATION
☞ ALCOHOL, SEX

PRESBYTERIANISM
☞ SPEARS

PRESLEY, Elvis (1935–1977)

The name Elvis comes from an Old Norse word meaning 'all wise'. Although Elvis's middle name on his birth certificate was 'Aron', his grave has it as 'Aaron', which was his own preferred spelling. Elvis had an identical twin brother Jesse who died at birth. Throughout his life Elvis maintained the belief that he could talk to his dead twin. Elvis's only TV commercial was for Southern Made Doughnuts in 1954. His only line of dialogue was: 'You get 'em piping hot after 4am'. Elvis had a pet chimp called Scatter, which developed a taste for Scotch whisky and bourbon.

Elvis collected badges from police departments, including a Federal Narcotics badge given to him personally by President Richard Nixon.

Elvis's motto was TCB – 'Taking Care of Business' – and his last words were 'OK, I won't', spoken to his last girlfriend, Ginger Alden.

☛ According to a CBS News Survey in 1989, 7 per cent of Americans believed that Elvis Presley was still alive.

☞ BOWIE, BURIAL, ICE CREAM

PRIME MINISTER

The title of Prime Minister was officially recognised in the UK only in 1937. The brass plate outside 10 Downing Street still bears only the title 'First Lord of the Treasury'.

☞ BAHAMAS, BUTE, DUELLING, GEORGE I, GHOSTS, LLOYD GEORGE, PALMERSTON, PARLIAMENT, PERCEVAL

PRUNE

The word 'prune' occurs only twice in the King James Bible, both in Leviticus. But 'pruned' turns up in Isaiah and 'pruninghooks' occurs twice more in Isaiah plus once each in Joel and Micah.

PSYCHOLOGY

☞ ALCHEMY, BABIES, MARSTON, POLAR BEAR, POSTMEN, TOURISM

PUCCINI, Giacomo (1858–1924)

Puccini's wife put bromide in his coffee and soaked his trousers in camphor when attractive women came to dinner.

PUERTO RICO
☞ HANGOVER

PUMPKIN
The world's biggest pumpkin weighed in at 1,385lb at a Pumpkin Fair in Canby, Oregon, in October 2003. The furthest a pumpkin has ever been shot from a cannon is 1,368m (4,491ft) at the Morton Pumpkin Festival, Illinois, in 1998. The world's fastest time to carve a face into a pumpkin is 54.72 seconds, by Stephen Clarke (USA), set on 23 October 2001 in New Jersey, USA.

The Hallowe'en practice of pumpkin-carving has its origins in an Irish folk tale about a drunkard named Jack who trapped the devil in an apple tree. This led to great problems when Jack died. Denied entrance to Heaven or Hell, he roamed the earth, lighting his way with a hot coal in a pumpkin.

PYRAMID
If all the Egyptian pyramids were dismantled, they would provide enough stone and mortar to build a wall 10ft high and 5ft wide from Baghdad to Calais.
☞ ALCOHOL, EGYPT, GARLIC

PYTHAGORAS (c.580BC–c.500BC)
☞ COMPUTATION, FORTY-SEVEN, LIVER

QATAR
☞ INCOME TAX

QUAGGA
Only one quagga was ever photographed alive. Five pictures exist of a London Zoo quagga taken around 1870. Related to the zebra, the quagga had stripes extending down head, neck and chest, but its back half was plain brown.

★ The last quagga in the world died in an Amsterdam zoo on 12 August 1883. It was not realised at the time that she was the last of her species.

QUANTUM MECHANICS
Max Born, co-winner of the 1954 Nobel Prize for Physics, and the man who coined the term 'quantum mechanics', was the grandfather of Olivia Newton-John.

QUEEN MARY
The liner *Queen Mary* was launched on 26 September

1934 by Queen Mary, wife of George V. The 28 words used by the Queen when she launched the ship are said to have been her only public utterance.

The ship is said to have received its name after Cunard went to George V asking for permission to name the ship after 'England's greatest queen' – meaning Victoria. The King said that his wife would be delighted, so the name became Queen Mary. The ship retired from passenger service in 1967 after 1,001 Atlantic crossings.

The *Queen Mary* can now be visited at Long Beach, California. It is supposed to be haunted: reports include sightings of women in vintage swimsuits. According to paranormal researchers, the first-class swimming pool is a vortex that allows ghosts from other realms to enter.

The *Queen Mary 2* was launched in 2004. It is called the 'Queen Mary 2' rather than 'Queen Mary II' because the numeral refers to the second ship rather than the second Queen Mary. The whistle on the *Queen Mary 2* can be heard for 10 miles. It was originally on the *Queen Mary*.

Henry IV, William III and George V all married women called Mary.

QUEENSLAND

There are 120 species of snake in the Australian state of Queensland. Most are venomous, 20 are classed as 'dangerous' and 16 are 'potentially fatal'. Since 1883, the box jellyfish has been responsible for 67 recorded deaths in Queensland. You can also be killed by the Irukanji jellyfish, stonefish, blue octopus, sharks, crocodiles or a wide variety of venomous spiders and insects in Queensland.

These are not the only natural hazards. In 2002, Queensland announced plans to replace its coconut trees following increased litigation by tourists hit or even killed by falling coconuts.

Aborigines were only finally given the vote in Queensland in 1965.

In 2006, researchers at the University of Queensland reported tests showing that wild goats can be frightened off by the smell of tiger excrement.

☞ CROCODILE, SARDINE

RABBIT

☞ BELGIUM, CHOCOLATE, MEMORY, SANTA CLAUS

RADISH

☞ ADULTERY, CELIBACY, PARAPSYCHOLOGY

RAILWAY

The gauge of the tracks on British Rail is equal to the distance between the wheels of a Roman chariot.

'National Rail Timetables' is an anagram of 'All trains aim to be late in'.

In 1988, two German inventors patented the 'toilet chute for railway carriages'.

☛ Four per cent of complaints made to British Rail operating companies concern the way they handle complaints.

★ British trains were first fitted with lavatories on 2 April 1873, but only in sleeping-cars.

☞ ALASKA, ELEPHANT, FLIGHT, HEALTH, KISSING, LAVATORIES, MOUSE, STEPHENSON, TOURISM, TRANSPORT, WELLINGTON

RAIN

The maximum speed of rain is 18mph. Raindrops are about one-fifth of an inch in diameter; drizzle is about one-fiftieth of an inch. Including drizzle, the total weight of rain falling on the British Isles in a year has been calculated as around 115 billion tons.

A 'shower' is officially 'precipitation from a convective cloud' (that's a bubble-type broken cloud). 'Rain' is precipitation from 'layered cloud'. If a shower lasts more than 20 minutes, it's probably rain.

'Scattered showers', in the language of weather forecasters, means around a one-in-10 chance of any particular place having a shower.

To reproduce the biblical description of Noah's Flood, one inch of rain would have to fall every second for 40 days without any evaporation.

☞ ANTARCTICA, COSTA RICA, HAWAII, MONDAY, PERU, SARDINE, SHAKESPEARE, St SWITHUN, THAMES, THOR, UGANDA, UMBRELLA, WEATHER

RAINCOAT

The waterproofing method that led to the creation of the raincoat was invented by the Scottish chemist Charles Macintosh. Nobody knows why the garment named after him, the mackintosh, has an extra letter 'k' added to its name.
★ Macintosh patented his waterproofing system on 17 June 1823.

RALEIGH, Sir Walter (c.1552–1618)

Until 1581, Walter Raleigh spelled his surname Rauley or Rauleygh. He then changed it to Ralegh. He never spelled it Raleigh. He founded Virginia and named it after Queen Elizabeth, the Virgin Queen. After he was beheaded, his head was sent to his widow in a red leather bag, which she carried with her for the rest of her life.

☞ BURIAL, HYENA, TOBACCO

RAPE
In English law, only boys over 14 can rape; there is no such limitation in Scotland.

☞ CAPITAL PUNISHMENT, SWAZILAND, YETI

RAT
Rattus rattus is black; *Rattus norvegicus* is brown.

The rat population in Taipei doubled in 1984 (the Chinese Year of the Rat) and they now outnumber the 2.3 million humans by four to one. Mainland China killed 526 million rats in 1984. A lottery was run in Shanghai that year with a dead rat as the price of a ticket.

In 2005, Spanish researchers showed that rats can be trained to distinguish spoken Japanese from spoken Dutch.

☞ BANGLADESH, CAMEL, EXAMINATIONS, HAMSTER, MARS, PARLIAMENT

REAGAN, Ronald (1911–2004)
Ronald Reagan was the first US president to have been divorced. His middle name was Wilson, which is also the only surname shared by a US president and a British prime minister; if you arrange all the US presidents in alphabetical order, Woodrow Wilson comes last.

☞ BUSH, GUITAR, UNITED STATES

RECRUITMENT
In June 2000, Swedish furniture chain Ikea began a new recruitment drive with handwritten job advertisements on lavatory walls. 'In the toilet people are more relaxed and receptive to our message,' a spokesman said. The ads on the walls of restaurant lavatories in Malmo cost one-tenth the amount charged by newspapers and initial response was encouraging. After only four days 60 applications had been received, which was four or five times as many as via a normal newspaper advertisement.

REINDEER
Duck droppings are a reindeer's favourite food. In 2001, Harrods department store in London had to replace Santa's reindeer and sleigh with a horse and carriage because the movement of reindeer in Britain was limited by an outbreak of foot-and-mouth disease. 'This is the first time in living memory Harrods has not used a reindeer,' a spokesman for the store said.
☞ SANTA CLAUS

REMBRANDT, Harmenszoon van Rijn (1606–69)
Rembrandt's favourite meal was simply bread and cheese or pickled herring.

He was declared bankrupt in 1656, when he even had to sell his wife's grave, and died penniless in 1669.

● Including paintings, etchings and drawings, Rembrandt is known to have composed almost 90 self-portraits.

RENOIR, Pierre Auguste (1841–1919)

Renoir said, 'A painter who has the feel for breasts and buttocks is saved.'

☞ OLIVE, PIGEON

RESTAURANTS

According to a survey in 1999, the top ten causes of arguments when dining out are:

1. Pinching your partner's chips
2. Eyeing up other diners
3. Loud and messy eating habits
4. Arguing over who pays the bill
5. Speaking too loudly
6. Complaints over food
7. Getting very drunk
8. Rudeness to staff
9. Spillages
10. Talking politics

☞ ALCHEMY, CHINA, CRISPS, DAVIDSON, DINOSAUR, IRELAND, RECRUITMENT, SINGAPORE, TOOTHPICK

REVOLVING DOORS

The International Revolving Door Association was established in 1991. It is based in California and listed 19 members on its website in 2004.

★ On 7 August 1888, Theophilus van Kannel of Philadelphia patented the Van Kannel Revolving Storm Door, the world's first revolving door.

RHINOCEROS

The white rhino is a dirty grey colour. Its name is a mistranslation from the Afrikaans *weit*, meaning wide –

it has a wider face and body than the more common black rhino.

A fully grown rhino may eat half a ton of grass a day. In courtship, the female partner is the active one.

The collective noun for rhinoceroses is a 'crash'.

☞ HIPPOPOTAMUS

RHUBARB

Botanically, rhubarb is a vegetable, but in 1947 the US Customs Court ruled it to be a fruit, since that is how it is normally eaten. Rhubarb first became known in England in the 16th century for its medicinal properties. It did not begin to appear as an ingredient in cookery books until the beginning of the 19th century.

On 11 January 1770, Benjamin Franklin sent a consignment of rhubarb from London to John Bartram in Philadelphia. This was the first rhubarb in the United States.

☞ SEX

RHYME

It has frequently been asserted that there are no English words that rhyme with purple, orange, silver or month. This is untrue:

- A curple is a strap on a horse's saddle (also known as a crupper), or a slang term for the buttocks.
- To hirple is to walk with a limp.
- To turple is to fall or tumble or, in the case of animals, to die.
- A sporange is a spore-containing sac in mushrooms (which also leads to the compounds hypno-

sporange, macrosporange, megasporange, micro-sporange, prozoosporange and tetrasporange).
- A chilver is a ewe-lamb.
- Grunth (or Granth) is a sacred Hindu scripture.

Mathematicians might also argue that if cardinal numbers are identified as 1, 2, 3, 4, 5... n, (n+1) and so on, the corresponding ordinals would be first, second, third, fourth, fifth ... nth, (n+1)th, the last of these being a perfect rhyme for 'month'.

☞ DONKEY

RICE
★ On 13 August 1997, the Laotian news agency reported that farmers had successfully completed trials using pig manure as a snail repellent on rice crops.

☞ CHOPSTICKS, SARDINE

ROBBERY
Listed below are brief details of some of the least successful robberies in recent years.

Israel: a bank robber in Tel Aviv in 1995 was foiled by a deaf cashier, who could not hear him whispering 'this is a hold-up'. He fled the bank in embarrassment.

Florida, USA: a bank robber waited in line for 20 minutes for a cashier to bring him a bag of money. He was arrested as he left the bank.

Netherlands: a Dutchman gave a shopkeeper a note

demanding money but fled when handed a reply saying: 'Sod off'.

Los Angeles, USA: in 1996, a 71-year-old grandmother pleaded not guilty to armed robbery, saying she had been driven insane by the Internal Revenue Service.

Colombia: a blood bank was robbed in Colombia in 1996.

Canada: a man was charged in 1997 after threatening to kill a racoon if people idn't hand over their money.

South Africa: in 2002, a thief at a South African zoo made a fatal mistake: he attempted a getaway via the tiger's cage. He died of a broken neck and a fractured skull.

★ The first time a getaway car was used in a robbery was on 27 October 1901 in Paris.

☞ CAPITAL PUNISHMENT, COLOMBIA, ICELAND

ROMANIA

In January 2005, the Bucharest daily newspaper *Libertatea* reported that a Romanian couple had named their baby Yahoo after the Internet website that brought them together. A week later, the same paper reported that it had sacked the journalist responsible, because the story had been invented. 'If it were real, it would have been a good story indeed,' said Simona Ionescu, *Libertatea*'s deputy editor-in-chief.

☞ CHRISTMAS, DRACULA, RUGBY

ROOSEVELT, Theodore (1858–1919)

When asked permission to lend his name to the 'teddy' bear, President Roosevelt replied, 'I don't think my name is likely to be worth much in the bear business but you are welcome to use it.'

☞ CAMP DAVID

ROSSINI, Gioacchino Antonio (1792–1868)

The composer Rossini was born on 29 February 1792. As 1800 was not a leap year, his second true birthday occurred when he was 12.

ROULETTE

If you add together all the numbers on a roulette wheel, the result is 666, the Number of the Beast in the Book of Revelation.

☞ EVEREST

RUBBER BANDS

★ The first elastic bands were patented by Stephen Perry & Co. of London on 17 March 1845.

☞ PORTUGAL

RUGBY

According to legend, rugby was invented at Rugby School in 1823 when William Webb Ellis, aged 16, picked up the ball and ran with it in a soccer game. A stone at the school bears the inscription: 'This stone commemorates the exploit of William Webb Ellis who with a fine disregard for the rules of football, as played in his time, first took the ball in his arms and ran with it, thus originating

the distinctive features of the rugby game A.D. 1823.'
William Webb Ellis went on to Oxford University, where
he won a blue not for rugby but cricket.

Rugby was included in the Olympics of 1900, 1908,
1920 and 1924. The United States are the reigning
Olympic champions, having beaten France in the final in
1924 (Romania was the only other entrant). Britain's
Olympic rugby record reads: played two, lost two. Despite
this, they won bronze in 1900 (last of three entrants) and
silver in 1908 (two entrants).

The Seventh Underwater Rugby World Championship was held in Denmark in 2003 and won by Sweden.

The Zulu for 'scrum half' is 'iskramuhhafu'.

RUSEDSKI, Greg (b. 1973)
Greg Rusedski is an anagram of 'Rugged kisser'.
☞ WIMBLEDON

RUSSIA
A kick-boxing school specifically for nannies opened in
St Petersburg in 1997 in response to the growing
problem of child-kidnapping.
☞ ALASKA, ALCOHOL, ALEXANDER I, St ANDREW,
ATLANTIC, CATHERINE I, CELIBACY, CHESS, CRIME,
CZECH REPUBLIC, DOG, ESTONIA, FISH, GEORGIA, HAIR,
HEALTH, St MATTHEW, MONDAY, MUSHROOM, OCTOBER,
OLYMPIC GAMES, PETER the GREAT, PREGNANCY,
TRANSPLANTATION

SAILORS

Mallemaroking means 'the carousing of seamen on an icebound ship'.

☞ DARWIN, WEATHER

St LUCIA

The Caribbean island of St Lucia has produced more Nobel Prize winners per head of population than any other country on earth – two Nobel Prizes from a population of 144,000.

SALAMANDER

Asbestos was originally believed to be the wool of the salamander.

SANDCASTLE

★ On 18 June 1997, science finally came to grips with sandcastles as physicists at the University of Notre Dame, Indiana, published their discovery of the 'sandcastle effect'. This solved the mystery of why sandcastles do not collapse when the water in them has dried out.

SANDWICHES

According to a poll among British schoolchildren in 2002, the five sandwich fillings children most liked to find in their lunchboxes are:

1. Ham
2. Chicken
3. Turkey roll
4. Cheese
5. Peanut Butter

while the five least favourite sandwich fillings are:

1. Egg mayonnaise
2. Salad
3. Pate
4. Salami
5. Marmite

☛ If you eat a sandwich for breakfast, lunch and dinner, it will take 168 days to get through the amount of bread produced from one bushel of wheat.

☞ CHEESE, CHICKEN, EXAMINATIONS, LINDBERGH, TELEVISION

SANTA ANNA, Antonio López de (c.1795–1876)

President Santa Anna of Mexico led the siege of the Alamo in 1836. His leg was amputated after a wound in battle in 1838. He kept it at his hacienda near Veracruz from 1838 until its ceremonial burial in 1842. The leg was stolen from the Pantheon of Saint Paula in Mexico City during the 1844 riot that toppled him.

SANTA CLAUS

According to tradition, Santa's reindeer will eat 360 different plants, but not carrots.

In June 1995, a New Zealand Santa Claus was sentenced to six months' detention for breaking the security glass at a petrol station the previous Christmas when they would not give him a free ice cream.

Another achievement by Santa the same year was the award of his personal postal code by the Canadian post office. Letters addressed to Santa Claus at the North Pole would be sped on their way if they carried the postal code H0H 0H0, officials of Canada Post promised.

In 1995 there was a great dispute at the 32nd World Santa Claus Conference in Copenhagen. The Finnish Santa, who claims to be the only true one, refused to attend unless the others acknowledges his uniqueness. 'This is the last straw,' an organiser of the Conference said. 'We had invited the Finnish Santa to attend and explain himself at this year's conference. Now we're going to strip him of his white beard and red robe and excommunicate him once and for all.'

In 1927, a Finnish radio programme pinpointed Santa's location on Lapland's Korvatunturi, or 'Ear Mountain'. The area resembles a rabbit's ears, from which Santa can hear if children are being naughty or nice.

In 1998, a man appeared in court in Finland for driving his car into a reindeer-drawn Santa sleigh. Although he was drunk, the jury recommended leniency on the grounds of his understandable surprise.

In Great Yarmouth in 2000, a street trader dressed as Santa was arrested for brawling. A police spokesman said, 'It was extremely upsetting for the young children to see Santa being nicked and handcuffed.'

In 2001 a Mother Christmas sued a store in America for $100,000 because she was sacked for having breasts. In the same year, two banks in Switzerland banned entry to anyone in Santa Claus costume for fear of robberies.

Two recent research studies throw light on the phenomenon of children's belief in Santa Claus. In 2002, the *Canadian Medical Association Journal* published a paper called 'Do Reindeer and Children know Something that we Don't? Pediatric Inpatients' Belief in Santa Claus', in which Claude Cyr reports the results of interviews with 45 children and their parents. His results show that there is no difference between girls' and boys' belief in Santa, but that belief decreases with age. Santa-belief is, however, directly proportional to the age at which their parents stopped believing in him. The author admits that the study has many limitations, including its timing (late April 2002) which, he says, 'might overestimate the rate of belief in the Easter bunny and underestimate the rate of belief in Santa'.

The second, more recent study is even less encouraging for Santa. At Christmas 2003, Prof. John Trinkaus observed and classified, on a six-point scale, the expressions on the faces of 300 children as they visited Santa in department stores in New York. Of the 300, one (0.3 per cent) was 'exhilarated'; two (0.7 per cent) were 'happy'; 247 (82 per cent) were 'indifferent'; 47 (16 per cent) were 'hesitant'; none (0 per cent) was sad; and three (1 per cent) were 'terrified'.

☛ It has been calculated that Santa would need 200,000 reindeer flying at 200,000 times the speed of sound in order to deliver presents to every child on earth.

☞ MANDELA, SONGS

SARDINE

According to a spokesman for the European Patent Office, the most frequently requested patent document is the one for sardine-flavoured ice cream. 'No one believes that it actually exists until they've called it up and seen it themselves,' patent examiner Bernard Delporte said in 1998.

The patent he referred to is numbered JP6233654 and was granted to Sato Shigeaki on 23 August 1994. According to the patent application, the purpose of the invention is: 'To obtain a delicious ice cream and to promote industries by expanding consumption of fishes by thoroughly removing a fish-like smell so as to make children who dislike fishes eat fishes.' The constitution of the product is given as follows:

> *Miso (fermented soybean paste) and Welsh onion are put on ground sardine meat, steamed with SAKE (rice wine), boiled with milk and alcohol, mixed with paste of walnut, paste of almond and paste of peanut and boiled. The cooked sardine is mixed with an ice cream base of chocolate taste and cooled to produce the objective ice cream of sardine.*

In 1989 it rained sardines over the town of Ipswich in Queensland, Australia.

SAUDI ARABIA

In recent years, Saudi Arabia has beheaded more
criminals than any other country. In 2002, 45 men and
two women were beheaded and a further 52 men and
one woman in 2003.

☞ CAMEL

SAUSAGES

The British spend around half a billion pounds on
sausages in a year, eating over quarter of a million tonnes
of them. Research shows that 6.8 per cent of people eat
sausages 'because they are convenient', 13.4 per cent 'for
a change', 8.4 per cent 'for a treat' and 30 per cent
because 'they are my favourite meal'. The world's longest
sausage was made in Britain in 2000. It weighed 15.5
tonnes and was 35 miles long. The British Sausage
Appreciation Society has over 6,000 members, and
sausages are the third most popular foodstuff taken on
holiday by Britons when travelling abroad.

Sausage-eating had a long tradition in Britain. King
Henry V is quoted as saying: 'War without fire is like
sausages without mustard', yet sausages are by no means
a British invention. The ancient Sumerians were eating
sausages 5,000 years ago.

☞ HOT DOG

SCARECROW

The gun-firing scarecrow was patented in 1913 (US
patent 1056602) by John Steinocher of West Texas 'for
scaring off birds, animals and such like as tend to prey
upon or devastate crops, stock or like property'.

SCENT

A fragrance called 'Madeleine' was introduced in a trial at three London tube stations on 23 March 2001 in an attempt to make the tube smell better. The experiment was abruptly terminated on 24 March 2001 as it was making people feel sick.

☞ St VALENTINE

SCHILLER, Friedrich von (1759–1805)

The German poet, dramatist and historian Schiller used to work with a bowl of rotting apples on his desk. He believed the smell stimulated his creative processes.

SCISSORS

The first open international championship at the game of Scissors–Paper–Stone was held in Toronto in November 2002 and was won by Canadian website operator Pete Lovering. More than 250 people took part and the top prize was $1,200, a video game system and a gold medal. Lovering said the secret to winning is maintaining a clear mind and judging each opponent individually.

SCORPION

☞ IBSEN, MEXICO

SCOTLAND

St Columba is not only credited with being the man who brought Christianity to Scotland, he is also thought to be the first person to claim a sighting of the Loch Ness Monster in AD565.

☞ ALCHEMY, St ANDREW, GOLF, IRELAND, NEWCASTLE, RAPE, TRANSPORT, UNIVERSITIES, VANUATU, WORM

SCOTT, Sir Walter (1771–1832)

Scottish author who wrote the novel *Ivanhoe*. 'Ivanhoe by Sir Walter Scott' is an anagram of 'A novel by a Scottish writer'.

☞ BULLOCK

SCOUTING

Robert Baden-Powell was persuaded, with great reluctance, to remove a section entitled 'Continence' from his *Scouting For Boys*. 'You all know what it is,' he wrote, 'to have at times a pleasant feeling in your private parts.' The excised section was a warning of what could befall a boy who gave way to the temptations associated with such a feeling:

> *The practice is called 'self-abuse'. And the result of self-abuse is always – mind you, always – that the boy after a time becomes weak and nervous and shy, he gets headaches and probably palpitation of the heart, and if he still carries it on too far he very often goes out of his mind and becomes an idiot. A very large number of the lunatics in our asylums have made themselves ill by indulging in this vice although at the time they were sensible cheery boys like any one of you.*

SCRABBLE

The game of Scrabble was invented by Alfred Butts in 1921, since when over 100 million Scrabble sets have been sold in 121 countries. Alfred Butts also produced another game, marketed under the title 'Alfred's Other Game'. It was not a great success.

There are 19 'A's in a Malaysian Scrabble set, the highest number of any single letter in any language.

In Finnish Scrabble, the letter D is worth seven points.

British Scrabble organisers were taken to court in 1995 by a player who complained that he was allowed insufficient time to go to the lavatory between games. Leicester Police once received a call from a five-year-old boy complaining that his sister was cheating at Scrabble.

☛ There are 121 permissible two-letter words in Scrabble, using every letter except V. The only number (in English) that scores its own value when played on a Scrabble board (excluding bonus squares) is TWELVE.

☞ AA

SCRATCHING

Studies have shown that right-handed people tend to scratch with their left hands and left-handed people with their right.

☞ ACNESTIS

SEAL

The study of seals and signet rings is called sphragistics.

- One way to tell a seal from a sea lion is that a sea lion's hind flippers can turn round to aid propulsion when moving on land, while a seal's cannot.

- The crabeater seal doesn't eat crabs. Its preferred food is the small shrimp-like creatures called krill. French explorers gave it the name of 'crabeater' in error.

- In 1951, two Italian journalists were fined for taking their pet seal for a swim in the Trevi Fountain in Rome.
- Under the old laws of Newfoundland, seal-hunting vessels were obliged to serve soup on a Saturday.
- The collective noun for a group of seals is a herd or a pod.
- The term for a breathing hole made in ice by a seal is an aglu.

☞ AUGUSTUS, DINOSAUR, SEA LION

SEA LION

- One way to tell a sea lion from a seal is that a sea lion has ear-flaps whereas a seal does not. Here are some more distinguishing features:
- Sea lions have no distinguishable nails on their front flippers, whereas seals have claw-like nails.
- Seals have nails on all digits of their hind flippers, but sea lions have nails only on the middle three digits.
- Sea lions' flippers are usually hairless, unlike those of seals.
- The front flippers of a sea lion are long and wing-like; the front flippers of a seal are short and blunt.
- The Chinese used to use sea lion whiskers to clean opium pipes.
- Sea lions are unable to see the colour red, which they cannot distinguish from grey.
- Sea lions can suffer from epilepsy.
- Research published in 2004 showed that a sea lion could remember things it has learned 10

years previously, the longest memory interval ever recorded in a non-human mammal.

• 'Sea lions' is an anagram of 'a lioness'. 'Pigeon' is an anagram of 'one pig'.

☞ SEAL

SECOND

A second of time was originally the ancient Roman's *pars minutia secunda* (second small part) of an hour, the first small part, or *pars minutia prima*, being what we now call the minute. The Romans in turn got the idea from the counting system of the Babylonians, which was based on the number 60. Our 60 seconds in a minute, 60 minutes in an hour and 360 degrees in a circle all stem from that source. Sixty was chosen for its ease of divisibility into two, three, four, six, 10 or 12 parts. The *pars minutia* was not just any small part but very specifically one-sixtieth.

Until 1960, a second was defined as 1/86,400 of a mean solar day (the average period of rotation of the Earth on its axis relative to the Sun). In that year, however, the General Conference of Weights and Measures adopted a more precise definition of 1/31556925.9747 of a tropical year. In other words, the definition changed from one based on the Earth's rotation on its axis to one based on its orbit round the Sun. That new definition only lasted seven orbits, however, for in 1967, following the development of super-accurate atomic clocks, another definition was adopted. Since then, a second has been equal to: '9,192,631,770 oscillations of the electromagnetic radiation corresponding to a particular quantum change in the superfine energy level of the ground state of the caesium-133 atom'. Thanks to this definition, a caesium clock is accurate to within one second in 316,000 years.

☞ BIRTH, BUGANDA, CHICKEN, CHOPSTICKS, COMPUTATION, CRIME, FISH, GARLIC, GOLDFISH, JIFFY, NAPOLEON BONAPARTE, PANCAKE, PATIENCE, POPULATION, POTATO, SUN, WHISKY

SEDUCTION

It is illegal to seduce the wet-nurse of an heir to the British throne.

☞ CASANOVA, TUESDAY

SEMI-COLON

The modern semi-colon first appeared in 1494 in the first edition of Pietro Mombo's *De Aetna*. Similar-looking punctuation marks had been used by the Romans, but the convention of using them to signify something stronger than a comma, but less than a full stop, was the idea of the printer Aldus Manutius the Elder (1450–1515) and Francesco Griffi his punch-cutter. Griffi went on to design the first italic type in 1500.

SEX

History, sadly, does not relate when humans first discovered how to make more humans, but they have been arguing about the details ever since. Indeed, as far as we have been able to ascertain, the only society which has never shown any interest in sex is the Dani tribe of Grand Valley, New Guinea.

The Egyptians and ancient Greeks believed that the father alone was responsible for the seed from which a child grew. The mother was at best responsible for providing it with warmth and nourishment. Aristotle challenged that view and accepted that the woman had more than a nursing role to play. She also gets twice the pleasure out of it: 'she having an enjoyment both by reception and ejection, by which she is more delighted in'.

Aristotle prefaced his remarks on the 'Organs of Generation in Women' with the following words: 'If it were not for the public benefit, especially for that of the professors and practitioners of the art of midwifery, I would refrain from treating the secrets of Nature, because they may be turned to ridicule by lascivious and lewd people. But as it is absolutely necessary that they should be known for the public good, I will not omit them because some may make a wrong use of them.' He went on immediately to point out that the bits he was talking about are collectively known as: 'the pudenda, or things to be ashamed of, because when they are exposed they cause a woman pudor, or shame'.

Among the secrets of nature that Aristotle then divulged was that the womb is divided into two halves, one for boy babies, the other for girls. A woman wishing to conceive a son should lie on her right side, or on her left for a girl. For the right side of the womb contains 'the greatest generative heat, which is the chief procuring cause of male children'. Hippocrates clearly had a similar opinion when he announced: 'If, in a woman pregnant with twins, either of her breasts lose its fullness, she will part with one of her children; and if it be the right breast which becomes slender, it will be the male child, or if the left, the female.'

Pliny the Elder believed that sexual intercourse is a good remedy for pains in the loins, dimness of sight, insanity and melancholia. Other strange beliefs concerning childbirth have persisted over the centuries. Irish magistrates in the late 19th century also recognised the old superstition that it was unlucky for a pregnant woman to take an oath in court. The subject began to be more scientifically studied in the same century with Sir Astley Cooper's 'Surgical Lectures', published in the *Lancet* in 1824, among the first to offer a serious account of sexual ailments. He was not sure that turpentine and rhubarb did any good for the treatment of premature ejaculation, which he blamed on debauchery, irritability and a bad diet. Impotence, he said, was due to 'general torpor' and 'sluggishness of constitution'.

A more recent study concluded that a single act of love-making expends the same energy as 45 minutes of frisbee-throwing, 1.5 hours of card-playing or 7.5 hours standing around at cocktail parties.

In Connorsville, Wisconsin, it is illegal for a man to fire a gun while his partner is in the throes of sexual ecstasy.

☞ BALI, CELIBACY, COCONUT, D'EON, DIVORCE, DRIVING, EDUCATION, INCOME TAX, ISRAEL, LOVE, LUTHER, MARRIAGE, PENGUIN, PREGNANCY, SEX EDUCATION, SEX TEST, SKIING, ZAMBIA

SEX EDUCATION

At Garissa, north-east Kenya, in October 1987, an elderly man who got a schoolgirl pregnant while pretending to give her private tuition was ordered in court to pay four camels in compensation.

SEX TEST

The first sporting disqualification on a sex test was of the Polish sprinter Ewa Klobukowska in 1967. The record she had helped set when winning the Olympic gold in the sprint relay in 1964 was struck from the record books. The extra chromosome which made her ineligible for female athletic events, however, did not prevent her from becoming pregnant a few years later and giving birth to a healthy baby.

SEXUAL HARASSMENT

In 2001, a Texas prisoner, David Joyner, sued *Penthouse* magazine for publishing what he said was a disappointing layout of Paula Jones, who had previously accused President Clinton of sexual harassment. Joyner's lawsuit alleged that the pictorial of Jones was not sufficiently revealing and caused the plaintiff to be 'very mentally hurt and angered'. He sought $500,000 in damages.

District Judge Sam Sparks dismissed the suit and fined Joyner (who was serving 14 years for robbery and assault) $250 for filing a frivolous legal motion. His judgment was accompanied by a 12-line poem which began: 'Twas the night before Christmas and all through the prison, inmates were planning their new porno mission.'

SHAKESPEARE, William (1564–1616)

William Shakespeare had red hair and bequeathed his second-best bed to his widow.

The only world heavyweight boxing champion to have lectured on Shakespeare at Yale University was Gene Tunney.

Shakespeare's play *Romeo and Juliet* contains the earliest recorded use of the word 'bump'.

Shakespeare's plays are generally models of accuracy. Here are some of his errors:

In *Julius Caesar*, Act II, scene i, Brutus says, 'Peace, count the clock' and Trebonius replies, 'The clock hath stricken three.' But the chiming clock was not invented until 1400 years after the time of Julius Caesar.

In *The Winter's Tale*, Act III, scene iii, Bohemia is described as a desert country near the sea and Antigonus says, 'our ship hath touch'd upon/The deserts of Bohemia'. But Bohemia is totally inland, about 160 miles from the sea at its closest point.

In *The Merry Wives of Windsor*, Act V, scene v, Falstaff says, 'Let the sky rain potatoes', but the potato had not been imported into Europe at the time the play is set.

In *Henry IV Part One*, Act II, scene ii, First Carrier exclaims, 'God's body, the turkeys in my pannier are quite starv'd.' But the play takes place almost a century before the discovery of America, from where the first European turkeys were brought.

'William Shakespeare' is an anagram of 'I am a weakish speller'.

☛ The role of Hamlet contains 11,610 words.

☞ ALCOHOL, BIBLE, BILLIARDS, CABBAGE, CRAB,
ENGLISH, FASHION, FEBRUARY, FOOTBALL, FORTY-SEVEN,
GARLIC, St GEORGE, LAVATORIES, STAMP

SHARK
Sharks keep growing new teeth to replace old ones.
A 10-year-old shark may well have gnawed and bitten
its way through about 24,000 teeth.

☞ FISH, QUEENSLAND

SHEEP
The fat from an average lamb can be used to make half
a gallon of diesel fuel. In 1986 a test fleet of 40 New
Zealand lorries averaged 10 miles per lamb.

In November 2001, the science journal *Nature*
published a paper entitled 'Sheep Don't Forget a Face'
by five Cambridge psychologists. The paper reported
research showing that a sheep can remember the faces of
50 other sheep for over two years.

On 25 June 1911, Sir John Throckmorton won a
wager of 1,000 guineas that a woollen coat could be
made between sunrise and sunset starting with the
shearing of the sheep.

☞ BALLOON, BIBLE, BURNS, CAPITAL PUNISHMENT,
CHAMOIS, CUCUMBER, HALIFAX, HANGOVER,
LIGHTNING, METHANE, RHYME, TEETH, WALES

SHOES
The feet of two kings played a crucial role in the
development of the modern shoe. Louis XIV of France
(1638–1715) was the first person to wear high-heeled

shoes; and George IV of Britain (1762–1830) was reputedly the first to wear a pair of shoes specially tailored for his right and left feet. Most common folk, however, had to wait until about 1850 before they could buy right shoes and left shoes, rather than two shoes that were equally uncomfortable on either foot.

In 14th-century France, there was a fashion for long shoes called Poulaines, which were also status symbols according to length. Princes and noblemen wore shoes up to 2ft in length. At the Battle of Nicopolis in 1396, French Crusaders hacked off the tips of their shoes so they could run away.

Other notable footprints in the history of shoes are as follows:

- *1790*: Invention of the shoelace (until then, we had to make do with buckles).
- *1891*: Whitcomb L. Judson invented his 'Clasp Locker and Unlocker for Shoes', the earliest known version of the modern zip.
- *1905*: Miguel y Villacampa of Argentina patented the ventilated shoe heel, with a pump circulating air to cool the wearer's feet.
- *1959*: The first recorded reference in print to stiletto heels, as *The Times* newspaper of 13 May thundered about 'the iniquitous effect of stiletto-heeled shoes on the modern woman's feet'.
- *1976*: Power-assisted boots were developed by the Ufimsky Aviation Institute in the USSR. With petrol-powered engines, they enabled the wearer to make 9ft strides and walk at 16mph.

- *1978*: The Goodyear Rubber Company reported the result of years of research: right shoes wear out faster than left shoes.

More recent improvements received at the European Patent Office include a 'shoe for bandaged foot' (1991) and a 'device for determining the fit of shoes when buying same' (1989).

Shoes tied behind the cars of newlyweds are a sign of good luck and prosperity – as long as you still have your shoes you can't be too badly off. At funerals, mourners used to go barefoot to avoid arousing the envy of the dead.

More superstitions:
Shoes left upside down under the bed will ward off attacks of cramp.

A girl's shoes may help her dream of her future husband: 'Hoping this night my true love to see, I place my shoes in the form of a "T".'

Pliny, in his *Natural History* in AD77, recommended spitting into your right shoe before putting it on, as an antidote to evil spells.

In AD396, St Augustine of Hippo mentioned the belief that you should go back to bed if anyone sneezes while you are putting your shoes on.

If you put your left sock and shoe on first in the morning you will not get toothache.

Useful tip: On average, high heels increase bottom protrusion by 25 per cent.

☞ AUGUSTUS, FRANCE, SUPERSTITION, WELLINGTON BOOTS

SHOPPING

Mr John Moore, a trader of Clapham High Street, was banned in the High Court in December 1984 from calling his shop 'Sellfridges' because he sold fridges. In November he had been banned from calling it 'Harrodds'.

☞ PORTUGAL, SHOPPING TROLLEYS, TOURISM, TRANSPORT

SHOPPING TROLLEYS

According to research in 1999 conducted by the psychologist David Smith, people in supermarkets are increasingly using the contents of other people's trolleys to assess their possible merits as romantic partners. Up to 11 per cent of single under-25s are believed to use this 'love-coding' to aid their judgements about others. The following foods were identified as sending out clear signals:

Asparagus – 'I am a sensual lover who loves exotic holidays.'

Bananas – 'Life is hectic but I love it.'

Brussels sprouts – 'I am down to earth and enjoy a stable lifestyle.'

Chocolate fudge cake – 'Let's have a wild time doing whatever pleases us.'

Cocktail cherries – 'I am rather shallow and pretentious.'

Cookery books – 'I am domesticated and want to look after someone.'

Fish fingers – 'I'm unadventurous between the sheets.'

Pasta – 'I am passionate and love romantic suppers for two.'

Percolated coffee – 'I am decisive and like to be in control.'

Stir-fry vegetables – 'I love to experiment.'

Tinned soup – 'Too many nights alone – tendency to be a bore.'

Tropical fruits – 'I am exotic and passionate.'

The album *Abandoned Shopping Trolley Hotline* was released by the rock group Gomez in 2000.

Physiotherapists have listed unco-operative shopping trolleys as a major cause of back pain.

The value of the shopping trolleys that go missing from UK supermarkets every year is around £8 million. Many of these end up in rivers, but British Waterways have deliberately put trolleys into the Forth and Clyde canal to protect Bennett's pond weed, a rare water plant.

☛ Recent research published by KwikSave reveals that 18 per cent of shoppers are too embarrassed to put budget items in their shopping trolleys.

★ The world's first shopping trolley first arrived on the aisles of a supermarket in Oklahoma, USA, on 4 June 1937.

★ On 26 August 1996, a man in Sweden became the first person to be charged with being drunk in charge of a shopping trolley. He was charged after hurtling downhill at 30mph, after which his trolley collided with a car. A police prosecutor said, 'He was certainly careless, but I suppose it's debatable whether he was driving. But he was rather drunk and his trolley wasn't showing proper lights.'

SHROVE TUESDAY
☞ BELGIUM, PANCAKE

SIAM
★ The original Siamese twins, Chang and Eng Bunker, were born on 11 May 1811.

On 11 May 1939, Siam changed its name to Thailand.

SIGN LANGUAGE
According to research in Tennessee published in 2001, people who use sign language are five times more likely to suffer hand and wrist injuries than people who don't use sign language.

SINGAPORE
Since 1992, it has been illegal to import chewing gum into Singapore. By then the war against chewing gum had already been raging for a decade. In 1983 the Singapore Minister of Culture announced that £50,000 had been spent in the previous year removing chewing gum from floors and walls of government buildings.

In 1996, Singapore passed a law imposing a fine of about £1,000 or a three-month jail term, or both, on anyone found guilty of appearing nude in a public or a private place but exposed to public view. In the same year, the Prime Minister of Singapore announced two markers of a gracious society. They were appreciation of music and clean public toilets.

Singapore law imposes heavy fines on people caught urinating in lifts. Thanks to CCTV and urine detectors, only 14 people were convicted of urinating in lifts in

Singapore in 1996, down from 40 in the previous year.

In 2002, Singapore's Changi Airport launched the world's first live airport game show.

The Imperial Herbal Restaurant in Singapore serves dried deer's penis soup.

☞ GHOSTS, TOILET

SKATES

The first recorded appearance of roller skates was not a success. They were worn by a Belgian entertainer, Joseph Mervin, who appeared on them, playing a violin, at a party in Carlisle House, London. Unfortunately, he lost control and crashed into a mirror, injuring himself and causing some £500 worth of damage.

★ The accident happened on 22 April 1760.

SKIING

Norwegian rock carvings dating back to 2500BC are the oldest known depictions of people skiing. A Siberian rock carving of roughly the same time illustrates a man on skis apparently trying to have sex with an elk.

By 1721, however, the Norwegians were definitely leading the world in skiing. In that year, the Norwegian army became the first to have a specialised ski unit. Norwegian army skis at that time were the first to have leather straps on the heel as well as toestraps. The most successful Olympic skier ever was also Norwegian: Bjørn Dählie of Norway won eight gold medals and four silvers in Nordic skiing between 1992 and 1998.

In Switzerland, 35.3 per cent of skiing accidents involve injuries to the knee. In snow boarding, the upper arm and shoulder are the parts most frequently injured.

In the USA in 2000, there were 94,883 skiing accidents serious enough for emergency hospital treatment.

The earliest known stretchers were made by stretching a piece of canvas between two skis. They were used to carry away wounded soldiers during a 1521 conflict between Denmark and Sweden.

Statistics show that skiing is 29 per cent more dangerous than being a policeman in Northern Ireland.

Your chance of being killed in five minutes' skiing is the same as that of winning the British National Lottery with one ticket.

☞ St BERNARD

SKIN
The skin of the average adult weighs about 6lb.
☞ ANORAK, AUGUSTUS, BANANA, BEAUTY, CHAMOIS, CUCUMBER, EGYPT, LIFETIME, MONEY, NAVEL, OSTRICH, PENGUIN, STRAWBERRY, TEETH, TIGER, St VALENTINE

SKUA
The skua dives at its victims and eats the food they sick up in fright, often even catching the food before it hits the ground.

SKUNK
A skunk can shoot its pungent spray a distance of 15ft. It is legal to kill a skunk at any time of year in Florida.

SLAVERY
'Do not obtain your slaves from Britain,' Cicero advised,

'because they are so stupid and so utterly incapable of being taught, that they are not fit to form part of the household of Athens.'

☞ BRANDING, BURIAL, CHOCOLATE, CUCUMBER, HUDSON, OSTRICH

SLIME
Blennophobia means 'fear of slime'.
☞ SNAIL, WORM

SLIPPERS
In 1995, Britain's most successful examination taker, Francis Thomason, gave credit to his warm slippers when explaining how he had managed to pass 70 O-levels, 16 A-levels, one S-level and gain an Open University degree. 'It is important to have comfortable feet,' he said.
☞ CINDERELLA

SLOANE, Sir Hans (1660–1753)
Hans Sloane was the man who invented milk chocolate. He succeeded Sir Isaac Newton as President of the Royal Society, and his private collection formed the basis for the British Museum.

SLOTH
The sloth can swim twice as fast as it can run – a mile in four hours. Each week it spends on average 10 hours awake motionless, 11 hours eating, 18 hours climbing and 129 hours asleep.
☞ KOALA

SLOVENIA
☞ PORTUGAL

SLUG
Slugs eat 36,000 tonnes of potatoes each year in Britain.

Slugs are hermaphrodite; vitamin B stunts their growth, shortens their lives, and inclines them towards cannibalism.

The record speed for a slug is 0.2mph.

A slug can smell a mushroom up to 2m away.

☞ COFFEE, HEDGEHOG, POTATO

SMELL
According to a survey in 2004, the top ten favourite smells are:

1. Bread	6. Babies
2. Frying bacon	7. The sea
3. Coffee	8. Real Christmas trees
4. Ironing	9. Perfume
5. Cut grass	10. Fish and chips

☞ ANORAK, CHEESE, BABIES, GARLIC, GOLDFISH, HITLER, MOOSE, NOSTRIL, ORANGE, POLAR BEAR, SARDINE, SCENT, SCHILLER, SLUG, URINE, VIRGINITY

SMILING
The often-repeated advice that smiling is to be preferred to frowning because 'it takes more muscles to frown than to smile' is false. A genuine (also known as 'zygomatic') smile uses the following muscles: *zygomaticus major*, *zygomaticus minor*, *orbicularis oculi*, *levator labii superioris*,

levator anguli oris and *risorius.* There are two of each of these, one on each side of the face, giving a grand total of 12 muscles.

To frown, you need the *orbicularis oculi, platysma, depressor anguli oris* and *corrugator supercilii,* of which there is again one on each side of the face, plus the *procerus, orbicularis oris* and *mentalis* which are all single muscles, giving a grand total of 11.

For most people, however, the smiling muscles are better exercised than the frowning ones, so using them may take less energy. The insincere smile is the most energy-efficient, and can be accomplished with the use of only the two *risorius* muscles.

The word for someone who never smiles is 'agelast'.

☞ ALBANIA, TENNIS

SMOKING
In January 2001, the University of Tokyo offered a new service to people who had made a New Year's Resolution to give up smoking. When the urge to light up became too strong, they could press a button on their mobile phone and receive a message encouraging them not to give up giving up. The price of the new service was designed to be the same as the cost of a packet of cigarettes.

☞ CARUSO

SNAIL
Thanks to the sticky carpet they exude, snails can crawl along the edge of a razor blade without injuring themselves. Sadly, however, they cannot crawl fast

enough to escape from the French, who eat 40,000 tonnes of snails every year. Indeed, at its top speed of two inches a minute, a snail would finish a marathon in just over 18 months.

The French are not the only ones to pose a threat to snails. Oribasius, a fifth-century Byzantine physician, used to treat wounds with an ointment made from crushed snails mixed with flour. If he ran out of snails, he would use earthworms instead. Snail-slime and sugar were once used to treat tuberculosis.

Before World War I, Bristol glassblowers used to eat snails to improve their lung power. By contrast, one of the safest places for snails is the Swiss canton of Valais, where snail-hunting is illegal.

In 1996, a Nottingham professor discovered that sexual activity among tropical snails could be increased by feeding them porridge.

The World Snail Racing Championship takes place every year at the Cricket Field in Congham, Norfolk. The world record for the 13in course was set by a snail called Archie who won in 1995 in a time of two minutes. L'Escargot (which is French for 'the snail') won the Grand National in 1975.

☛ A snail can have up to 25,600 teeth.

☞ COFFEE, HEDGEHOG, RICE

SNAKE
In March 2006, a Malaysian set a world record by kissing a poisonous snake 51 times in three minutes.

☞ AUSTRALIA, BARCELONA, IRELAND, KOMODO, MEXICO, QUEENSLAND

SNORING

Around a quarter of the people in the UK are believed to snore habitually and about 45 per cent snore sometimes.

More than 300 devices are registered in the US Patent and Trademark Offices as cures for snoring. A typical anti-snoring patent was the one taken out in 1955 consisting of a hinged board beneath the pillow which would shake the sleeper awake when a microphone positioned above his nose detected snoring noises.

There is also no shortage of folk remedies for snoring. One says that the best way to stop someone snoring is to pinch their big toe, while another theory is that a gold coin hung around your neck will stop you snoring. This is said to work on dogs too.

In Massachusetts, snoring is prohibited unless all bedroom windows are closed and securely locked.

According to Mark Twain (in *Tom Sawyer Abroad*, 1894): 'There ain't no way to find out why a snorer can't hear himself snore.'

☛ The noise of a really rasping snore can register 69 decibels – a pneumatic drill is 70–90 decibels.

☞ GORILLA, KOALA, TENNIS

SNOW

More useless disinformation has been spread about the number of Eskimo (now Inuit) words for snow than almost any other subject in linguistics. For a detailed account, the reader is referred to Geoffrey Pullum's highly entertaining paper 'The Great Eskimo Snow Hoax' in *Natural Language & Linguistic Theory*, vol. 7, No. 2, 1989. What follows is a summary of Pullum's research.

The story begins in 1911 when Frank Boas, writing about the development of North American Indian language, cited four apparently distinct Eskimo words for different types of snow. His point was that diversity of language may stem from diversity of experience. The condition of snow is important to Eskimos, so they develop a wide range words for it.

This topic was taken up in 1940 by an amateur linguist named Benjamin Lee Whorf, who was actually a fire prevention officer in Connecticut and who had probably never met an Eskimo. Writing in a popular science journal *Technology Review*, he borrowed Boas's example and, without actually mentioning any Eskimo vocabulary, suggested seven different types of snow for which he asserted they had different words. This article was picked up in all sorts of places, and the Eskimo snowmobile rapidly gathered momentum.

In a 1984 trivia encyclopedia, the number of Eskimo words for snow is asserted to be nine; in a *New York Times* editorial the same year, it is given as 100; in a Cleveland weather forecast, it was confidently announced to be 200. In the science section of the *New York Times* in 1988, a paper on snowflake formation adjusts the earlier figure in saying: 'The Eskimo have about four dozen words to describe snow and ice.'

So what is the true figure? The short answer is: it is impossible to say. What counts as distinct words anyway? Are 'snow', 'snowman', 'snowflake' and 'snowdrift' four words, or just four versions of the same word 'snow'? And what do we mean by 'Eskimo' anyway? There are, after all, a number of different Inuit dialects, each of which may have its own snow vocabulary. Pullum, however, offers a good piece of advice to anyone who is subjected to ill-informed assertions regarding Eskimo snow. After mentioning his own behaviour of cringing and creeping away when such things happen, he says: 'Don't be a coward like me. Stand up and tell the speaker this: C.W. Schultz-Lorentzen's *Dictionary of the West Greenlandic Eskimo Language* (1927) gives just two possibly relevant roots: *qanik*, meaning "snow in the air" or "snowflake"; and *aput*, meaning "snow on the ground". Then add that you would be interested to know if the speaker can cite any more.'

☞ ANTARCTICA, BACON, BUTTOCKS, CHRISTMAS, DWARF, KIPLING, POTATO, SKIING, SPAIN, TIGER, YETI

SOAP OPERAS

According to a paper in the Christmas 1997 issue of the *British Medical Journal*, characters in soap operas have a considerably higher mortality rate than almost any other professional group. Not only that, but they were three times more likely to have a violent death than the average person. 'Death Rates of Characters in Soap Operas on British Television: is a Government Health Warning Required?' by Tim Crayford, Richard Hooper and Sarah Evans was, in the words of its authors, 'a hard-hitting analysis of mortality in British television soap operas'.

Their findings are startling. A character aged under 30 in *Coronation Street*, for example, has a 10 per cent chance of dying within five years of being introduced into the series. The figure for the general population is 0.3 per cent. Indeed, being a character in *Coronation Street* is more hazardous than being an oil-rig diver or bomb-disposal expert. Only Formula One drivers had a greater chance of dying, and even they were better off than *EastEnders* characters.

'Characters in these serials,' the writers conclude, 'would be advised to wear good protective clothing... and to receive regular counselling for the psychological impact of living in an environment akin to a war zone.'

SOCIALISM
☞ EDUCATION

SODOMY
In November 1998, the Supreme Court of the US state of Georgia ruled by a six-to-one majority that the state's sodomy law violates the right to privacy guaranteed by the Georgia Constitution.

SOMALIA
In Somalia, there are about two hundred times as many camels as cars.
☞ CAMEL

SONGS
According to the American Society of Composers, Authors and Publishers, the most performed songs of the 20th century were as follows:

1. 'Happy Birthday'
2. 'Tea For Two'
3. 'Moon River'
4. 'Over The Rainbow'
5. 'White Christmas'
6. 'Hello, Dolly!'
7. 'As Time Goes By'
8. 'Blue Moon'
9. 'Rhapsody In Blue'
10. 'Night And Day'
11. 'Santa Claus Is Coming To Town'
12. 'Misty'
13. 'Raindrops Keep Falling On My Head'
14. 'Mack The Knife'
15. 'The Christmas Song'
16. 'Unchained Melody'
17. 'Sweet Georgia Brown'
18. 'Winter Wonderland'
19. 'I Left My Heart In San Francisco'
20. 'I Only Have Eyes For You'
21. 'I Got Rhythm'
22. 'The Way We Were'
23. 'Stardust'
24. 'I Could Have Danced All Night'
25. 'That Old Black Magic'

☞ CHRISTMAS, CONDOM, EUROVISION SONG CONTEST, FUNERALS, INDONESIA, PHOENIX, TEXAS, THAILAND

SOUTH AFRICA

Although South Africa has only 5.2 per cent of Africa's total population, it has over 45 per cent of the continent's Internet users.

The male life expectancy in South Africa is 46.57, while the female figure is 46.54 – which means that the average man lives 11 days longer than the average woman. There are 11 official languages in South Africa: Afrikaans, English, Ndebele, Pedi, Sotho, Swazi, Tsonga, Tswana, Venda, Xhosa and Zulu.

There are 727 airports in South Africa, of which 143 have paved runways.

Every year, South Africa moves about two inches farther away from South America, including Colombia, which is the only country on earth with a higher murder rate than South Africa. Despite this, there are only 220 prisons in South Africa, placing it 14th in the world league table of most jails.

☞ ELEPHANT, GOLD, HIPPOPOTAMUS, OSTRICH, PIZZA, ROBBERY

SOUTH KOREA
The South Korean delicacy known as poshintang (literally: 'body preservation stew') is considered very good for your health. The main ingredient is dog meat.

South Korea has more heliports (204 in 2002) than any other country in the world.

SPAIN
With 12.41 robberies per 1,000 people per year, Spain is the place you are most likely to be robbed according to official figures.

In 1995, the Spanish village of Berchules in Granada celebrated the New Year on 5 August. The village had been hit by a 13-hour power cut on the previous 31 December, which had ruined their festivities. So they rescheduled them. At 12 noon, in a very un-Christmassy temperature of 39°C, the church bells sounded 12 times to ring in the New Year while villagers danced around Christmas trees and barrels churned out artificial snow made of white mousse.

☞ BARCELONA, BLYTON, CELIBACY, CHOCOLATE, COLOMBIA, COW, EUROVISION SONG CONTEST, MICKEY MOUSE, NUDISM, POPEYE, TUESDAY, VICTORIA

SPEARS, Britney (b. 1981)

Britney Spears is an anagram of 'Presbyterians'.

☞ NOSE

SPECTACLES

Until 1902, soldiers in the British army were not permitted to wear spectacles off duty.

SPEED LIMIT

In 1864, the speed limit for a steam-driven car in the UK was 2mph.

☞ MOTORING

SPIDER

It has been estimated that the total weight of insects eaten each year by spiders is greater than the weight of all the humans on earth. Each acre of land in Britain contains approximately two million spiders, which adds up to about 200,000 billion spiders in total.

The Harvestman spider may distract predators by detaching one of its own legs. The sacrificed limb twitches to keep the predator interested, while its former owner scuttles away on the other seven.

In 1973, a spider named Arabella became the first to spin a web in space, thus providing an answer to the question of whether webs can be spun in zero gravity.

In 1994, Edward Doughney patented a latex ladder to enable spiders to climb out of baths.

In 1996, it was reported that US army trials showed that silk from the Golden Orb Weaver spider is twice as strong as the current US army body armour, Kevlar.

☞ AUSTRALIA, CHRISTMAS, MEDICINE, QUEENSLAND

SPIRITUALISM

In 1942 the American National Association of Spiritualists resolved that for the duration of war no medium should ask the spirit of a departed serviceman any question whose answer might furnish military information to enemy agents in the audience.

☞ PARAPSYCHOLOGY

SPORT

★ On 14 June 1906, the British Parliament passed a bill banning women from dangerous sports after a female parachutist had fallen to her death. Three months earlier, any woman interested in sport had been urged to confine herself to 'the lighter and more graceful forms of gymnastics and athletics and to make herself supreme in those'. Sports to be avoided included hockey, lacrosse and netball.

☞ AFGHANISTAN, ALBANIA, ASHES, BASEBALL, BILLIARDS, FISHING, FOOTBALL, GOLF, HAMSTER, SEX TEST, SWEDEN, TUG-OF-WAR, URINE

SRI LANKA

Formerly Ceylon, but once known as Serendip, Sri Lanka (when it was still Ceylon) became in 1960 the first country to have a woman prime minister.

The 1995 winner of the Best Female Entrepreneur award in Sri Lanka was subsequently arrested for being a man.

☞ TRANSVESTITES

STALLION

The following extract is the summary of UK patent No.2073 from 1897, granted to E. de Pass. It is accompanied by the picture of a horse wearing an appliance with various numbered parts:

Self-abuse, preventing, *by administering electricity. An appliance to be worn by stallions for preventing masturbation consists of a surcingle 1, carrying a battery 2 and an induction coil 3, the secondary terminals of which are connected, one to the bit 10, and the other to an insulated contact-plate 15, attached to the body of the animal. When the penis is erected, it makes contact with the plate 15 and completes the secondary circuit of the induction coil. To prevent current passing when the animal is lying down, an automatic mercury switch is arranged in the primary circuit.*

STAMPS

Britain introduced postage stamps in 1840 with a standard rate of one penny for up to half an ounce.

As the originator of stamps, Britain has kept the distinction of never putting the country's name on them. The first non-royal person displayed on a British stamp was William Shakespeare in 1964. The first country to depict flying saucers on its postage stamps was Equatorial Guinea in 1975. Bugs Bunny was the first cartoon character to appear on a stamp.

Bosnia introduced the world's biggest postage stamp at a philatelic fair in Germany in 2002. It was a 50-euro stamp measuring 500 x 630mm (about 20 x 25in).

The world record for sticking stamps on envelopes is

held by Dean Gould of the UK, who stuck 309 stamps on to envelopes in five minutes. According to the US Postal Union, he is unlikely to have put on much weight by doing this: the gum on each stamp contains about one-tenth of a calorie.

By weight and size, the most valuable thing ever sold is the three-skilling Swedish stamp sold at auction for $2.3 million (about £1.5 million) in 1996. The reason it is so valuable is that it was misprinted as yellow instead of green.

☛ Throughout the world, each person posted an average of 73 items in 2001. That is a total of about 44 billion letters, cards and parcels. The country where most letters were sent per head of population is the Vatican – almost 10,000 per person every year, mostly official messages from the Holy See.

☛ DINOSAUR, FLYING SAUCERS, FORD, OKAPI, TREASON, TRISTAN DA CUNHA, St VALENTINE

STEPHENSON, George (1781–1848)

In 1825, railway pioneer George Stephenson assured a parliamentary inquiry that trains would never go faster than 25mph.

On 15 September 1830, the first fatal rail accident occurred as William Huskisson, President of the Board of Trade, stepped in front of Stephenson's *Rocket* at the opening of the Manchester–Liverpool Railway. The train had stopped to take on water and several of the passengers alighted to stretch their legs or chat. When the train restarted, most of them got out of the way but, in the words of one witness: 'Poor Mr Huskisson, less active from the effects of age and ill-health, bewildered, too, by the frantic cries of "Stop the engine! Clear the track!" that resounded on all sides, completely lost his head, looked helplessly to the right and left, and was instantaneously prostrated by the fatal machine, which dashed down like a thunderbolt upon him, and passed over his leg, smashing and mangling it in the most horrible way.'

Another contemporary account recalls: 'His first words, on being raised, were, "I have met my death," which unhappily proved true, for he expired that same evening in the parsonage of Eccles. It was cited at the time as a remarkable fact, that the Northumbrian engine, driven by George Stephenson himself, conveyed the wounded body of the unfortunate gentleman a distance of about 15 miles in 25 minutes, or at the rate of 36 miles an hour.'

STEVENSON, Robert Louis (1850–94)
☞ DONKEY

STEWART, James Maitland (1908–97)
The real name of the English actor Stewart Granger was James Stewart. He had to change it because Jimmy Stewart (whose real name was James Stewart) was already acting under that name.
☞ YETI

STOCKINGS
★ On 7 July 1942, the Vatican allowed bare-legged women to enter St Peter's in Rome for the first time.

STOMACH
☞ COW, CZECH REPUBLIC, DINOSAUR, DOLPHIN,
FROG, NAVEL

STONE
The pastime of skimming a stone across the surface of
water has been known since the time of the ancient
Greeks and the world record of 38 bounces was
achieved by J. Coleman-McGhee in 1992. Physicists,
however, had little advice to offer to stone-skippers until
2004 when Clent, Hersen and Bocquet published a
paper in *Nature* on the subject. Their conclusion, based
on monitoring the collision of a spinning disc with
water, was this: 'An angle of about 20 degrees between
the stone and the water's surface is optimal with respect
to the throwing conditions and yields the maximum
possible number of bounces.'
☞ ALCHEMY, ANORAK, BILLIARDS, FIZZY DRINKS,
PYRAMID, RUGBY, STRAW

STRAW
★ Paper drinking straws were patented by Marvin C.
Stone of Washington DC on 3 January 1888. The ideal
straw, in his opinion, was 8.5in long, with a diameter just
narrow enough to stop lemon pips being sucked up.
☞ DRUNKEN DRIVING, SANTA CLAUS

STRAWBERRY
Grown on every continent except Antarctica, the
strawberry is technically a 'false fruit'. Strictly speaking,
each of the seeds on its outside is a fruit in its own right.

On average, there are 200 seeds on every strawberry.

Nobody known why they are called 'strawberries'. The name comes from the Old English *streawberige*, where the *streaw* may refer to the straw-like runners sent out by the plant, or it may have been a reference to the seeds 'strewn' round the fruit.

American strawberries: The 'World's Largest Strawberry' can be seen atop City Hall in Strawberry Point, Iowa. In 1995 the Nebraska Supreme Court ruled that strawberries may be sold either by weight or volume, but not both by the same store at the same time.

European strawberries: The town of Wépion, Belgium, is home to the 'Musée de la Fraise' or Strawberry Museum.

Medicinal strawberries: Pregnant women used to avoid strawberries, for fear their babies would have strawberry birthmarks. Strawberry juice combined with honey is said to be a good treatment for sunburn: rub it into the skin and rinse with warm water and lemon juice.

Strawberry quotation: 'Doubtless God could have made a better berry, but doubtless God never did' – William Butler, physician, writing in praise of the strawberry in around 1600.

☞ WIMBLEDON

STRIKE
★ The longest strike in history was that of apprentice barbers in Copenhagen. It began in 1938 and was finally called off on 4 January 1961.

☞ MICKEY MOUSE

STRING

The correct word for a fear of string is 'linonophobia'. Sufferers would be well advised to steer clear of Cawker City, Kansas, where there is a ball of string that measures over 38ft in circumference and weighs more than 16,750lb.

☞ ARCHERY, FORTY-SEVEN, GARLIC, GUITAR

STRIPTEASE

The scientific term for a striptease artiste is 'ecdysiast'.

SUDAN

☞ PALINDROME

SUICIDE

In 1985 in New York, Mr Jay Shaheri, 34, filed a $20 million suit against the estate of a banker's widow who landed on him in a suicide leap from her 19th-floor apartment. He said Mrs Mildred Walker jumped 'without regard for human safety'.

According to a study in 1991, countries with high chocolate consumption have more suicides but fewer murders than non-chocoholic nations.

In 1996, psychologists reported that suicide rates in different regions of the United States correlated with the amount of country music being played on the radio: the greater the amount of country music playing, the more likely it was that suicide rates would be higher.

According to research published in 1996, women who drink coffee are less likely to commit suicide than those who do not. Though presumably if they are eating chocolate and listening to country music with their coffee, the odds could shift against them again.

In 1989 David Lester found that suicide rates by drowning were higher in American states that bordered on oceans or the Great Lakes. In 1993, however, he found no correlation between suicide rates in 27 different nations and the lengths of their coastlines. More research is clearly needed.

On 13 June 1995, an unsuccessful novelist in Taiwan, 38-year-old Huang Chia-yuan, attacked six cars with a hammer in the hope that their owners would kill him. Apparently he got the idea from a publication called *The Complete Suicide Book*. He had already unsuccessfully tried other methods it recommended. This one failed too: he was rescued from the irate car-owners by police and taken to hospital with severe bruising.

☞ CHERRY, CHOCOLATE, DISNEYLAND, HANGING, MONDAY

SUN

The Sun is 93,000,000 miles away, weighs 332,946 times as much as the Earth (meaning that the Sun amounts to 99.87 per cent of the entire mass of the solar system) and its light takes 500 seconds (8min 20sec) to reach us. It is about 75 per cent hydrogen and 25 per cent helium but about 700,000,000 tons of hydrogen are converted to helium in nuclear reactions every second. The Sun is about 4.5 billion years old and should continue burning for about another five billion years.

☞ ASTRONOMY, CUCUMBER, DOG, EUROPE, GALILEI, LAVATORIES, LOUIS XIV, MAY, MONET, PANAMA, PENGUIN, PERU, PHOENIX, SECOND, SHEEP, THIRTEEN, UMBRELLA

SUPERSTITION

According to a recent survey, shoes, trainers, necklace, T-shirts, socks and football shirts, in that order, are the most popular items worn for good luck during driving tests. Other items worn for luck by learner drivers included a tutu, clean Y-fronts and a silk G-string.

☞ BREAD, HAIR, MAY, PREGNANCY, SHOES, TEETH, THIRTEEN, VIRGINITY

SWAHILI

Swahili (the word means 'coasts') was originally a language of the coastal people of Africa. Useful phrases include:

Hakuna matata (the catchphrase of Timon and Pumba in Disney's *The Lion King*): 'No worries.'

Shikamoo!: literally meaning: 'I touch your feet', this is the respectful greeting from a young person to an old one.

Wapi choo: 'Where are the toilets?'

'Wednesday' in Swahili is *Jumatamo*, which means fifth day of the week. Confusingly, the word for 'Thursday' is *Alhamisi*, which is Arabic for fifth day of the week.

SWAT

Swat is a principality on the Northwest Frontier, which has been a part of Pakistan since 1969. The principality was ruled by the Wali of Swat (great-grandson of the Akond of Swat) until his death in 1987. Wali Miangul Jahan Zeb always wore a felt hat and an English suit. He kept Swat free from practising lawyers (up to 80 cases a day were decided by personal audience), and ate three-course meals, always starting with mulligatawny soup and ending with apple pudding.

SWAYING

To wintle is to sway gently from side to side. To shoogle is to rock back and forth with small rapid movements.

☞ BEETHOVEN

SWAZILAND

When a King of Swaziland dies, his successor is chosen from among his younger sons and must be a right-handed man with no full brother.

In 1985, a Swaziland MP said that anyone found possessing human flesh or bones without reasonable cause should be hanged in public. He claimed that the practice of human sacrifice was harming Swaziland's reputation.

In 2002, Swaziland was reported to have lost track of its only ship. The transport minister was quoted as saying, 'Our nation's merchant navy is perfectly safe. We just don't know where it is; that's all.' He went on to say, 'We believe it is in a sea somewhere.'

★ On 6 November 1995, a group of Swaziland MPs called for new laws to protect men and boys from being raped by women. They argued that the current rape laws were sexually discriminatory.

☞ GHOSTS

SWEDEN

History

In the Middle Ages the Swedish town of Hurdenburg elected its mayor by seeing which candidate's beard was selected by a louse. In the 17th century, Queen Christina of Sweden had a miniature cannon made, which she used for firing tiny cannonballs at fleas.

Culture
The town of Ystad in Sweden hosts a game of Cow Bingo every year at which visitors place bets on which of 81 squares in a field a cow will first drop a cow pat on.

Food and drink
The Swedes drink more coffee per head than any other nation and spend more per head on tomato ketchup. In Sweden, the second Thursday in August is the beginning of the crayfish season, and the third Thursday in August is the first day for selling surströmming, a dish of fermented herring. Sweden is the only country where the consumption of Coca-Cola drops at Christmas. This is due to production of a local festive drink called Julmust.

Sport
Sweden is the only country to have participated in every men's handball world championship since 1938.

Crime
A man was fined £9 for striking his 11-year-old son in Gallivare, Sweden, in 1984. The child had taken a bicycle ride in defiance of his father. It was the first conviction under the anti-child-spanking law of 1979.

Gender issues
Sweden has a lower rate of male smokers than any other European country; and, in the year 2000, was the

only country where a majority of government ministers were women.

★ On 8 May 1921, Sweden abolished capital punishment. Twelve years later, to the day, on 8 May 1933, the USA first used a gas chamber to carry out a death sentence.

Anyone born in Sweden on the last day of February in 1812 never had another birthday. Uniquely, as the country dithered between Julian and Gregorian calendars, February had 30 days in Sweden that year.

☞ ANORAK, BALLOON, BERGMAN, MILK, NAMES, PRAYER, RECRUITMENT, RUGBY, SHOPPING TROLLEYS, SKIING, STAMPS, VICTORIA

SWIMMING

'*Fornication avec l'onde*' was how Paul Valéry described swimming, and humans have been fornicating with the waves for as long as history records. 'And he will spread out his hands... as a swimmer spreads his hands out to swim,' says Isaiah (Ch. 25 v. 10). In Greek mythology too, we have the lovelorn Leander drowning in his attempt to swim the Hellespont in order to be with his girlfriend Hero. The trouble with the Hellespont is that, while it is only about a mile and a half across, the currents are so strong you have to swim five or six miles to get to the other side. Byron managed it in an hour and 10 minutes on 3 May 1810 and wrote, when he had dried himself off: 'I plume myself on this achievement more than I could possibly do any kind of glory, political, poetical, rhetorical.'

Other notable names in the history of swimming include the following:

Robert Hawker, a late-19th-century vicar of Mortenstow, who liked to sit on a rock off the coast at Bude, wearing only a seaweed wig and an oilskin wrapped around his legs, trying to persuade holidaymakers he was a mermaid.

Matthew Webb (1848–83), known as 'Captain Webb', who, even before he became the first man to swim the Channel, had won a wager that he could remain in the sea longer than a Newfoundland dog. After Webb had remained in the water for an hour and a half, it was reported that 'the poor brute [the dog, presumably] was nearly drowned'. His Channel swim took him nearly 22 hours and a distance of about 40 miles. He was coated in a protective layer of porpoise fat.

Mercedes Gleitze (1900–79), the first Englishwoman to swim the Channel, was also the first person to swim the Straits of Gibraltar. In 1932, she broke her own endurance record, swimming for 46 hours in municipal baths, supported by the community singing of well-wishers. The money she earned from swimming enabled her to set up the Mercedes Gleitze Homes for Destitute Men and Women.

Sir Arthur Elvin (1899–1957), who joined the Royal Flying Corps in World War I, was shot down and taken prisoner. He escaped, but was recaptured 'because he knew neither French nor German and could not swim'. This gave him the ambition to build a public swimming pool, which he realised with the launch of the Empire Pool, Wembley, and led to his later founding Wembley Stadium.

Christopher Middleton (1560–1628), author, in

1595, of 'A Short Introduction for to Learn to Swimme, gathered out of Master Digbies [Everard Digby] Booke of the Art of Swimming, and translated into English for the better instruction of those who understand not the Latin tongue.'

As the quotation from Isaiah testifies, early swimmers used the breaststroke. The 'overarm' stroke was considered effective only over short distances. In 1902, however, J.A. Jarvis wrote: 'I am firmly convinced that the present records at all distances will be wiped out and fresh ones put in their place by "trudgers".' Trudgers were practitioners of the trudgen (or trudgeon), a cumbersome overarm stroke introduced into Britain by John Trudgen, who had been taught it by the natives of Buenos Aires in 1863. In the same year that Jarvis made his prediction, however, Richard Cavill, an Australian, demonstrated the front crawl, and trudging vanished forever. The next major improvement came with the invention of the butterfly stroke by the German Eric Rademacher, in 1926. Nobody took much notice, however, until 1933, when an American, Henry Myers, used it as a means of legal cheating in breaststroke races. It took the authorities until 1953 before the laws were sorted out and butterfly was recognised as a distinct stroke.

More dates:

1377: First appearance of word 'swymmynge'
1742: England's first indoor pool opened
1961: Channel swum both ways without stopping
1962: Channel swum under water

1970: Rules of water polo drafted
1981: First triple-crossing of the Channel

☞ ALEXANDER III, BUFFALO, BYRON, CHANNEL, DUCK, GIRAFFE, GOLDFISH, ISRAEL, MOOSE, OLYMPIC GAMES, POLAR BEAR, QUEEN MARY, SEAL, SLOTH

St SWITHUN (or Swithin, c.800–62)

'St Swithin's Day, if thou dost rain,
For forty days it will remain;
St Swithin's Day, if thou be fair,
For forty days 'twill rain na mair.'

★ The legend connecting St Swithin's Day with the weather dates back to 15 July 971, when the bones of St Swithun, bishop of Winchester (the *Dictionary of National Biography* firmly castigates 'Swithin' as a misspelling) were scheduled to be moved from an unmarked grave outside his church to a consecrated site within the walls of the building. On that day, however, it is said to have poured with rain, and continued to do so for the next 40 days, which was taken as a sign that his bones preferred to remain where they were.

That account, however, seems to be a piece of 16th-century romanticism at variance with contemporaneous accounts of the event. Back in the 10th century, it was generally thought that Swithun had been overjoyed at having his bones reburied, and he was credited with hundreds of miracles supposedly performed in gratitude.

The long-range weather forecast associated with Swithun also fails to stand up to scrutiny. An analysis was published in 1894 calculating the number of rainy days in the 40 days following 15 July. After a wet St Swithun's Day, there were an average of 18.5 rainy days, while for a dry 15 July, the rainy score was slightly higher at 19.25.

Whatever the statistics show, St Swithun did give Britain its own meteorological saint's day to match those of St Medard (8 June) in France, St Godelieve (6 July) in Belgium, and the Day of the Seven Sleepers (27 June) in Germany, all of which carry a similar tradition of 40-day, long-range weather forecasts. And none of those works either. In fact, records suggest that it has not rained for forty days since the Great Flood.

☞ CELIBACY

SWITZERLAND
Genetically modified chocolate is illegal in Switzerland.
★ On 16 July 1661, Switzerland became the first country in Europe to issue banknotes.
☞ COW, MICKEY MOUSE, MOUNTAINEERING, SANTA CLAUS, SKIING, SNAIL, VATICAN

SYDNEY
Sixteen men died during the building of Sydney Harbour Bridge. The only one to survive a fall from the bridge into the water was Vincent Kelly, who was awarded a medal for 'Preserving His Own Life'.
☞ AUSTRALIA, LATVIA

SYPHILIS
☞ BAUDELAIRE, St GEORGE

TABLE MANNERS
Louis XIV of France ordered that table knives have rounded, not pointed ends, to stop them being used as daggers during mealtime arguments.

TABLOID
★ The word 'tabloid' was originally coined and registered on 14 March 1884 as a trademark by Henry Solomon Wellcome; at the time it was a proprietary brand name for pills, medicine chests, food, tea and publications. The phrase 'tabloid journalism' was first used in 1901.

TAIWAN
In 1995, the Taiwanese government announced that it would allow people to omit the number four from their addresses because the word for 'four' sounds like the word for 'death'.

The following year, the Taiwanese government appealed to the people to eat more garlic. Excess production had caused a drastic fall in prices.

The first nude wedding in Taiwan was held on 19 October 1997. The bride was a stripper and former parliamentary candidate.

☞ LAVATORIES, MONKEY, SUICIDE, VATICAN

TANZANIA
☞ LION

TARANTINO, Quentin (b. 1963)
The word 'fuck' occurs 155 times in Quentin Tarantino's *Pulp Fiction* and 177 times in *Reservoir Dogs*. All of the clocks on the wall in the pawn shop scene in *Pulp Fiction* are stuck at 4:20.

☞ ANCHOVY

TATTOO
The first tattoos were carried out by the Egyptians, possibly as early as 4000BC. The word 'tattoo' (signifying body-art) comes from a Samoan word *ta-tau*. This has nothing to do with the word 'tattoo' (meaning a military drum or bugle signal), which comes from the Dutch *taptoe* – to close the tap (of a wine cask).

Statistics show that during World War II, a tattooed American was one-and-a-half times more likely to be rejected for military service than an untattooed one, and a man with a tattoo of a naked woman was more likely to be rejected than a man with a flag or landscape tattoo.

This is quite the opposite of the traditional view in New Zealand, where Maoris regard a tattooed chin as a sign of high rank.

King Harold of England, who was slain at the Battle of Hastings, had a tattoo over his heart that read: 'Edith and England'.

Bookkeeper, bookkeeping and tattooee are the only English words with three consecutive pairs of double letters – but tattooee is not in most dictionaries.

First-time receivers of a tattoo are known to tattooers as 'Freshcuts'.

TAX

Police in Poland hunting the killers of a taxman whose dismembered body was found in two suitcases in 1986 arrested a man and a woman he visited just before disappearing. They owed more than 12,000 zlotys (£50) in arrears. In 2006, the Australian tax office ruled that sex toys are tax deductible for prostitutes.

The total UK government income from all forms of taxation in 1900 was £108,336,193. This is less than half the cost of running Scottish prisons in 2000.

'In this world, nothing can be said to be certain except death and taxes' – Benjamin Franklin.

☛ The Greek grammarian Julius Pollux (180–238) listed 33 terms of abuse for tax collectors in his *Onomasticon*.

☞ ALBANIA, BERGMAN, BISCUIT, GODIVA, HAIR, HAT, INCOME TAX, ITALY, St MATTHEW, OSTRICH

TAXI

Until 1976, when the relevant piece of old legislation was finally repealed, London taxi drivers were breaking the law if they did not carry a bale of hay and a sack of oats in their cabs to feed the horses.

TAXIDERMY
The oldest stuffed bird in existence is a parrot buried in Westminster Abbey. It was the companion of Frances Theresa, Duchess of Richmond.

TEA
According to legend, tea was discovered by the Chinese emperor Shen Nung in 2737BC.

Since the Way of Tea was established in the 16th century, there have been only 15 grand masters of Japanese tea.

Iced tea was first served during a heatwave at the St Louis World Fair in 1904, which was also the year of invention of the banana split and the paper plate.

☞ BISCUIT, BRAZIL, COCOA, COFFEE, SONGS, TABLOID, ZAMBIA

TEETH

Famous teeth
Only one in 2,000 babies is born with teeth, though Richard III, Napoleon Bonaparte, Louis XIV and Julius Caesar shared that distinction. George Washington soaked his dentures in port overnight to improve their taste. He had several sets, in which elephant tusks, lead, cow teeth, hippo teeth, human teeth and possibly a walrus tusk all played their parts. He had two of his own teeth when he died, which is one fewer than Stalin.

Brushed teeth
A world record for simultaneous tooth-brushing was set in 2006 in Manila by 10,800 schoolchildren.

Teeth in literature
'The husband was a teetotaller, there was no other woman, and the conduct complained of was that he drifted into the habit of winding up every meal by taking out his false teeth and hurling them at his wife' – Arthur Conan Doyle, 'A Case of Identity'.

Misquoted teeth
'My bone cleaveth to my skin and to my flesh, and I am escaped with the skin of my teeth' – Job, 19:20. Not *by* the skin of my teeth.

Miscounted teeth
'Males have more teeth than females in the case of men, sheep, goats and swine' – *Aristotle, History of Animals*. As Bertrand Russell pointed out, Aristotle could have avoided the error by the simple expedient of 'asking Mrs Aristotle to open her mouth'.

Ominous teeth
Dreaming about teeth falling out foretells the death of a friend (old English superstition). Dreaming about teeth falling out indicates fear of sexual impotence (modern Freudian superstition).

A gap between the front teeth is a sign of future richness or a propensity to travel.

When a milk tooth falls out, you should burn it to prevent a dog finding and eating it, which would ensure that a dog's tooth grows in its place. (This superstition long pre-dates that of the Tooth Fairy, who is a modern import from the United States.)

DENTAL HEROES

Sir Edwin Saunders (1814–1901), who in 1883 became the first dentist to be knighted. He also invented a machine for sweeping city streets.

Mrs Hamilton, actress (fl. 1745–72), a leading lady of the English stage until, according to the *Dictionary of National Biography*: 'An accident to her false teeth as she played Lady Brumpton turned applause into ridicule.' She died in poverty and obscurity.

Edwin Thomas Truman (1818–1905), whose work on gutta-percha for insulating an Atlantic cable led to a patent for gutta-percha tooth fillings. He was also famed for his surgical success at correcting a cleft palate.

➤ The numbat, a west Australian marsupial, has 52 permanent teeth, the most of any land mammal. It doesn't use them, but swallows ants and termites whole.

☞ AARDVARK, St APOLLONIA, AUGUSTUS, COSMETICS, DINOSAUR, ELIZABETH I, HEDGEHOG, LIECHTENSTEIN, LOUIS XIV, MARQUESAS ISLANDS, MONKEY, PLATYPUS, SHARK, SNAIL, TOOTHPASTE

TELEPHONE

There are over a billion telephone lines in the world.

☞ BELL, BURNT FOOD, EDISON, LUXEMBOURG

TELEVISION

The UK record TV audience was achieved by the wedding of Prince Charles and Diana Spencer in 1981. Diana's funeral is fifth on the list of most-watched programmes. Numbers two, three and four are all football matches.

People in the UK aged over four spend an average of 26 hours a week watching television – which adds up to over 11 years in an average lifetime.

The average American sees 13,000 deaths on television between the ages of five and 14. Including the murders, the crimes committed on-screen in an average week's viewing would merit 6,000 years in prison. Despite this, a survey in the 1980s reported that 44 per cent of American children prefer the television to Daddy.

According to a poll in 2001, the top ten favourite snacks to eat while watching television are:

1. Crisps
2. Chocolate bars
3. Fresh fruit
4. Sandwich
5. Ice cream
6. Nuts
7. Bread or toast
8. Other sweets
9. Savoury biscuits
10. Cheese

★ The first UK television advert was for Gibbs SR toothpaste on 22 September 1955.

☛ There are 844 televisions per 1,000 people in the US. According to a survey in the UK in 2004, the number of televisions equalled the number of people.

☞ CINEMA, CLARE, DIANA, MANILOW, MONKEY, MOZART, POTATO, SOAP OPERA, TUNISIA

TEMPERATURE
The highest temperature ever recorded in the shade

was 57.8°C (136°F) in Libya on 13 September 1922.
☞ CRICKET, CUCUMBER, LION, MARS, SPAIN, WIMBLEDON

TENNIS

Lawn tennis was patented under the name 'Sphairistike' by Major Walter Wingfield in 1874, though it grew out of the much older game of real (or royal) Tennis, which was played indoors in long, narrow rooms. The word tennis probably comes from the French *tenez!* ('take' or 'receive'), a warning shouted by the server.

Wingfield's game was much as we know it today, but it was played on an hour-glass-shaped court, 30ft across at its widest but only 20ft at the net. He sold Sphairistike sets, comprising ball, four racquets and netting to mark out the court, for five guineas. The rectangular court arrived in 1875 when the All England Croquet Club at Wimbledon decided to add tennis (as it was by then being called) to its repertoire. Twenty-two players paid a guinea (£1.05) each to enter the first tournament and Spencer Gore became the first Wimbledon champion. He said he didn't think this new game would catch on.

When lawn tennis was introduced by the British to the King and Queen of Korea in 1892, Queen Min is said to have commented, 'These Englishmen are becoming very hot. Why do they not have their servants do it?'

Goran Ivanisevic is the only Wimbledon champion whose entire name is a strict alternation of consonants and vowels. A smile by him at Wimbledon won a punter £1,000 in 1995. Ladbroke's had offered good odds against the Croatian smiling on Centre Court.

Sewing a tennis ball into the back of a person's pyjamas is a recommended remedy for snoring.

Charles VIII of France died in 1498 after hitting his head on a lintel above a door leading to a tennis court.

According to research published in 1998, drinking caffeine-laced fluids between points improves the accuracy and results of women tennis players but has no effect on men.

In a Scottish Gas survey in 1999, 1 per cent of women said Tim Henman was the man they would most like to share a bath with.

☛ The ball is only in play for about 20 minutes of an average two-and-a-half-hour tennis match.

★ Elizabeth Ryan, winner of 19 Wimbledon titles, died on 6 July 1979. The following day, Billie-Jean King overtook her record by taking her 20th title.

☞ ALBANIA, AUSTRIA, CUBA, FISHING, GEORGE VI, THAILAND, WHITE HOUSE, WIMBLEDON

TENNYSON, Alfred Lord (1809–92)

Tennyson's last words were: 'I have opened it.' Nobody knows what he was talking about.

★ He spoke them on 6 October 1892.
☞ BABBAGE

TERRAPIN

The name of the terrapin comes from an Algonquin Indian word meaning 'edible'.

TESTICLE

Greek statues of naked males are anatomically inaccurate,

according to a paper in the science journal *Nature* in 1976. In a short contribution entitled 'Scrotal Asymmetry in Man and in Ancient Sculpture', Chris McManus pointed out that the left testicles in Greek statues are always larger and lower than their companions. They were correct about the left being larger, but it is the smaller right testicles which are lower. The scientific instrument for gauging the size of testicles is called an orchidometer.
☞ BEAVER

TEXAS
Texas is the only state in the USA that was a country in its own right. That is why the Texan state flag is the only one permitted by federal law to be flown at the same height as the Stars and Stripes. The third line of the Texas state song is: 'Boldest and grandest, withstanding every test'. The first word was changed from 'Largest' to 'Boldest' when Alaska became a state in 1959.
☞ BUSH, FERRARI, POPEYE, SCARECROW, SEXUAL HARASSMENT, WORM

THACKERAY, William Makepeace (1811–63)
☞ DONKEY, TOURISM

THAILAND
The official name of Bangkok is 'Krung Thep Maha Nakhon Amon Rattanakosin Mahinthara Yutthaya Mahadilokphop Noppharat Ratchathani Burirom Udom Ratchaniwet Maha Sathan Amon Phiman Awatan Sathit Sakkathattiya Witsanukam Prasit' (usually abbreviated to 'Krung Thep'). Loosely translated, this becomes 'The

City of Angels, the Great City, the Residence of the Emerald Buddha, the Capital of the World Endowed with Nine Precious Gems, the Happy City Abounding in Enormous Royal Palaces which Resemble the Heavenly Abode wherein Dwell the Reincarnated Gods, a City Given by Indra and Built by Witsanukam'. This name is generally accepted as the longest name of any capital city in the world, though there is debate about precisely how many letters it has, because it is itself a transliteration from the Thai alphabet and several different versions are in circulation. The one used above results in 169 letters; other sources suggest a total of 167, which by coincidence equals the number of singles tennis titles won by Martina Navratilova.

The song 'One Night in Bangkok', from the musical *Chess*, was banned in May 1985 from a TV channel and government radio station in Thailand because the lyrics could 'cause misunderstanding about Thai society'.

A world record for vasectomies was claimed in Bangkok in December 1983 when 50 doctors held a nine-hour state-sponsored vasectomy session that attracted 1,190 patients.

★ Thailand, appropriately enough, unveiled the world's longest tie on 15 May 1995. It was 99.6m long and 6m wide, and had been made to honour King Bhumibol's 50 years on the throne of Thailand.

☞ BUFFALO, CAT, SIAM, VALENTINE

THAMES
The Debris Clearance Operation of the Port of London Authority removes around a thousand tonnes of litter

each year from the Thames. In the 19th century, sewage in the Thames was so bad that 1858 was known as the year of the Great Stink. Since recent cleaning of the river, 119 species of fish have been found in the Thames. There are 396 sewage works along the Thames, cleaning the sewage and returning the water to the river. This is necessary because a drop of rain falling into the Thames at its source will have been drunk by as many as eight people before it reaches the sea.

☞ POLAR BEAR, UNIVERSITIES

THATCHER, Margaret Hilda (b. 1925)
☞ BUSH, MANDELA

THERBLIG
A therblig is the basic unit used in time-and-motion studies of operational efficiency. A therblig may be any one of 18 standard proto-activities as listed by the American psychologists Frank and Lillian Gilbreth around 1920. (The word 'therblig' is, give or take a lisp, their surname spelled backwards.) The complete list is as follows: search, find, select, grasp, hold, position, assemble, use, disassemble, inspect, transport loaded, transport unloaded, pre-position for next operation, release load, unavoidable delay, avoidable delay, plan, and rest for overcoming fatigue. Every operation is a combination of these basic components and the number of them is its rating in therbligs.

THIRTEEN
Fear of the number 13 is called triskaidekaphobia. Fear of Friday the 13th is paraskevidekatriaphobia.

Fear of the number 13 was known in both Old Norse and Ancient Babylonian myths. Old Norse mythology tells of a banquet that ended in disaster after Loki arrived as an uninvited guest, raising the total number from 12 to 13. For the Babylonians the fear was linked to a belief that the Sun needed to be kept separate from the 12 Zodiac signs.

According to the 1894 edition of *Brewer's Phrase And Fable*: 'The Turks so disliked the number 13 the word is almost expunged from their vocabulary.'

In Christian tradition, fear of Friday the 13th stems from the day of the Crucifixion (Friday) and the number at the Last Supper (13). Despite these origins, the Friday the 13th superstition dates back only to the Middle Ages.

No more than three Friday the 13ths can occur in a single year. The last year that had three Friday the 13ths was 1998; the next time it will happen is 2009.

Louis XIII of France (1601–43) was so fond of the number 13 that he married 13-year-old Anna of Austria. By the 19th century, however, the number had become so feared that a society of French aristocrats was formed called the quatorziennes ('14ths'), who were available to come at short notice to dinners where 13 had turned up.

Even in the modern supposedly enlightened age, it has been estimated that fear of the number 13 costs the US economy a billion dollars a year in absenteeism, cancellations and reduced commerce on the 13th days of the months.

Anyone seeking supporting evidence for the superstition, however, need look no further than the British National Lottery, where the number 13 has been picked less frequently than any other.

The wedding anniversary corresponding to 13 years' marriage is called a Lace Wedding.

☛ The spoil from digging the Channel Tunnel would have filled Wembley Stadium 13 times.

☞ BAR CODES, CALENDAR, FASHION, FRUITCAKE, HOUSEWIVES, KANGAROO, LOVE, OLYMPIC GAMES, PREGNANCY, SNAIL, TIE KNOTS, St VALENTINE

THOR

The Norse god Thor, after whom Thursday is named, was the eldest son of Odin, the chief of the gods. He was primarily god of thunder but also god of strength, agriculture, farmers, free men, rain and fertility. He had a really bad temper.

His main weapon was a hammer called Mjollnir, which returned to his hand after being thrown. This hammer is a symbol of fertility and a model of it is placed in the lap of the bride in traditional wedding ceremonies in Nordic countries. Thor couldn't throw his hammer without the aid of his magic belt Megingjardir, which doubled his power.

Thor was the only god not allowed to cross Bifrost, the bridge connecting the world of men with the world of the gods. It was feared that his lightning, or the very heat of his presence, might destroy it.

Thor rode in a chariot drawn by two fierce billygoats named Tanngniost ('Toothgnasher') and Tanngrisnir ('Toothgrinder'). These goats could be killed and eaten, and they would be revived, good as new, the next day. The rolling of the wheels of Thor's goat-drawn chariot is said to create thunder.

In the great end-of-the-world battle at Ragnarok, Thor fights the Wyrm of Midgard, a serpent whose body encircles the whole world. Both are killed.

THUNDER

If you want to hear the sound of thunder, the best place to go is Tororo, Uganda, where it thunders for 251 days a year.

☞ DINOSAUR, HIPPOPOTAMUS, THOR, WEATHER

TIBET

Bumping foreheads is part of a traditional handshake in Tibet.

☞ YETI

TIE KNOTS

According to the Cambridge physicists Thomas Fink and Yong Mao, there are 85 possible ways to knot a conventional tie, but only 13 of them are aesthetically pleasing. Those found to pass the aesthetic tests are the knots known as the Oriental, the Four-in-Hand, the Kelvin, the Nicky, the Victoria, the half-Windsor, the St Andrew, the Plattsburgh, the Cavendish, the Windsor, the Grantchester, the Hanover, and the Balthus. The Pratt and the Christensen are excluded from the list as they are less well-balanced than knots of comparable complexity.

A book entitled *L'Art de la Toilette*, published in 1830, listed 72 ways to tie a cravat.

'A well-tied tie is the first serious step in life' – Oscar Wilde (1891).

'There is no time, sir, at which ties do not matter' – Jeeves to Bertie Wooster in P.G. Wodehouse's 'Jeeves and the Impending Doom' (1926).

TIGER
The tiger not only has striped fur, its skin is striped too. ★ On 6 December 1995, the Isle of Wight Zoo announced that in view of the bad weather it would be giving special training to its Siberian tigers because they had never seen snow before.

☞ BRONTE, PREGNANCY, QUEENSLAND, ROBBERY

TINS
Tinned food originated with a prize offered by Napoleon Bonaparte in 1795 for a method of food preservation to feed his armies on long campaigns. Although modern tinned food for general consumption had begun to appear in 1810, the modern tin-opener was not invented until 1870.

☞ BISCUIT, FOOD, NAPOLEON BONAPARTE, SHOPPING TROLLEYS

TOAST
According to research at Leeds University, to produce a perfect slice of buttered toast, the bread needs to be heated to at least 120°C, and the butter should be used straight from the fridge, applied unevenly within two minutes of the bread coming out of the toaster. The amount of butter should be about one-seventeenth the thickness of the bread.

☞ BURNT FOOD, MOLE, TELEVISION

TOBACCO

Walter Raleigh brought the first tobacco from Virginia to England on 27 July 1586.

☞ BEAVER, BURIAL

TOGO

In 1984 the Togo Cabinet passed a law forbidding sexual relations with schoolgirls because of the growing number of teenage pregnancies.

TOILET

Some 200 delegates from Europe, North America and Asia attended the first World Toilet Summit of the World Toilet Organisation in Singapore in 2001.

There is a French patent of 1987 for a 'Personal weighing device on toilet seat'.

☞ BRAZIL, LAVATORIES, LIGHT BULB, PAPER, RAILWAY, RECRUITMENT, SUN

TOKYO

If all the household garbage produced in one day in Tokyo were piled into a square column with base 1ft wide, it would be three times as high as Mount Everest.

☞ HORSE, HOT DOG, JAPAN, PAPER, SMOKING, TUNA

TOMATO

The first tomatoes imported into Europe were golden in colour, which led to them being nicknamed 'golden apples'. The Italian for tomato is still *pomodoro* – 'apple of gold'. Until 1820, North Americans believed that tomatoes were poisonous.

☛ There are nine main varieties of tomato: beefsteak, globe, plum, green, cherry, pear, currant, purple and striped.

☞ HANGOVER, PIZZA, SWEDEN

TOOTHPASTE

Washington Wentworth Sheffield of Connecticut is generally credited with inventing the toothpaste tube in 1892, but while his company was the first to sell toothpaste in squeezable tubes, his claim to have invented the tubes themselves is highly dubious. The collapsible metal tube was in fact patented in 1841 by John Goffe Rand, an American artist living in England. He used it as a handy way of storing his paints. It was only after Washington Sheffield's son Lucius had seen such paint tubes in use in France that the idea was adapted for toothpaste.

Toothpaste and toothbrushes themselves have an even vaguer history. William Addis is often credited with the invention of the toothbrush around 1771. Some say he came up with idea while in Newgate Prison, but at best this was a reinvention of an idea that had been known to the Chinese since around 1500.

In ancient Egypt, teeth were rubbed clean with various concoctions. Among the ingredients listed were the ash of burned ox hoofs, powdered egg shells, pumice and myrrh. The ancient Romans preferred powdered fruit, dried flowers and talcum powder, but were also known to use powdered flint, pumice and crushed oyster shell, often in a suspension of urine.

Fingers were used to apply the concoction, then

twigs, then twigs with cloth wrapped round them, and from this the toothbrush evolved.

☞ TELEVISION

TOOTHPICK

There is evidence that the use of toothpicks goes back to Neanderthal times, but the mass production of toothpicks began in 1869 with the invention by Charles Forster of Boston, Massachusetts, of a toothpick-making machine. He created demand for his product by having Harvard students loudly ask for toothpicks after eating their meals at local restaurants. Forster set up a wooden toothpick factory in Maine in 1887, where he found good supplies of white birch, the favoured wood for toothpicks.

Great toothpick achievements include Joe King's feat of building a 23ft-high likeness of the Eiffel Tower out of 111,000 toothpicks, and a 16ft-long replica of the luxury liner *Lusitania* made by Wayne Kusy of Evanston, Illinois, with 193,000 toothpicks.

☞ AGATHOCLES

TORTOISE

In 1997, Australian scientists announced an important discovery concerning the Fitzroy River tortoise, *Rheodytes leukops*: it breathes through its mouth on land and through its bottom when under water.

☞ AESCHYLUS

TOURISM

Tourism began on 5 July 1841, when Thomas Cook organised his first trip for fellow members of his local temperance association in Market Harborough to attend a gathering in Loughborough. He arranged, with the Midland railway, the running of a special train, and 570 passengers went on the first publicly advertised excursion to Leicester and back, for a shilling each.

There had been tourists before Thomas Cook, however. There is some evidence of island-hopping in the Pacific some 20,000 years ago, though the sea levels may then have been low enough for them to have walked over. Also, since tourism may be defined as 'travelling for pleasure' we can never be sure that our ancestors were true tourists.

Marco Polo was definitely a tourist, even taking three and a half years over his sea voyage home in 1292 rather than going back to work. Ibn Battuta (1304–77) was another inveterate traveller, who went on a pilgrimage to Mecca in 1326, then spent the next 30 years wandering around the entire Islamic world.

The industry of tourism, however, undoubtedly began with Thomas Cook. His inaugural one-shilling trip to Leicester soon grew into regular jaunts and a one-guinea excursion to Glasgow in 1845, where the first tourists were welcomed with salutes from cannon and band music. His first package holiday abroad was a six-day trip to Paris, starting at London Bridge on 17 May 1861.

The growth of tourism met with some initial resistance, however, and one journalist maintained in 1865 that an early party of British holidaymakers were in fact convicts whom the Australians had refused to accept and whom the British government were dropping surreptitiously in Italian cities. The Italians did not see the joke, and Cook appealed to Lord Clarendon, the foreign secretary, for redress for the damage to his business caused by the journalist's remarks. His Lordship offered only sympathy.

Curiously, tourism is one area where language appears to have moved faster than technology. The word 'tourist' dates back at least as far as 1780 and the word 'tourism' was established by 1811. Writing of the West of Ireland in 1843, Thackeray commented: 'No doubt, ere long... the rush of London tourism will come this way.' The first 'day-tripper', however, was spotted in 1897.

Tourism now earns Britain about £8 billion a year in foreign currency, is responsible for about 4 per cent of our GDP, and provides about 1.5 million jobs. The annual value of the Loch Ness monster alone to Scottish tourism is estimated at £5 million.

The United States earns more than any other country from tourism (close to $55 billion a year) but its tourists also spend most (about $40 billion). The Japanese, however, spend most on shopping when they go abroad. The most popular tourist attraction in Britain is Alton Towers, followed by Madame Tussaud's and the Tower of London.

Why do they do it? Psychology has little light to throw on the subject. Sandor Ferenczi, a follower of Freud, wrote of the thrills and challenge of tourism, but it seems he was concerned primarily with mountain climbing. More recent research has shown that terrorism significantly reduced Spanish tourism between 1970 and 1988, but statistical analysis has shown that tourism has no measurable effect on terrorism. When the average tourist stays in a hotel, he or she is most likely to leave behind a nightdress, break a glass and steal a towel.

At any given moment there are approximately 350,000 people flying in aeroplanes. Most of them are tourists.
☞ DRACULA

TRAFFIC LIGHTS

The world's first traffic lights were a gas-powered contraption erected just off Parliament Square in London in December 1868 and designed to make it easier for MPs to reach the House of Commons. They took the form of a revolving lantern with red and green signals, controlled by a lever that had to be operated by a police constable. This was not without risk and, on 2 January 1869, the whole thing exploded, causing severe injuries to the policeman. This experience did not encourage a repeat of the experiment elsewhere. It was finally removed in 1872, and it took over half a century before Britain was prepared to put its trust in traffic lights again.

The United States had her first set working on 5 August 1914 in Cleveland, Ohio, at the crossroads formed by Euclid Avenue and 105th Street. They were red and green, with a warning buzzer too. By 1918, New York had a set with red, green and amber, a colour scheme Britain also adopted for its first electric traffic lights at the junction of St James's St and Piccadilly in 1926.
☞ ALBANIA, LIFETIME

TRANSPLANTATION

The World Transplant Games have been organised under

the aegis of the World Transplant Games Federation (WTGF) since 1978. The 14th such Games were held in Nancy, France, in 2003 and attracted 1,500 athletes and competitors from 70 countries. Sadly these Games also saw the first death during the series when a contestant in the badminton event, who had recovered from a successful kidney transplant, collapsed and died of a heart attack.

The first hand transplants were in France and the United States in 1999.

After Russian surgeon Valery Agafonov had part of his pelvic bone transplanted in 1997 to replace a thumb mangled in an accident, bank officials said his signature was exactly the same as before.

In 1979 the *National Enquirer* offered Dr Christian Barnard $250,000 to transplant a human head.

☞ DONKEY, GRAPEFRUIT, KNEES

TRANSPORT

The earliest known wheel is to be seen on a pictogram in Uruk, Mesopotamia, dating back to around 3500BC. A picture of a sled is followed by another of an almost identical sled on wheels. Sailing ships, however, had already been around for much longer. Some say that the Aborigines reached Australia by sea in around 40,000BC.

The next important invention was the Sedan chair, a closed one-seater vehicle supported on poles and carried by two bearers. There is considerably less support, however, for Dr Johnson's suggestion of a connection with the town of Sedan in France. An etymological link with the Latin *sedere*, to sit, is more likely.

In 1634 an exclusive right was granted to Sir Sanders Duncome to supply 'covered chairs (called sedans)' for British use, though they had been in use in Naples since the late 16th century. Jane (or Jean) Elliott (1727–1805), poet and third daughter of the second baronet of Minto, was said to have been the last woman in Edinburgh to make regular use of her own sedan chair.

In 1818, Denis Johnson of Long Acre took out an English patent for the Velocipede – at the time, a sort of hobby horse, though by 1850 the word was also being used to describe something closer to a bicycle or tricycle. The first word for cyclists appeared in 1869: they were called 'Velocipedestrians'.

Although the invention of the pedal bicycle was commonly attributed to one Gavin Dalzell of Lesmahagow, the credit is really due to Kirkpatrick MacMillan (1812–78), whose half-a-hundredweight pedal, rod and crankshaft mechanism hit the roads of Dumfries in Scotland in 1839. Three years later, he rode the 70 miles into Glasgow, becoming, in the course of his trip, one of the first traffic felons when he was fined five shillings for causing a slight injury to a girl who ran across his path.

In 1888 an Act was passed classifying the bicycle as a carriage, thus giving it full rights to use British roads. From then until 1930, however, it was mandatory, while riding a bike, to ring your bell non-stop.

The petrol-driven car arrived in 1896 (with the invention of the electric starter responsible, more than anything else, for driving steam-powered vehicles off the roads). About 10 years earlier, a Frenchman, Monsieur

Huret, had invented a vehicle powered by dogs on treadmills, but early animal liberationists objected too strongly for it to gain popular acceptance.

All this time, however, the trains had been speeding ahead, with the world's first passenger service causing the world's first railway fatality on its inaugural run in 1830 between Liverpool and Manchester (see STEPHENSON).

Which brings us to underground trains (1890), escalators (1911), commercial airliners (1938) and Concorde (which came into service in 1976).

And the future? Well, here are some recent transport improvements registered at the European Patent Office:

- Foldable and portable bicycle convertable into a shopping cart (1981).
- Sail propulsion bicycle (1983).
- Support for suspending a bicycle or the like from a wall (1984).
- Means for exercising dogs from a bicycle (1986).
- Bicycle tent (1992).

☞ BISCUIT, GLADSTONE, JAPAN, MOTORING, SWAZILAND, THERBLIG, TURKEY (country)

TRANSVESTITES

★ On 20 June 1995, the Cultural Bureau in the city of Shen-yang, China, banned transvestite shows on the grounds that they had no artistic merit.

★ On 12 April 1997, Sattambije Sriyaratne, a 36-year-old Sri Lankan, was reported to have been arrested for being a man. He had posed as a woman for three years and had won an award as his country's best female entrepreneur.

☞ ALCOHOL, CAMBODIA, D'EON

TRAPPIST
☞ FRUITCAKE

TREASON
Under the 1848 Treason Felony Act, it is a serious offence to publish an article advocating the abolition of the monarchy. A challenge to the legality of this Act was rejected by the House of Lords in 2003.

It is officially an act of treason to stick a stamp with the Queen's head on it upside down on an envelope.

☞ CAPITAL PUNISHMENT, PARLIAMENT

TREVINO, Lee (b. 1939)
Golf champion Lee Trevino was struck by lightning during the 1975 Western Open golf tournament in Chicago.

TRISTAN DA CUNHA
Potatoes were used as currency on the island of Tristan da Cunha until 1942. Even four years later when the island issued its first stamps, each stamp still bore a value in potatoes.

TRIVIA
If you wish to praise this book, the word you seek may well be 'adoxography' – fine writing on a trivial subject.

☞ SNOW

TROUSERS

In October 1812, St John's and Trinity Colleges in Cambridge issued orders that students appearing in hall or chapel in pantaloons or trousers should be considered as absent.

★ On 24 June 1985, Colonel Patrick Baudry of Air France, travelling on the space shuttle *Discovery*, announced his own discovery that: 'In zero G you can put your trousers on two legs at a time.'

Under the earth's gravitational pull, the question of which leg to put into trousers first has long been a matter of dispute. According to old Sussex folklore, putting your socks and trousers on right-leg first can prevent toothache. According to old Shropshire folklore, however, putting your trousers on right-leg first invites bad luck. Research has shown that right-handed men generally put trousers on with the right leg leading; left-handed men go left-leg first.

Although the word 'trousers' dates back to 1599, the singular 'trouser', meaning one leg of a pair of trousers, dates back only to 1893.

'You should never have your best trousers on when you go out to fight for freedom and truth' – Henrik Ibsen.
☞ ALEXANDER I, POSTMEN, PUCCINI

TRUMAN, Harry S (1884–1972)

The middle initial of Harry S Truman did not stand for anything. Both his grandfathers had names beginning with 'S', so he was given the bare initial to avoid having to choose between them.
☞ WHITE HOUSE

TUESDAY

Tuesday is named after the Norse God Tiw or Tyr. The Romans called it dies Martis, after Mars the God of War (the French, Spanish and Italians still call it Mardi, Martes and Martedi respectively), but, when the German tribes ousted the Romans, they renamed Tuesday after their own God of War, which was Tiw or Tiwaz. The Angles and Saxons brought Tiwasdaeg (Tuesday) to England in the sixth century.

Tuesday is considered a lucky day in Wales, but unlucky in Greece and Spain. In northern England it is considered unlucky for a traveller to meet a left-handed person on a Tuesday. On other days, it is good luck to do so.

Research has shown that in Somerset between 1640 and 1659, fewer seductions took place on a Tuesday than any other day of the week. Sunday was most common.

Californians have barbecues less often on Tuesday than any other day of the week and are also least likely to use a petrol-driven lawnmower on a Tuesday.

The actress Tuesday Weld was born on a Saturday.

'He respects Owl, because you can't help respecting anybody who can spell TUESDAY, even if he doesn't spell it right' – A.A. Milne, *The House At Pooh Corner*.

TUG-OF-WAR

According to international rules, the rope in a tug-of-war contest must be between 100mm and 125mm in circumference. Tug-of-War featured as an Olympic sport between 1900 and 1920 and resulted in one of the most notable disputes of the 1908 Games in London.

The medal table for the event tells a tale of British dominance with gold, silver and bronze all going to teams from British police forces: the London City Police won, Liverpool Police came second, and K Division Metropolitan Police were third. The real battle, however, came in the first round when the Liverpool Police scored a quick win over the US team. The Americans immediately lodged a protest against the footwear of their opponents. According to them the boots were equipped with illegal steel spikes, cleats and heels. The British insisted that they were standard-issue police boots and the protest was disallowed. The Americans then stormed out of the competition. Later the winning City Police team challenged the Americans to a contest in stockinged feet, but the challenge was not taken up.

Three members of the winning team, James Shepherd, Edwin Mills and Frederick Humphries, went on to represent Britain in two later Olympics, winning silver at Stockholm in 1912 and gold again at Antwerp in 1920.

TUNA

A Japanese seafood distributor paid £120,000 for a 445lb blue-fin tuna at an auction in Tokyo in January 2001, setting a new record for a tuna. The price, which works out at about £270 a pound, almost doubled the previous all-time high set in 1998.

TUNISIA

When the film *Raiders of the Lost Ark* was shot in Tunisia, crew members had to remove 300 television antennas from homes in Kairouan, Tunisia, for one scene to make a rooftop shot look like 1936.

☞ AGE OF CONSENT

TURING, Alan Mathison (1912–54)
☞ COMPUTATION

TURKEY (bird)
In Turkey, the turkey is called the 'American bird'. The correct collective noun for turkeys is a 'rafter'.

☞ CALIFORNIA, HUDSON, SANDWICHES, SHAKESPEARE

TURKEY (country)
In June 1984 Turkey banned the screening of videotapes in buses after a driver tried to censor a love scene while behind the wheel. Seventeen people died in the ensuing accident.

Turks eat more bread per head of population than any other nation – 199.6kg each in a year.

There is only one irregular verb in the Turkish language.

☞ COFFEE

TURKMENISTAN
In 2001, 39 women and one man from the state carpet company in Turkmenistan completed the world's largest carpet, weighing more than a ton and covering about 3,200sq ft. The carpet was decorated with sayings of Turkmen president Saparmurat Niyazov.

TURTLE
Turtles mate at four in the afternoon and lay eggs at six.
☞ WATER-SKIING

TUSSAUD, Madame (Anne Marie Grosholtz) (1761–1850)
☞ TOURISM

TWELFTH NIGHT
The British used to celebrate Twelfth Night (6 January) with a special drink called Lamb's Wool made from roasted apples, sugar and nutmeg in beer. The Dutch celebrate it with a midwinter horn-blowing competition dating back to 2500BC.

Henry VIII, George Washington and George Bush (the elder) all celebrated Twelfth Night by getting married on that day, in 1540, 1759 and 1945 respectively. When Henry VIII saw his wife for the first time on that day, he is said to have commented, 'You have sent me a Flanders mare.' Apparently he had been taken in by an over-flattering portrait of his bride by Hans Holbein the Younger.

TYPEWRITER
The left hand of a skilled typist does 56 per cent of the work.
☞ BLYTON, ENGLISH, LAVATORIES, PERU

UGANDA

According to a news report from Kampala on 13 November 1988, Ugandan villagers lynched a local rainmaker after crops and homes in the Kabale district were destroyed by hailstones and torrential rain. Villagers beat Festo Kazarwa to death because he had threatened to summon up hailstones if people did not show him more respect.

Uganda is the only country on earth in which more than half the population are under 15.

☞ EXAMINATIONS, THUNDER

UKRAINE

Shortly after the Ukraine gained independence from the old Soviet Union, it changed its currency from the karbovanets to the hryvna.

In the Ukraine, ducks go 'krya-krya'.

On 3 October 1995, the city council in the Ukrainian capital, Kiev, established a commission to ease confusion among postmen and delivery workers by renaming the 38 streets in the city that were all called 'Vostochnaya' (East).

ULCER
☞ ENGLISH, MOUSTACHE

UMBRELLA
The original ancient Chinese and Egyptian umbrellas protected against the sun, not the rain, while in ancient Egypt, an umbrella was a sign of rank. Jonas Hanway (1712–86) is said to have introduced umbrellas into England in the 1750s, but they were generally used only by women until the mid-19th century. Significant events in the history of the umbrella include the following:

- In the Peninsular War (1808–14), the Duke of Wellington issued an order forbidding officers to take umbrellas with them into battle.
- 1903 saw the invention of 'Pardoe's Improved Umbrella', an umbrella with mosquito net attached to protect from insects and rain.
- In 1969, an Italian was charged with selling as Parmesan cheese a substance identified on analysis as being grated umbrella handles.
- In September 1978, Bulgarian writer and broadcaster Georgi Markov was fatally stabbed in London by an assassin using a poisoned umbrella.
- The world's first Umbrella Cover Museum opened on Peaks Island off the coast of Maine in

1996. The curator is Nancy Hoffman, whose collection of umbrella covers now contains exhibits from 30 countries. Ms Hoffman's middle initial is '3', which she adopted after a mistyping.

- In 2002, the number of umbrellas left behind on London's tube trains and buses was 11,277.

★ The folding umbrella was patented in Paris on 4 May 1715.

☞ ELASTIC

UNDERGROUND

Forty-two per cent of the London Underground is under ground. The entire system serves 275 stations and includes 408 escalators (including 25 at Waterloo) and 112 lifts. The number of escalators is equal to the number of kilometres of route covered. The busiest station is Victoria, with 76.5 million passengers a year.

☞ DUCK, LONDON, MACKEREL, MONOPOLY, PIGEON, TRANSPORT, WELLINGTON

UNICORN

The Greek physician Ctesias wrote a classic description of the unicorn around 400BC. He described it as an Indian fleet and fierce wild ass with a white body, purple head, and a straight horn, a cubit long, with a white base, black middle and red tip. The unicorn is also mentioned in the writings of Aristotle, Pliny and Aelian.

☞ MARY, QUEEN OF SCOTS

UNITED ARAB EMIRATES
☞ INCOME TAX

UNITED NATIONS

There are 191 members of the United Nations. Seychelles is the only one of them whose name has no letters in common with 'Britain'.

☞ VATICAN

UNITED STATES

The first US president to be born a US citizen was the eighth president, Martin Van Buren (held office 1837–41). The seven before him were born British.

The first US president to have been born in a hospital was Jimmy Carter (born 1924, elected 1977).

The last US president to have had a beard was Benjamin Harrison, who left office in 1893.

The tallest US president was Abraham Lincoln (held office 1861–5) at 6ft 4in. The shortest was James Madison at 5ft 4in.

The only US president to have appeared in a shirt advertisement is Ronald Reagan.

The only US president to have been arrested and fined $20 for speeding on a horse was Ulysses S. Grant.

The only US president to hold a patent was Abraham Lincoln. It was awarded in 1849 for 'A Device for Buoying Vessels Over Shoals'.

The heaviest president was William Taft (held office 1909–13), who weighed between 300lb and 350lb. When he once got stuck in the bath at the White House it took six men to lift him out. He promptly ordered a bigger bath.

Since 1840, every US president elected in a year ending in zero has died in office except for Ronald Reagan – and he survived an assassination attempt.

George W. Bush was elected in 2000.

According to a retired FBI agent, there are 300 to 500 threats on the President's life each month.

☞ APPLE, BACHELORS, BEER, BUSH, CALIFORNIA, CLINTON, COMMUNISM, CRIME, DUBLIN, FLIES, MAINE, MONEY, MOSCOW, OBESITY, OLYMPIC GAMES, RHUBARB, RUGBY, SUICIDE, TEETH, TOURISM, TRAFFIC LIGHTS, TRANSPLANTATION, WILSON

UNIVERSITIES

No one can say when university education began. Indeed, they cannot even give a definite date for the inauguration of Oxford or Cambridge as seats of learning. Universities in general, and Oxford and Cambridge in particular, simply evolved into formal institutions from very informal beginnings.

The Greeks, of course, knew all about further education. Plato opened his Academy around 387BC and the orator Isocrates founded a rival school at about the same time. Both set their sights firmly on the study of philosophy and the acquisition of wisdom, but, while Plato concentrated on abstract thought, Isocrates took a more practical point of view and even accepted fee-paying customers.

The modern universities have their origins in medieval European schools known as *studia generalia*. As scholars began to travel more widely, a need was felt for institutions of learning whose prestige would have more than purely local significance. The *studia generalia* were meant to satisfy that need, opening their doors to students from all parts of Europe and providing teaching qualifications that would be accepted anywhere. The guild of students and teachers within a *studium* was known as *universitas* which, in due course, became the word for the entire institution.

The first university was, according to which authority you consult, established either at Salerno in the ninth century or, more reputably, at Bologna in the 11th. Dante, Petrarch and Copernicus went there, and the institution received a charter from the emperor Frederick I Barbarossa.

While Bologna began as a guild of students in pursuit of learning, the University of Paris adopted a different fashion. Founded some time between 1150 and 1170, it began as a guild of teachers in pursuit of students and that became the model for later universities, beginning with those at Oxford and Cambridge.

In the 12th century, scholarship was becoming trendy in England, and scholars naturally gathered at Oxford simply because roads from all over the country met there – it was a good place to cross the Thames by ford. In 1167, Henry II, during a squabble with Archbishop Becket, forbade English scholars and students to go to Paris, so they all went to Oxford instead. In 1209, a crisis was provoked by murderous quarrels between townsfolk and students, which was finally resolved by a papal settlement in 1214 – which could be considered the first charter for the university. The first formal college to be opened there was University College in 1249, which is often given as the date of the founding of Oxford University, though teaching had been going on there already for more than a century.

Meanwhile, at another river crossing, the University of Cambridge was growing and was boosted by an influx of disaffected Oxford students in 1209. Their first college was Peterhouse, founded in 1284. Already in 1231, however, Henry III had sent letters to the sheriffs and mayors of both Oxford and Cambridge, urging them to co-operate with university officials in suppressing 'rebellious and incorrigible' students.

In late medieval and Tudor times, Oxford and Cambridge argued about who had come first, with supporters of Cambridge claiming that the university had been founded by an ancient Spanish prince called Cantaber, with a later charter from King Arthur, and Oxford countering that it had been founded by the legendary first Briton, the Trojan exile Brutus. In more recent years of peaceful coexistence, Oxford has produced most of our prime ministers, while Cambridge has given us more Nobel Prize winners and spies. Of the 53 British prime ministers, 40 went to Oxford or Cambridge, two went to other universities and 11 did not go to university at all.

While Scotland (St Andrews in 1411) and Ireland (Dublin in 1591) were quick to open new universities, no more appeared in England until the 19th century. With the recent elevation of polytechnics to university status, the UK now has 97 universities.

☞ ABORIGINE, ADOLESCENCE, ANAESTHETICS, St ANDREW, BEAUTY, BENTHAM, CANADA, CHEESE, CHOPSTICKS, CREATION, DWARF, FIDGETING, FISH, FOOTBALL, GALILEI, HAIR, HALITOSIS, HAMSTER, INDIA, KOALA, MEMORY, MOSQUITO, MOUSTACHE, PANCAKE,

POTATO, RUGBY, SANDCASTLE, SHAKESPEARE, SLIPPERS, SMOKING, TOAST, VOICE, WELLS, WORM

URINE

According to Francis Bacon: 'We find also that places where men urine commonly have smell of violets. And urine, if one hath eaten nutmeg, hath so too.'

Urination was an early word for the sport of diving.

☞ ANORAK, DANDELION, HORSE, MOOSE, SINGAPORE, TOOTHPASTE

UZBEKISTAN

Liechtenstein and Uzbekistan are the only other countries that are doubly landlocked: not only are they totally inland, but none of the countries they border on has a coastline either.

Uzbekistan is the only county surrounded entirely by other countries whose names end in '-stan'.

In January 2006, the authorities in Uzbekistan banned the sale of a range of fur-lined underwear because of the 'unbridled fantasies' it could provoke.

St VALENTINE

There are at least 13 saints named Valentine, of whom two have their feast days celebrated on 14 February. Both were Romans, one a priest and physician who was beheaded on 14 February 269, the other a bishop who was martyred around the same time. Or it may have been a few years later. Or they may both have been the same person. Nobody is at all sure, and it's not at all clear that either had much to do with courtship, but the romance business may be tied in with two other mid-February rituals.

The first is an old British belief, mentioned by Chaucer, that 14 February is the date when birds choose their mates. The second is an even older Roman festival called Lupercalia, which was celebrated on 15 February. At Lupercalia, young men, dressed only in wolf-masks and loincloths, ran through the city hitting people with strips of goat skin. According to tradition, women who wanted to become pregnant could improve their chances by being hit by goat hide. Pope Gelasius officially instigated the romantic celebrations of St Valentine's

Day in AD496 as the Christian answer to Lupercalia.

An unexpected connection between this ritual and the romance of St Valentine was revealed in a letter to the *New England Journal of Medicine* in 1987. Apparently the disease known as brucellosis may be spread from goats to humans by contact with freshly killed skins. The symptoms include depression, dizziness, loss of weight, insomnia and general malaise. As the writer of the letter pointed out, these are precisely the symptoms of lovesickness. He concluded that the Valentine's/Lupercalian tradition of lovesick young men in mid-February was nothing more than an annual outbreak of brucellosis caused by too close a contact with goat skins.

The world's first Valentine message is believed to have been sent by a Norfolk woman, Margery Brews, to her fiancé John Paston in 1477. Her letter 'unto my right well-beloved Valentine' was lost for centuries but was rediscovered at the British Library in 1999.

Thailand issued the world's first rose-scented stamps in February 2002 for Valentine's Day.

In Mexico, 14 February is a Day of National Mourning.

☛ Forty-six per cent of the flowers sent in Britain on Valentine's Day are roses.

VALENTINO, Rudolph (1895–1926)

Valentino's first job when he came to the United States in 1913 was as a gardener. He went on to take the romantic lead in many films, including *The Sheik* (1921), which was written by Mrs E.M. Hull who was married to a pig-breeder named Percy.

☞ BURIAL

VAMPIRES

The earliest reference to vampires in England occurs in Walter Map's *De Nagis Curialium*, written in 1190. This was some 700 years before Bram Stoker created Dracula.

Recent research links references to vampirism to outbreaks of rabies, of which the symptoms may include sensitivity to light and garlic and a tendency to bite people.
☛ In 1999 in the United States, 907 people took out insurance against turning into vampires or werewolves.
☞ GARLIC

VAN GOGH, Vincent Willem (1853–90)

Van Gogh's 1889 *Self-Portrait with Bandaged Ear and Pipe* shows the artist apparently with his right ear bandaged, whereas it was the left ear which he partially cut off. The explanation seems to be that the self-portrait was done in a mirror. Van Gogh had sliced off part of the earlobe after an argument with Paul Gauguin. He took the piece of ear to the local brothel where he thought he might find Gauguin, but in his absence he gave it to a prostitute called Rachel.

Although van Gogh painted some 750 canvasses and 1,600 drawings, he is said to have sold only one during his lifetime. *Red Vineyard at Arles* was bought by his younger brother Theo, who was an art dealer, for 400 francs. Four of the ten most expensive paintings ever sold at auction are by van Gogh.

VANUATU

The first European to discover the islands of Vanuatu was the Spanish explorer, Captain Pedro Ferdinand De Quiros in 1605. He named them 'Tierra Australis del

Espiritu Santo', believing he had discovered the great southern continent. The island he landed on is still called Espiritu Santo.

The next European to land there was the French explorer Louis Antoine de Bougainville in 1768. He called the islands the 'Cyclades' after the Greek islands and named a strait between the islands after himself.

In 1774, Captain James Cook arrived and renamed the archipelago the New Hebrides after the islands off Scotland, by which name it was known until Independence in 1980. It is estimated that diseases brought to the country by missionaries and traders were responsible for the population dropping from about a million in 1800 to 45,000 in 1935.

☞ INCOME TAX

VATICAN

With an area of 0.44 sq km and a population of 911, Vatican City is the world's smallest state. It has no coastline, no waterways, no natural resources and no airport but has one heliport.

The uniform of the Swiss Guard of Papal defenders was originally designed by Michelangelo but, according to the Vatican tailor Ety Cicioni, there were no patterns and no instructions on how to make it when he arrived in 2000. By examining an existing uniform, he discovered that it can be made from 154 pieces. The uniforms weigh approximately 8lb each, which is more than twice the weight of US army battle dress.

Vatican City and Taiwan are the only countries that are not members of the United Nations.

☞ GALILEI, MISOGYNY, POPES, STAMPS, STOCKINGS

VENEZUELA

Venezuela was given its name, which means 'little Venice', by Alonso de Ojeda (1468–1515).

☞ AMERICA

VENICE

On 6 May 1996, gondoliers in Venice stopped serenading passengers following a ruling that singing would turn them into freelance musicians and therefore liable to contribute to a state pension fund.

In 2005, Venetian gondoliers became subject to breathalyser tests.

☞ BIRMINGHAM, VENEZUELA

DE VERE, Edward, Earl of Oxford (1550–1604)

'This Earle of Oxford, making of his low obeisance to Queen Elizabeth, happened to let a Fart, at which he was so abashed and ashamed, that he went to Travell, 7 yeares. On his returne the Queen welcomed him home and sayd, "My Lord, I had forgott the Fart"' – John Aubrey, *Brief Lives*.

VIBRATOR

According to Rachel Maines, author of the academic study *The Technology of Orgasm: Hysteria, the Vibrator and Women's Sexual Satisfaction*, the vibrator was the fifth common domestic item – after the sewing machine, fan, kettle and toaster – to be powered by electricity. Electric vibrators first appeared around 1880 but, until the 1920s, they were considered respectable items of medical equipment and were used by physicians to treat cases of alleged hysteria in women. Only when vibrators began to appear in blue movies did attitudes towards them change.

VICTORIA, Queen and Empress (1819–1901)

The flowers at Queen Victoria's funeral cost £80,000. Her direct descendants include Kaiser Wilhelm II, Alexandra (wife of Tsar Nicholas II), Elizabeth II, the Duke of Edinburgh and the present monarchs of Spain, Norway, Denmark and Sweden. According to the editor of *Burke's Peerage*, Queen Victoria had terrible handwriting.

☞ CARROLL, CHOCOLATE, COW, EDWARD VIII, HANDKERCHIEF, QUEEN MARY, TIE KNOTS

VIOLENCE

★ On 14 April 1989, police in Huddersfield, England, reported that research had confirmed that violent criminals could be calmed down by putting them in pink cells.

☞ FOOTBALL, SOAP OPERAS, WEATHER

VIRGIN ISLANDS

There are 100 women to every 82 men in the Virgin Islands, the highest female to male ratio in the world.

VIRGINITY

According to mediaeval superstition, a woman could recover her virginity by giving birth to seven illegitimate children.

A male Emperor moth can smell a virgin female up to seven miles away upwind.

☞ CELIBACY, GALILEI, LOVE, RALEIGH

VIVALDI, Antonio (1678–1741)
☞ BACH

VOICE
According to research at Nottingham University published in 2001, men with deep, sonorous voices are thought by women to be more attractive, older, heavier, more muscular and more likely to have a hairy chest than men with higher voices. A sample of women were played tapes of the voices of 34 men and asked to judge their attractiveness, age, weight, muscular development and whether they had a hairy chest. While women tended to agree with one another quite strongly in their assessments, measurements showed they were wrong on all counts except one: men with deep voices tend to be heavier than higher-pitched men.

☞ AIR HOSTESSES, BLANC, CLEOPATRA

VOLTAIRE (1694–1778)
The French writer/philosopher Voltaire (born François Marie Arouet) was 5ft 3in tall and had a long nose. He is said to have drunk 50 cups of coffee a day.

VOWELS
Abstemious and facetious are frequently alleged to be the only two words in English that include all five vowels once each, in their correct alphabetical order. This is far

from true: the full *Oxford English Dictionary* includes 16 such independent words. Here are the other 14:

Acheilous: without a lip.

Adventious: an old form of adventitious.

Aerious: of the nature of air.

Affectious: affectionate.

Anemious: of plants, growing in a windy situation.

Annelidous: of the nature of a worm.

Arsenious: of the nature of arsenic.

Arterious: of an artery.

Caesious: bluish or greyish green.

Camelious: of a camel's hump.

Fracedinous: pertaining to putrid fermentation.

Materious: material.

Placentious: disposed to please.

Tragedious: full of tragedy.

Of the words in this list, the *Oxford English Dictionary* classifies arterious as 'archaic'; camelious as 'jocular'; annelidous and anemious as 'rare'; adventious, aerious, affectious, fracedinous, materious and tragedious as 'obsolete'; and placentious as 'obsolete and rare'. But acheilous, arsenious and caesious are perfectly good modern words fit to hold their vowels high alongside abstemious and facetious.

☞ MACKEREL, TENNIS

WAGNER, Richard (1813–83)

The composer Richard Wagner wore pink underwear. According to Mark Twain, his music was better than it sounds.

WALES

An Englishman has the right, granted a millennium ago, to shoot a Welshman from a distance of 12yd using a longbow in the grounds of Hereford Cathedral on a Sunday... if only he could do it without breaking laws passed more recently.

In the 19th century nearly 14 per cent of the Welsh population had the surname 'Jones' and more than half the population were covered by only 10 surnames. There are four times as many sheep as people in Wales.

WALNUT

☞ AUGUSTUS, SARDINE

WALRUS

According to research published in 2003, walruses use their right flippers eight times as much as their left when eating. Analysis of videotapes of walruses scooping up molluscs from the sea bed showed that the acts of scooping and flicking the molluscs to clean them were performed 89 per cent of the time with the right flipper and only 11 per cent with the left.

☞ DINOSAUR, TEETH

WASHINGTON, George (1732–99)

Washington had a horse called Nelson and was said to have been the first American to breed jackasses and mules. Having suffered from smallpox in his youth, he had his entire army inoculated against it in 1777. Among his other innovations was the feat of sending the first airmail letter – carried from Philadelphia to New Jersey by the balloonist Jean Pierre Blanchard.

The first First Lady, Martha Washington, would never have occupied that post if Betsy Fauntleroy had accepted on either of the occasions on which George Washington proposed to her first.

☞ AUSTRALIA, ICE CREAM, TEETH, TWELFTH NIGHT

WASP

In November 2001 Dutch scientists announced that they had found a way of using wasps to detect drugs or explosives. The antennae of wasps are more sensitive than sniffer dogs' noses and wasps can be trained in an hour to detect drugs, whereas dogs take six months. The disadvantage, as one of the researchers

pointed out, is that wasps only live for a couple of months.
☞ CHRISTMAS

WATER

To survive indefinitely in a hot, exposed desert, an average human requires 1.5 gallons of water a day.
☞ ALCHEMY, ANORAK, ATLANTIC, BEAR, BELL,
BUFFALO, BULGARIA, CAMBODIA, CAMEL, CHAMOIS,
CHANNEL, CHOCOLATE, CUCUMBER, ELEPHANT, FISH,
FIZZY DRINKS, FORTUNE-TELLING, GOLDFISH, HAIR,
HUDSON, LAVATORIES, LINDBERGH, MARS, MONOPOLY,
PARA-PSYCHOLOGY, PENGUIN, POLAR BEAR, RUGBY,
SANDCASTLE, STEPHENSON, STONE, STRAWBERRY,
SWIMMING, THAMES, TORTOISE, WIFE-CARRYING, WINDOW

WATERFALL
☞ BULLOCK

WATERMELON

The first recorded watermelon harvest took place around 5,000 years ago in Egypt. Pictures of the fruit have been found in paintings on the walls of ancient buildings.

The seedless watermelon was developed in 1939.

Cordele, Georgia, claims to be Watermelon Capital of the World. The average American eats over 17lb of watermelons a year.
☞ LIBYA

WATER-SKIING

In 1972 an elephant named Bimbo, aged seven, was awarded $4,500 damages by the Californian Supreme

Court after his owner claimed that a road accident caused the elephant to lose interest in dancing and water-skiing. Bimbo was travelling in a trailer that was involved in the accident. The case was heard by Judge Turtle.

WEATHER

In the UK the weather forecast 'It'll be much the same as yesterday' is right three days out of four.

According to Petronius, writing in AD65: 'No living man has the right to cut his nails or hair on a ship; that is, unless the wind is blowing a hurricane.' If there is a hurricane at sea, however, an observation by Charles Darwin may help establish its cause. In 1831, he recorded that the sailors on HMS *Beagle* believed that strong winds were caused by someone on shore keeping a cat shut up. Since there are, at any moment, about 2,000 thunderstorms going on somewhere on earth, those who shut cats up may have a good deal to answer for.

Research published in 1990 showed that most violent crime rates increase in hot weather, while property crimes are unaffected.

Useful weather verb: to driffle, which means 'to rain fitfully or in sparse drops'.

★ Britain's worst ever storm was on 26 November 1703, when high winds and torrential rain killed an estimated eight thousand people in southern England.

'When two Englishmen meet, their first talk is of the weather' – Samuel Johnson (1758).

☞ CHRISTMAS, St CLARE, METEOROLOGY, PENGUIN, RAIN, SNOW, St SWITHUN, TIGER

WELLINGTON, Duke of (1769–1852)

Arthur Wellesley, later the first Duke of Wellington, signed his name as Arthur Wesley until May 1798. Although he was married and is believed to have had several lovers, he maintained that 'no woman ever loved me; never in my whole life'. One of his lovers is said to have been the French actress Mlle George, who also slept with Napoleon. When asked to compare the two, she reputedly replied, 'The Duke was by far the more vigorous.'

As Prime Minister, he rejected the idea of an underground railway in London on the grounds that the French army might use it to launch a surprise attack.

He is probably the only man to have had a school (Wellington College), a tree (*Wellingtonia*) and a pair of boots (Wellingtons) all named after him.

☞ DUELLING, HAIR, UMBRELLA

WELLINGTON BOOTS

Wellington boots with individual toes were first seen at the Chelsea Flower Show in 1995, where they were modelled by the Japanese garden designer Koji Ninomija.

WELLS, Herbert George (1866–1946)

H.G. Wells, author of such science fiction novels as *The Invisible Man*, *War of the Worlds* and *The Time Machine*, gained a Doctorate of Science as an external student at London University at the age of 77 with a thesis entitled: 'Personality of the Mesozoics'. His last words are said to have been: 'Go away. I'm all right.'

The 2002 remake of the film *The Time Machine* was

directed by Simon Wells, the great-grandson of the author.

On 26 June 1862, Joseph Wells, father of H.G. Wells, became the first bowler to take four wickets in four balls in a county cricket match. He was playing for Kent against Sussex.

WEREWOLVES
Between 1520 and 1630, some 30,000 people were reported to the French authorities for being werewolves.

WESSEX
The origins of Wessex date back to the year 495 when the region was settled by Saxons under King Cerdic. His son Cynric became King of the West Saxons in 519. King Cerdic is believed to be the great-great-great-great-great-great-great-great-great-great-great-grandfather of Alfred the Great.

The full name of Prince Edward, Earl of Wessex, is Edward Antony Richard Louis: his initials spell his title: E.A.R.L.

WHALE
The large blue whale eats 3 tons of food a day. Its penis is 7–8ft long. Man, hoofed mammals, most marsupials and whales don't have a penis bone.

WHISKY
In Scottish Gaelic, the word *sgriob* means the itchiness felt on the upper lip just before taking a sip of whisky.

More Scotch whisky is sold in one month in France

than cognac in a year. Worldwide, Scotch whisky exports earn Britain £68 every second.

☞ ALCOHOL, BOXING, PRESLEY

WHISTLING
Marie-Augustin, Marquis de Pelier of Brittany, spent 50 years in jail from 1786 for whistling at Marie Antoinette in a Paris theatre.

☞ BURIAL, OYSTER, QUEEN MARY

WHITE HOUSE
Originally called the 'President's Palace', the official residence of American presidents was officially named the 'Executive Mansion' in 1810, and renamed the 'White House' in 1902. It is 168ft long, 152ft wide (including porticoes) and 70ft high with six floors, 132 rooms, 35 bathrooms, 147 windows, 412 doors, 12 chimneys, eight staircases and three lifts and it requires 570 gallons of paint to cover its outside surface. It also has a tennis court, jogging track, swimming pool, cinema and bowling lane.

While the interior of the building was being renovated in the 1940s, President Harry S. Truman lived across the road in a building called Blair House.

The White House is claimed to be the only private residence of a head of state that is open to the public, free of charge.

☞ UNITED STATES

WIFE-CARRYING
The annual Wife-Carrying Championships in Sonkajarvi,

Finland, have been held every year since 1992 and have been World Championships in Wife-Carrying since 1996. The important rules are as follows:

- The length of the official track is 253.5m, and the surface of the track is partially sand, partially grass and partially asphalt.
- The track has two dry obstacles and a water obstacle, about one metre deep.
- The wife to be carried may be your own, the neighbour's or you may have found her farther afield; she must, however, be over 17 years of age.
- The minimum weight of the wife to be carried is 49kg. If it is less than 49kg, the wife will be burdened with such a heavy rucksack that the total weight to be carried is 49kg.
- All the participants must have fun.
- The winner is the couple who completes the course in the shortest time.
- If a contestant drops his wife that couple will be fined 15 seconds per drop.
- The only equipment allowed is a belt worn by the carrier.
- Each contestant takes care of his/her safety and, if deemed necessary, insurance.

Since 1998, the Championship has been dominated by the Estonians, who that year introduced a new and efficient style of carrying their partners. In place of the traditional piggyback or fireman's hold, they carried their wives upside down over their backs. In 2003, Margo Uusorg and

Egle Soll of Estonia used this hold to capture the world title for the third successive year. Traditionally, the first prize is the wife's weight in beer. More recently, this has been accompanied by a cash prize.

☞ FINLAND

WIG

The word 'wig' only appeared in the English language around 1675. Before that, it was always called by its full name, 'periwig'.

Among the great wig-wearers of history, we should mention:

The ancient Egyptians around 350BC, who wore wigs to cover their heads which had been shaven to be free of vermin.

Mozart, who had a deformity of his left ear that he kept covered by a wig.

Queen Elizabeth I, who owned 150 wigs.

In 1765, wigmakers petitioned George III for financial relief, following a steep drop in demand for men's wigs. Demand was high, however, at the beginning of the 21st century when more wigs were made for *The Two Towers*, the second part of Peter Jackson's *Lord of the Rings* trilogy, than for any other film in history.

The word 'bigwig' comes from the old tendency for the most important officials to wear the biggest wigs.

☞ HAT, LOUIS XIV, MERKIN, SWIMMING

WILLIAM IV, King of Great Britain (1765–1837)

William IV became King in 1830 at the age of 64, on

the death of his brother, George IV. He is the oldest person to have acceded to the British (or English) throne. He had a reputation for eccentric behaviour, which was enhanced by his habit of spitting in public.
☞ EDWARD VIII

WILSON
The only surname to have been held by both a US president and a British prime minister is Wilson: Woodrow Wilson, who was President from 1913 to 1921, and Harold Wilson, who was Prime Minister from 1964 to 1970 and from 1974 to 1976.
☞ REAGAN

WIMBLEDON
An average four-set match in the men's singles at Wimbledon lasts two-and-a-half hours, of which the ball is in play for just 20 minutes. The average length is 3.68 sets (2.26 for women); the average set is 9.86 games (8.92 for women); the average game is 6.35 points (6.56 for women). In men's matches, 81.8 per cent are won by the server. For women the figure is 64.3 per cent. The grass on the courts is cut to a height of exactly 8mm.

During Wimbledon fortnight, spectators are expected to consume more than 27,000kg of strawberries, covered with 7,000 litres of cream, while the players are working their way through some 40,000 balls. Until needed the balls are stored at a temperature of 68°F.

The Austrian Hans Redl played at Wimbledon from 1947 to 1956 despite losing an arm during World War II. He served by tossing the ball up with his racket.

If a Greg Rusedski serve kept going at full speed, it would take 72 days to reach the moon.

☞ ARCHERY, KUWAIT, TENNIS

WINDOW

The world record for window-cleaning is held by Terry Burrows of South Ockendon, Essex, with an official time of 9.91 seconds for cleaning three standard 45-sq-in office windows using a standard 11.75in-long squeegee and two gallons of water at the NEC, Birmingham, on 7 March 2001. His actual cleaning time was 8.91 seconds, but he incurred two half-second penalties for faults.

☞ HAT, LAVATORIES, SNORING, WHITE HOUSE

WINE

St Vincent, the patron saint of wine, was teetotal.

☞ ALCOHOL, BEETHOVEN, BULGARIA, CORK, ELEPHANT, GRAPE, SARDINE, TATTOO

WISCONSIN

☞ BULL, CHEESE, HAMBURGER, ICE CREAM, MEMORY, POTATO, SEX

WITCHCRAFT

The word 'witch' comes from the Saxon 'wicca', meaning 'wise one'.

WOLF

The last person to be killed by a wolf in Britain died in 1743.

☞ COMPUTATION, COSMETICS, St VALENTINE

WONDER WOMAN
☞ MARSTON

WOODPECKER
According to research carried out in 1936, if you attach a false moustache on to the face of a wild female woodpecker, a male woodpecker will attack her just as if she were a rival male.

WORM
Linnaeus longissimus, the bootlace worm, is the longest animal on earth. In 1984 one found on the beach at St Andrews, Scotland, measured 55m.

Research has shown that earthworms learn fastest between 8pm and midnight. Experiments on the learning abilities of earthworms date back to work carried out in 1920 by the Dutch psychologist Van Oye, who taught worms to find food lowered into their bowls on pieces of wire. For more than 30 years, no further progress was made until two researchers at the University of Texas began some significant experiments in 1953. James V. McConnell and Robert Thompson first re-established Van Oye's finding that worms can indeed learn. They did this by turning a light on, then giving the worm an electric shock. After several repetitions, the worm began to contract – its normal reaction to pain – when the light came on. This simple condition experiment was evidence that the worm had a memory.

'It was while we were running our first experiment,' McConnell later wrote, 'that Thompson and I wondered aloud, feeling rather foolish as we did so, what would happen if we conditioned a flatworm, then cut it in two and let both halves regenerate. Which half would retain the memory?'

That apparently foolish thought launched a long series of experiments. Worms were taught something, then cut in half. When they had grown back, both halves were found to have retained some of the memory. They forgot a little during the time needed for re-growing, but then needed less training than before to reach the same level.

The researchers then tried teaching a worm something, cutting it in two, waiting for the front end to regenerate, then slicing that in two and this time waiting for the back end to grow into a full worm. Result: a worm none of which was present for the initial experiment. But still it seemed to remember.

All this seemed to confirm the 'Molecular Theory of Memory', which had been proposed at the time. The idea was that every new memory corresponds to a new molecule of RNA, which can be reproduced and spread through the organism. And that is what led to the most dramatic experiments of all: worms were taught something, then minced and fed to uneducated worms. A string of papers appeared in the early 1960s with titles ranging from: 'Memory transfer through cannibalism in planarians' to 'Is knowledge edible?'.

The answer appeared to be 'yes', which was unfortunate, because the scientific community was about to ditch the entire Molecular Theory of Memory as totally misconceived. Another string of papers followed explaining why the earlier ones had reached the wrong conclusions. One explanation was that the worms weren't really learning anything: they were just following the slime trails of earlier worms. The whole topic was then quietly dropped and minced worm dropped from the menu of laboratories.

☞ PHOBIAS, SNAIL, VOWELS

WRIGHT, Orville (1871–1948) and Wilbur (1867–1912)

The first time Orville and Wilbur called themselves 'The Wright Brothers' was in 1889 when they started a printing firm. They moved into bicycle repair in 1893.

The Wright Brothers made the first flight of a heavier-than-air machine on 17 December 1903. Orville's inaugural flight of 120ft was less than the distance between the wing-tips of a Boeing 747.

WRISTWATCH

☞ DOG

WYCLIFFE, John (c.1320–84)

The religious reformer John Wycliffe died in 1384 of natural causes. Despite this, he was condemned as a heretic in 1415 and burned at the stake posthumously in 1428.

YETI

Reports of a large, human-like creature in the Himalayas date back to 1832 when B.H. Hodgson wrote in *The Journal of the Asiatic Society of Bengal* of a hairy man-like biped that walked erect.

The Sherpa guides, however, seemed familiar with the creature. Some claim there are two yetis: 'dzu-teh', which is 7–8ft tall, and 'meh-teh', which is only 5–6ft tall. Both have long arms that almost reach to the knees.

In 1889, Major L.A. Waddell found footprints in the snow one morning. His Sherpa guides matter-of-factly told him they were the prints of a hairy wild man that was often seen in the area. Reports of sightings continued and in September 1921, on a mountaintop near Tibet at 20,000ft, Lt Col C.K. Howard-Bury found strange footprints in the snow. He described the prints as being three times the size of a man's. The Sherpas told him that they were from 'a man-like thing that is not a man'. This description was mistakenly translated by a *Calcutta Statesman* columnist as 'abominable snowman' and the name stuck.

The alternative name of 'yeti' came as a result of a sighting in 1925 by N.A. Tombazi, a British member of the Royal Geographical Society. He saw a creature stooping to pick at some bushes, then found 16 footprints, shaped like a man's, six or seven inches long and four inches wide. After this report, the creature became known as 'Yeti', from the Sherpa 'yeh-teh', meaning 'the thing'.

In 1959, mountaineer Peter Byrne visited a lamasery in Pangboche, Nepal, where the monks allowed him to examine something that was supposed to be the hand of a yeti. Byrne had come prepared and stole a finger and thumb from the hand, replacing them with a human finger and thumb that he had brought with him. The supposed yeti parts were smuggled into India where the actor James Stewart, and his wife Gloria, wrapped them in underwear to smuggle them to England. Tests were inconclusive and the samples subsequently vanished.

★ On 30 June 1969, the headline appeared in the *US National Bulletin*: 'I was raped by the Abominable Snowman'.

YODELLING
On 4 October 1988, the Bavarian Minister for the Environment requested people not to yodel in the Alps because it might frighten the mountain eagle and the chamois.

YORK
In York it is still legal to shoot a Scotsman with a bow

and arrow, but only if you see him within the city walls after dark. And, of course, if you can do it without breaking any other more modern laws.

☞ OSTRICH

YO-YO
The yo-yo was originally a Philippine jungle weapon, to be thrown at its target, then returned for re-use.

ZAMBIA

President Kaunda of Zambia once threatened to resign if Zambians did not cut down their consumption of beer. It is illegal for tourists to photograph pygmies in Zambia. Oral sex is also illegal in Zambia. In 2001, a 65-year-old German tourist was sentenced to six years in jail for breaking this law. In his defence Wolfgang Seifarth pleaded that he was not aware that oral sex was illegal in Zambia, but the magistrate ruled that ignorance of the law was no defence.

In October 2001, a Zambian man was granted a divorce after he found a frog in a cup of tea his wife made him. Andrew Nyoka, 28, told a community court, 'One time I found a frog in a cup of tea she had served me. That is the reason I went for another woman.' The judges granted him a divorce, saying it was clear the marriage could not be saved.

This seems fully in line with the advice given by Governor Welshman Mabhena of Zambia in March 1996 when he warned men against washing nappies or cooking, saying, 'Our culture and tradition have a clear division of labour. There are certain household chores that just cannot be done by men.'

ZIMBABWE
☞ BANANA

ZIPF, George Kingsley (1902–50)
The Harvard linguistics professor George Zipf made some profound discoveries on the statistical distribution of words. Here are some of the laws Zipf discovered:

Zipf's First Law
If the words in any large body of text are ordered according to the number of times they appear, then the position of each word in the list is multiplied by its frequency, the result settles to a more or less constant figure.

Example: In one large database of spoken language, the 35th most common word is 'very' which occurs 836 times; the 45th most common is 'see' with 674 hits; while the 55th, 65th and 75th are 'which' (563), 'get' (469) and 'out' (422) respectively. If we multiply 35 x 836, and 45 x 674, and 55 x 563 and so on, the answers are 29,260, 30,330, 30,965, 30,485 and 31,650 respectively, which are as close as makes no difference. Only with the top and bottom few items on the list would one expect there to be any great divergence from this pattern.

Zipf's Second Law
In general, the shorter a word is, the more often it will be

used. Zipf puts this down to the 'Principle of Least Effort'.

Example: Studies have shown that roughly 50 per cent of words used in any extended sample have only one syllable.

ZOO
☞ CARUSO, CHIMPANZEE, FLAMINGO, HIPPOPOTAMUS, MONKEY, PENGUIN, PIGEON, PLATYPUS, POLAR BEAR, QUAGGA, ROBBERY

ZYWOCICE
Alphabetically, the last place on earth is Zywocice in Poland.